William Carey Richards

Harry's Vacation

Or, Philosophy at Home

William Carey Richards

Harry's Vacation
Or, Philosophy at Home

ISBN/EAN: 9783337069667

Printed in Europe, USA, Canada, Australia, Japan

Cover: Foto ©ninafisch / pixelio.de

More available books at **www.hansebooks.com**

HARRY'S VACATION;

OR,

Philosophy at Home.

BY
WILLIAM C. RICHARDS, A. M.

AUTHOR'S REVISED EDITION.

NEW YORK:
D. APPLETON & CO., 549 & 551 BROADWAY.
LONDON: 16 LITTLE BRITAIN.
1873.

ENTERED, according to Act of Congress, in the year 1868,
BY WILLIAM C. RICHARDS,
In the Clerk's Office of the District Court of the United States for the District of Rhode Island.

PREFACE.

The first appearance of this volume dates back nearly nine years, at which time one or two editions of it were speedily exhausted, and many most flattering notices of it appeared in the papers and periodicals. It was hailed and welcomed as a novel and valuable contribution to the literature for the young.

Circumstances beyond the control of the author prevented its continued publication, and it has been out of print for several years, while its popularity, with the class for which it was designed, has undergone no diminution. It is deemed proper, therefore, to reprint the book, and the author has subjected it to such revision as was necessary.

It was his original purpose to follow the book with other volumes upon the same general plan, which contemplates the diffusion of valuable instruction in popular philosophy in the pleasing guise of story and with the accessories of fictitious incidents. A second volume may be expected next year.

PROVIDENCE, *Aug.* 25, 1863.

CONTENTS.

CHAPTER I.

The School-fellows, Harry and Herbert—The Invitation—Arrival at Beechwood—Doctor Sinclair and his Family—Herbert's Welcome—An Afternoon's Amusement—The Library—Evening Worship—Herbert's Dream, . . . 9

CHAPTER II.

Getting up Late—Dr. Sinclair's Plan—Jack Frost's Exploits—The Ice-bottle—Crystallized Breath—Breakfast Conversation—Fanny's Experiment—Alice's Explanation—Heat and Cold—Frost-burn, ... 23

CHAPTER III.

The Microscope—Frost-work—Stars and Diamonds—A Fluid Globe—Why the Frost-Crystals Disappeared—The Ice-Bottle Arraigned—Its Defence—A Wonderful Exception—The Lead Tree—Affinity Illustrated, ... 34

CHAPTER IV.

Mr. Oldbuckle—A Rock of Alum—Salts—A Disaster—Why the Dish Fell—Gravitation—Sir Isaac Newton's Discovery—Mutual Attraction of Bodies—An Experiment Proposed, ... 43

CHAPTER V.

The Walk to the Well—The Yellow Leaf—Gravitation Resisted—The Guinea and Feather Experiment—Velocity of Falling Bodies—A Rule—The Deep Well—The Pebble thrown in—The Result—Preparation for the Sabbath—How the Day was Spent, ... 52

CHAPTER VI.

A Surprise—William Sinclair—His Welcome—Mary—A Mother's Joy—Table-Talk—Evening Amusement—Music—A Charade-Play Proposed, ... 60

CHAPTER VII.

The Charade in Three Acts—Mew—Sick—Music—Old Hundred, ... 71

CHAPTER VIII.

Snow—Congratulations—Snow in the City—Snow-Crystals—Uses of Snow—The Snow-Blanket—Travellers in the Alps—Harry's Wise Resolution—Why Snow-Crystals are Opaque—Why Lofty Mountain Tops are Covered with Snow—Sledding—An Upset, ... 82

CHAPTER IX.

An Accession to the Party—Mr. Oldbuckle Declines an Adventure—A Sleigh-Ride Proposed—Early Dinner—The Sleigh—The Start—Ten Miles an Hour—Viviandale—The Vivians—William Sinclair's Desertion—A Pardon and its Conditions—Gertrude Vivian—The Return Home, . . 93

CHAPTER X.

Tea-table Chat—Alliteration—Herbert's Acknowledgment—Fanny's Wish—Papa's Consent—The Laboratory—The

Magic Lantern — Its History — Lenses — The Darkened Room — A Mistake which was not a Mistake — Optical Illusions — Fanny Frightened at her Shadow — Spectral Images — Fanny's Gratitude, ... 102

CHAPTER XI.

The Arrival — Gertrude Vivian's Welcome — Her Dilemma — Mr. Oldbuckle — Fire-works — The Relations of Pyrotechny to Science — History of Fire-works — A Sad Story — Memorable Displays — Ixion's Wheel — Mr. Oldbuckle's Apology, 113

CHAPTER XII.

Preparations for the Fire-works — Waiting for the Darkness — Amusement for the Interval — Playing Proverbs — Nine o'clock, ... 125

CHAPTER XIII.

A Compromise — The Signal — Flight of Rockets — The Rocket's Path — Why the Rocket rises — Its Rudder — Roman Candles — Sea Signals — A Catharine Wheel — Courantines — A Dragon — A Spiral Rocket — Serpents — Loaded Rockets — The Daft Boy — Chinese Fire — A Mock Sun — Alice — Thanks, ... 137

CHAPTER XIV.

Fanny's "Merry Christmas" — Old Jacob Fletcher — Alice's Greetings — Mr. Oldbuckle's Memories — Morning Worship — A Christmas Hymn — Christmas in America — Why Not Generally Observed — Chronology at Fault — Wishes — Christmas at the South — Negro Festivals — The Southern "Yule Log" — Christmas-greens — Mr. Oldbuckle's Proposition — Its General Acceptance, ... 146

CHAPTER XV.

Christmas Dinner—Church Decoration—Wordsworth—Snap-Dragon—Evening Amusement—Charade Plays—Infirm—Wedlock, ... 157

CHAPTER XVI.

Adieus—Departures—More Snow—Fanny's Balls—Science in Soap-bubbles—Elasticity—Form—Inertia—Variable Colours, ... 168

CHAPTER XVII.

The Return—Anecdote of the Iron Duke—Napoleon and Wellington—Sir Humphrey Davy—A Chemical Process, 179

CHAPTER XVIII.

Hydrogen Gas—Its Levity—More Soap-bubbles—Miniature Balloons—Origin of Balloons—Dr. Sinclair's Balloon—Its Ascent—Effect of Hydrogen upon the Voice, . . . 189

CHAPTER XIX.

The Aurora Borealis—Mr. Oldbuckle's Appearance—Polar Phenomena—Cause of the Aurora—Dr. Sinclair's Illustration—The Electrical Theory Triumphant, ... 200

CHAPTER XX.

A Gift for Alice—Narrow Escape of the Æronaut—The Fugitive Bubble—Making a Noise in the World—A Wonderful Change—Water at Firms—Illuminating Gas—Elements—Carbon, ... 211

CONTENTS.

CHAPTER XXI.

The Pond—Skating—A Collision—Harry's Mysterious Departure—Sledding on the Pond—An Upset—Inertia—Dr. Sinclair on the Ice—A Surprise at Home—More Sport on the Ice—The Skating Trio—A Novel Sleigh-ride, . . 222

CHAPTER XXII.

Better Late than Never—Christmas Gifts—Their Distribution—Fanny's White Swans—The Magic Wand—Feeding the Swans—Fanny's Wonder—Magnetism—The Mariner's Compass, ... 233

CHAPTER XXIII.

The Fairy Balloon—William Sinclair's Magic—The Spell Explained—Alice's Ink-stand—The Canary's Water-bottle—Alice in Spangles—The Diamond Necklace—Electrical Light, ... 242

CHAPTER XXIV.

A Cold Day—Electrical Apparatus—History of Electricity—Origin of the Term—Electrics—Conductors—Insulation—Harry Declines the Rod—William and Mary Conductors—How Franklin Caught the Lightning—Lightning Rods—The Leyden Jar—Induction—Harry's Gift, . . . 256

CHAPTER XXV.

The Miser's Plate—Harry's Avarice Outwitted—Gertrude Vivian Shocked—William Sinclair's Stratagem Detected—The Penalty—Fanny's Hair on End—A Bright Kiss—Harry on the Stool—A Pistol Fired by his Nose—Ether set on Fire by an Icicle—The Fatal Stroke, ... 268

CHAPTER XXVI.

The Afternoon—Tea-time—Music—Capping Verses—Verse *versus* Stanza—The Play—Conundrums, ... 279

CHAPTER XXVII.

Why Natural Science is often a Dull Study—Harry's Experiment—The Sucker—The Atmosphere—Winds and Hurricanes—Weight of the Air—Alice Raised by the Air—The Difference, ... 291

CHAPTER XXVIII.

The Air-Pump—Harry Made Prisoner—Cupping—The Fly's Foot—The Barometer—The Grand Duke's Well—Toricelli—Measuring Heights, ... 303

CHAPTER XXIX.

More Philosophy for Miss Vivian—The Laboratory—Empty Jars—Oxygen—The Magic Taper—Combustion—Burning a Watch-spring—Oxyd of Steel—Sparkling Carbon—Carbonic Acid Gas—The Grotto del Cane—The Martyred Mouse, ... 314

CHAPTER XXX.

The Resuscitation—Too Much of a Good Thing—Atmospheric Air—Supply of Oxygen—Producing an Alkali—Fire from Ice—The Mock Sun—Sulphurous Acid—The Compound Blow-pipe—Burning a Ten-penny Nail—The Drummond Light—The Bude Lamp—A *Feu de Joie*, . . . 329

CHAPTER XXXI.

The New Year—Fanny's Regrets and Reasons—Childish Philosophy—The Bent Spoon—An Optical Illusion—Bring-

ing a Sovereign to Light—Explanations—Twilight—The
Spectre of the Brocken—Departures, ... 339

CHAPTER XXXII.

A Sleigh-Ride—A Snow Landscape—The Railroad Station—
A Late Train—Rate of Speed—Railways in England and
America—English Engines—Brother Jonathan's Railroads
—The Locomotive—Its History—The Return, . . . 351

CHAPTER XXXIII.

Snow-Sports—The Telescope—The Tower-Chamber—History of the Telescope—Varieties—Lord Rosse's Telescope—
The Moon—Her Revolutions—Telescopic Views—Surface
of the Moon—The Moon-Hoax—A Star—Jupiter and his
Moons—Addison's Hymn, ... 361

CHAPTER XXXIV.

Alice's Wish—Dr. Sinclair's Consent—Waiting for Mr. Oldbuckle—His Arrival—Lord Rosse's Telescope Again—The
Microscope—The Wonders of a Fly—The Spider's "Hand"
—A Flea—Wonderful Leaping—Various Woods—The
Skin and its Pores—Fanny's Hair—Points Contrasted—
Other Objects—Animated Nature Displayed, . . . 374

CHAPTER XXXV.

Infusioræ—Wheel Animalculæ—Flint-Shelled Infusioræ—
Fossils—Flint—Chalk—Polishing Slate—Fossil-Flour—
Dirt-Eaters—Eating Slate-Pencils—Microscopic Blood—
The Wisdom of God—Thoughts of To-morrow—Pleasant
Intelligence—Mr. Oldbuckle's Adieus—The End of Harry's
Vacation, ... 387

Harry's Vacation.

CHAPTER I.

The School-fellows, Harry and Herbert—The Invitation—Arrival at Beechwood—Doctor Sinclair and his Family—Herbert's Welcome—An Afternoon's Amusement—The Library—Evening Worship—Herbert's Dream.

"HERBERT, you must go to Beechwood with me, and spend the vacation; indeed you must. I am sure papa and mamma and the girls will be delighted to have you, and brother Willie will be home at Christmas. Would n't we have rare fun, though! Really, Herbert, you must go. Ask your papa this very night, to let you go—won't you?"

"You forget, Harry, that even if papa would consent, I could not go until you had asked your parents about it."

"Oh! never mind about that," returned Harry. "Only say that you will go, and I will write to mamma to invite you."

"That's one way of disposing of the matter anyhow!" said Herbert, laughing; "but truly, Harry, I should like, of all things, to go with you; and I will promise you to ask my parents about it, when you have succeeded in getting an invitation for me."

This conversation took place between two lads of almost the same age, who were attending school together in the city of ———. The first speaker was Harry Sinclair, whose parents resided at a considerable distance from the city. The other was Herbert Russel, whose father was a clergyman residing in the city. They were both amiable and intelligent boys, and that sort of intimacy had sprung up between them which often exists between school-fellows, especially when there is congeniality of temper. Harry Sinclair was the younger son of a physician, who had formerly practised his profession in the city; but fortune having showered her favours upon him, soon after the birth of Harry, in the shape of a legacy from a distant relative in England, he relinquished his profession, and purchased a farm in the interior of the State, where he devoted himself to agricultural pursuits, and gathered around him the comforts and luxuries of life. Among the latter were some for which most people, unfortunately, care very little—a large library of choice books, and a collection of philosophical instruments, in the use of which Dr. Sinclair was exceedingly well skilled.

The doctor had five children—two sons and three daughters. For the education of the latter, he employed a governess at home—both he and Mrs. Sinclair agreeing in the opinion, that home education is the best for girls, at least during the earlier years of their studies. His sons, however, were sent to the best schools, and his eldest had nearly completed his course at ———— University.

A few days after the conversation recorded above, as Harry and his friend met at school, the former thrust into Herbert's hand an open letter, exclaiming joyously:

"There, Herbert, mamma has written to invite you to spend the vacation with me at my home, and sister Ally—Alice, my eldest sister, you know, Herbert—says in a postscript, 'I should be happy to see your friend and school-fellow, Master Russel, and hope you will prevail upon him to come home with you, as Mary and Fanny and myself are to have vacation, too—Miss Maurice wishing to pass the Christmas holidays with her friends. I am anticipating your return with great pleasure.'

"Now, Herbert," continued Harry, "let us take this letter and get your papa's consent at once, for you know school breaks up next week, and I am to start immediately after."

Herbert needed very little persuasion—he was only too happy, indeed, to consent to his school-fellow's proposition. At noon, therefore — for they were both too good boys to miss being present at the opening of the school—they went together to Herbert's home, and eagerly made their plans and wishes known to the good clergyman, whose consent was very soon obtained, as well as that of Herbert's excellent mamma. They had been well acquainted with Dr. Sinclair and his family in previous years, and a very strong mutual regard existed. So it was settled that Herbert should go home with his schoolmate; and neither of them could talk of any thing else for the brief interval which was to elapse before the close of the term.

I will not weary my readers with details of their anticipations—their preparations for the journey— the excellent counsels which Herbert received from his parents, or even with the journey itself, which was performed partly by railway, and partly in the family carriage of the Sinclairs, which was sent to meet our travellers at the nearest station to their residence. All these things I will pass over, and introduce the reader at once to Beechwood.

Externally it was a very pleasant place. The house, which was built of stone, was large, and had an exceedingly picturesque appearance with its steep Gothic roofs, twin gables, and a tower which rose at the extremity of the east wing of the building. This tower and a large part of the front of the house was nearly covered with ivy, the dark luxuriant foliage of which gave an appearance of age to the house far greater than that which justly belonged to it.

Immediately behind the house, and rising with a gentle slope, was a fine extent of woodland; in which the beech trees so greatly predominated that they gave their name to the domain. These woods, so beautiful in summer with their wealth of verdure, and so resplendent in the fall with the varied tints which the early frosts give to the leaves of the beech, until they seem to be dyed in the colours of the rainbow, were now, of course, all bare and brown. The grounds in every direction were tastefully laid out, and embellished with choice trees and shrubbery. The brilliant sward of the summer was not now to be seen, however, and the spacious garden in front of the hall wore no attractive dress. The broad gravelled carriage-road which swept circuitously through the garden was fringed upon both sides with a hedge of evergreen shrubbery, the still shining verdure of which, together with that of the ivy upon the house, and also of some fine laurels, greatly relieved the wintry aspect of the scene.

A closer approach to the dwelling brought into view, upon the west side, a handsome conservatory, in which was a multitude of rare and beautiful plants in full verdure and in gay bloom. A glimpse of this floral paradise helped very much, I think, to banish from Herbert's mind a feeling of regret which had just entered there in spite of his pleasure at having reached the home of his favourite companion —a regret that it was not summer instead of winter, that he might see Beechwood in all its glory.

He had not time to think more about it, or perhaps he would have recollected the matchless sports of the season, in the snow and upon the ice, and the charms of the winter fireside, and so felt glad, after all, that it was winter! He had not time to think of all this, for the carriage now stopped at the very door of the hall. A pair of bright and joyous faces appeared for an instant only at one of the parlour windows; and while Herbert was giving them the names he already knew so well, he and Harry had passed up the steps and were in the presence of those who, after all, had much more to do with the beauty and charm of Beechwood than the season, or the trees, or the flowers, or any other external thing.

Herbert's introduction to his new friends took place in the order in which I shall briefly describe it. Dr. Sinclair received him with tokens of the most affectionate regard. He was a tall and handsome man, with a very benevolent look, and easy, agreeable manners. He was about forty-five years of age, but did not seem so old. Mrs. Sinclair was several years younger than her husband, and her countenance was singularly handsome and charming, so that Herbert thought her, next to his own dear mother, the most winning person he had ever seen. Her face was lighted up with a sweet smile, as she bade her guest welcome, and her voice—which was gentle to every one—sounded like a familiar strain of music to the young boy's ear.

Alice Sinclair was just fourteen—and the very embodiment of grace and beauty. Her hair, which was very dark, hung in rich curls adown her neck, and the outline of her face was absolutely perfect. Her eye was bright to dazzling, and the colour on her exquisitely rounded cheek was as delicate as the flush of a young rose. She was not bashful, and when her mother spoke to her, holding Herbert kindly by the hand, and saying, " Alice, my daughter, this is your brother's playmate, Herbert Russel,—welcome him to Beechwood," she said sweetly, at the same time extending her hand,

" I am sure, mamma, I am pleased to see Master Russel, and hope he will be happy with us at Beechwood."

I suppose my little readers will be inclined to laugh at Herbert, if I tell them that he lost his heart at first sight to Alice, but I can't help it if they do, for I am obliged to tell them the truth, and, for my part, I don't at all wonder that he did.

Mary was only a year younger than Alice. She was almost as tall as her sister, but her childhood had been shadowed by a long and serious illness, which had so enfeebled her that she was far behind Alice in the development of her mind. She was, moreover, exceedingly reserved and even bashful in her manners, seeking generally to hide her pale face from the gaze of strangers. That face, however, was full of expression and even of beauty, particularly when lighted up with interest. She received Harry with evident delight, and when Herbert was introduced to her she extended her hand to him, and the soft but warm colour that overspread her face expressed, perhaps as well as words could do, that he was welcomed by her, also, to Beechwood.

I must not omit to mention little Fanny. She was a gentle blue-eyed child of nine summers—like her mother, as every one said—and she, too, put her hand in Herbert's, in token of welcome.

Had he been ever so timid he could not long have resisted the kindness which was manifested to him by every one, both in look and tone. Herbert was not shy, however. His manners were as gentle and as genial as his feelings, and these responded immediately to the tokens of regard which he received.

It was two o'clock when Harry and his friend reached Beechwood, and before dark Herbert was acquainted with every body there, from Dr. Sinclair to the old gardener, Jacob Fletcher, who had lived with the family ever since their removal from the city. With his young friends he had visited every object of interest—admired the noble watch-dog, praised the handsome pony and ridden on his back; played with Bob, Fanny's pet squirrel; thrown crumbs to the geese in the pond; raced with the tame deer that wore a collar embroidered by Alice; and, in short, had done a hundred boyish things, quite natural and innocent.

After tea was over, the whole party repaired to the library, which was so important a part of Beechwood

Hall that I must describe it very briefly. It was quite a spacious room, occupying that wing of the hall which was flanked by the tower. The extremity of the room was formed by the tower itself, which being hexagonal, with three of its sides projecting beyond the wing, afforded a charming recess. This was furnished with lounges on both sides of the central window, which opened like folding-doors upon a terraced lawn and the garden. The library was the handsomest room in the hall. It was fifteen feet high, and was lighted with deep windows upon the front side and in the tower. The opposite side was fitted up with handsome book-cases of oak-wood in the Gothic style. There were also similar cases between the three windows upon the front. A neat chandelier was suspended from the ceiling of the room, and bracket lamps were placed at the opposite corners of the recess. Heavy curtains of crimson damask draped the windows, and the recess could be secluded at pleasure by similar hangings.

The books, which constituted the chief excellence of this delightful place, had been selected with exceeding care and with admirable taste. While no department of English literature was entirely overlooked, works of history, biography, travels, *belles lettres*, and poetry, were the principal objects of favour. Nor were fiction and romance excluded from the library. Here, however, Dr. Sinclair had exercised great and becoming caution. He had given place to the delightful books of Miss Edgeworth and Mrs. Sherwood and Miss Bremer. The time-honoured fictions of Miss Porter were there also, although I must confess that the doctor's approval of these was somewhat influenced by his recollections of their charm to his own childhood. No such apology is needed for the works of that still unrivalled master of fiction, the admirable Sir Walter Scott. His novels, his miscellaneous works, and his poetry, so fascinating to the young, were all to be found in the library at Beechwood. There, too, our own Irving and Cooper and Simms had a welcome place, and the agreeable stories of James were prime favourites with the young people. Nor was Dickens excluded. His "Household Words" had insured his welcome to every happy and intelligent home; and he had won sympathy also, at Beechwood, by his matchless portrayals of character, his loving sympathies with the wronged, and his beautiful delineations of child-life and spirit, in his world-renowned fictions. These were the principal masters of fiction who were admitted at Beechwood. The introduction of new claimants for favour was sparing and judicious. Dr. Sinclair knew too well the rapid and insidious effect of moral poison upon the young mind, to run the risk of administering it to his children through negligence. When a new book contained healthful instruction, whether in the guise of fact or fiction, he admitted it to the companionship of his treasures in the library.

There were there, however, books which he did not consider it judicious for his children to read indiscriminately, and they were too well trained, and too dutiful, to indulge stealthily in reading which they knew their father did not approve for them. But for this confidence in them, he would have excluded many volumes of poetry and some prose works which claimed admission to his library, as parts of the great classic family of British standard literature. His selections from German, French, and Italian authors were far less numerous than the extent of his library would have led one to suppose. He did not overlook them altogether, but he preferred the tone of English to that of foreign literature.

The library was *well* supplied with periodicals, though here also judicious care and economy were practised. The current literature of Great Britain was represented in the American reprints of the leading reviews, and Blackwood's inimitable magazine. Of home literature, he contented himself with two or three leading newspapers, while the Lady's Book proved a welcome visitor to mamma's boudoir, and one or two juvenile magazines afforded delight to the young people. It is worthy of mention here, that a generous portion of the library was appropriated to the children, and they were denied no new book which had sufficient merit to entitle it to a place upon their shelves. The modern stories of Hawthorne and Mrs. Neal and Abbott were found side by side with the juvenile books of Mary Howitt, Mrs. Barbauld, and Maria Edgeworth.

In this pleasant library, and in the examination of its various attractions of books and prints, the time passed swiftly to our young friends, until nine o'clock, the hour for family worship, arrived.

Then, at the summons of a bell, the servants came into the library and took the places assigned to them. Dr. Sinclair read a portion of the sacred volume, after which he offered brief but fervent thanksgiving and prayer to our Heavenly Father—thanksgiving for past mercies, and prayer for a continuance of them. Herbert Russel had ever been accustomed to such devotional acts in his own Christian home, and he felt a glow of pleasure at his heart—for which, perhaps, he could have given no particular reason—when he found that he was still to enjoy the houschold worship he had been taught to regard of so much importance.

After prayers, the family party separated for the night, earlier than usual, in order that our young travellers might have the rest which Mrs. Sinclair insisted they must stand in need of.

It will hardly be supposed that Herbert went to sleep immediately after his head rested upon his pillow. He was gratified to be permitted to share the room of his friend, and they talked eagerly for at least an hour after they retired. When Harry at length fell asleep, Herbert continued wakeful from excitement; and although he closed his eyes, he saw over again the pleasant sights of the afternoon and evening. He looked forward, too, in his wakeful dreams, to the delight in store for him during his winter's vacation. He filled whole sheets of paper, in his active imagination, with glowing letters to his beloved parents—describing the beauty of Beechwood, and more particularly of his school-fellow's sister, the lovely Alice Sinclair.

It was while he was drawing her portrait that he actually fell asleep, and he did not tell Alice, the next day, that he dreamed that he was a famous artist, and that he was sought after by the most distinguished people in the land, to paint their portraits; but that every body was surprised to find that his female portraits were all alike—yet every sitter was satisfied, because the picture was so very beautiful.

CHAPTER II.

Getting up Late—Dr. Sinclair's Plan—Jack Frost's Exploits—The Ice-bottle—Crystallized Breath—Breakfast Conversation—Fanny's Experiment—Alice's Explanation—Heat and Cold—Frostburn.

THE morning after the arrival of the school-fellows at Beechwood was clear and frosty, and the temptation to lie in bed was too strong to be resisted by them; for they were not a little wearied with the travel and excitement of the previous day, notwithstanding their protestations of the night before that they did not feel the least bit tired.

It was, therefore, eight o'clock before the family was collected in the library for prayers, with which the day was commenced, as well as closed, in the happy home of Harry Sinclair. When the pleasant exercises of devotion were ended, and while the family was awaiting the summons to the breakfast-room—the younger members of it and their guest being eagerly engaged in planning amusements for the day, and indeed for days before them—Dr. Sinclair lifted up his eyes from the book he was reading, and addressed them as follows:

"Now, my children, I have something to suggest to you that may possibly contribute to your pleasure during the holidays—which I am anxious shall be as delightful as your most sanguine anticipations."

"What is it, papa?" said two or three eager voices in a breath.

"It is this," he replied: "I propose that we occupy a portion of every day in scientific amusements, which, I think, may be made as charming as they will be novel."

The young people had most of them some idea of what these amusements were, for their father had often gratified them by simple philosophical experiments, and they were therefore prepared to listen to the proposal with interest.

"I wish," continued Dr. Sinclair, "to make these amusements as natural as possible, and I think we may find most pleasure in converting the little incidents of life into lessons of wisdom. In other words, we may find philosophy in play, and science in the simplest events which happen to us. What say you, Herbert? What say you, Harry? And you, my daughters—are you pleased with my plan?"

Every one expressed delight with the suggestion; and little Fanny, springing from her chair to papa's side, exclaimed with child-like eagerness:

"When will you begin, papa?"

"At any time, Fanny—now, if you will give me a subject."

The little girl shook her head, till the bright curls fell over her rosy face, and made her quite a picture of beauty. She then ran laughing away to the window, in the tower, that looked out into the garden, and found the glass covered with a pure white crust, that sparkled very much, and presented a great variety of beautiful and fanciful shapes. She had seen this, however, so many times before, that, without thinking at all about it, she put her rosy little mouth against the cold glass, and, breathing warmly, melted away some of the frosty deposit. She then peeped through the clear glass, and rejoiced to see the earth bright with sunshine.

Her father, who had resumed his book, and happened to look up from it for a moment, observed her at the window, removing the coat of ice from the panes; and it immediately occurred to him that this would be a suitable incident with which to begin the very plan he had proposed. So he called Fanny; and the little girl, bounding gleefully to his side, he said to her:

"What is it, my little girl, that so completely covers the window-panes this morning?"

Little Fanny was puzzled what to answer; but presently, with a sweet little blush upon her cheeks, she said:

"I think it is Jack Frost, papa."

At this reply, Alice and Mary, and both the boys laughed heartily; and Dr. Sinclair joined them, but he immediately said:

"True, my little pet, it *is* Jack Frost; or, at all

events, it is all his doings; and I should like Alice to repeat the beautiful verses of Miss Hannah Gould, in which she describes the proceedings of the said Jack Frost. Can you not do so, my daughter?"

"Yes, sir," replied Alice, "I think I can;" and she immediately recited the following lines in a clear, sweet voice:

"He went to the windows of those who slept,
    And over each pane like a fairy crept;
Wherever he breathed, wherever he stept,
    By the light of the moon were seen
Most beautiful things. There were flowers and trees;
There were bevies of birds, and swarms of bees;
There were cities, thrones, temples, and towers—and these
    All pictured in silver sheen!"

"That," said Dr. Sinclair, "was quite unexceptionable conduct in Mr. Jack Frost; but, if I mistake not, Alice, Miss Gould attributes some mischief to him, which I hope he has not repeated here during the night."

"What was the mischief, Ally?" said her brother. "Do tell us."

Alice resumed her recitation

"But he did one thing that was hardly fair:
He went to the cupboard, and finding there
That all had forgotten for him to prepare—
    'Now just to set them a-thinking,

I'll bite this basket of fruit,' said he;
'This bloated pitcher I'll burst in three;
And the glass of water not left for me,
Shall tell them what I am drinking!'"

"No, that was hardly fair," said Harry, "I confess. I'll go and see if he has served us the same shabby trick;" and the young lad bounded out of the library. In a few moments he came running back, and in his hands he bore a lump of clear ice in the shape of a wine-bottle, with a cork frozen fast to the top of the neck.

"See!" he exclaimed, "Jack Frost has actually been at his mischievous tricks in the kitchen. I left a bottle full of water last night, just out of the kitchen-window where I was washing it. I put the cork in it, and forgot all about it; and now it is broken all to pieces, and this ice-bottle stood up in its place."

"This is certainly quite a singular coincidence," said Dr. Sinclair; "but if I had known that you had left the bottle out of doors, and full of water, I could have told you that you would find it changed into a bottle of ice this morning."

"But one thing at a time," he resumed. "Put the ice-bottle out of doors, Harry; it won't melt in an hour; and meanwhile I want to know, more particularly than Fanny has told us, what it *is* that we see upon the windows, on frosty mornings like this. Can *you* tell, Harry?"

"I thought it was frost, sir. Did you not say so?"

"I did; but what is it that is frozen?"

Harry was at fault; but Alice came to his help by asking—"Is it not our breath, papa, that settles on the cold glass, and freezes?"

"Precisely, my dear; it is the human breath—or rather the moisture which it holds—rendered visible by a very curious and beautiful process called crystallization. Would you all like to know something about this process?" he added, looking at the group now gathered about him.

Their eager response of "Yes, sir; oh! yes, indeed we should!" chimed in with the musical tones of the breakfast-bell, which rang out, at that moment, its welcome invitation to the hot rolls, the fresh eggs, and the piping buckwheat cakes, which graced the table that morning.

During the meal a lively conversation, on the subject of heat and cold, was kept up. Dr. Sinclair asked Harry why he poured his coffee into his saucer.

"To cool it, of course, papa," was his quick reply.

"But how does that cool it, my son?"

Harry was less ready with an answer to the latter question, and his father turned to Alice for a reply.

"I suppose it is cooled by being spread over a larger surface," she said after a moment's hesitation.

"Exactly, my daughter; the heat which the coffee contains is carried off more rapidly by the atmosphere—the particles of which, in contact with the hot liquid, abstract a portion of the heat, and then rise to be succeeded by cold particles which in turn become heated. In this way the heat of the coffee is rapidly diminished."

Here Mrs. Sinclair called the attention of the little inquirers by directing Fanny to put her finger upon the silver urn, in which the coffee was kept hot, by means of a spirit-lamp burning beneath it. The little girl placed her finger upon it, as her mamma directed, but instantly withdrew it with a slight exclamation.

"What is the matter, Fan?" said her papa.

"It burnt me, papa."

"Well now, Fanny," said her mamma, "put your finger upon the ivory handle of the faucet," pointing to it as she spoke.

The little girl obeyed with a slight degree of hesitation in her manner. She, however, did not immediately withdraw her hand, as she did when she touched the metallic part of the urn; and she looked up to her mamma with an expression of wonder that I think was shared by some of the others.

"There, Alice," said Mrs. Sinclair, "Fanny has illustrated a very important fact in relation to heat. Do you know what it is?'

"Thanks to Mrs. Marcet, mamma, I think I do. Is it not this: that some substances conduct heat much better than others? The silver is a good conductor, and lets the heat of the coffee pass through it freely. The ivory is a poor conductor, and so it is made use of instead of a silver handle."

Mrs. Sinclair's approving smile, and her father's spoken commendation, rewarded Alice well for her correct explanation of what puzzled Fanny; and greatly increased Herbert's admiration of his schoolfellow's lovely and intelligent sister.

"But Alice said just now," resumed Dr. Sinclair, "'that some substances conduct *heat* much better than others.' Suppose the urn were filled with iced water, instead of coffee, and Fanny were to put her finger upon the silver, as she did just now, would it burn her?"

"No, papa;" said Mary, venturing, in spite of her bashfulness, to answer so simple a question as that.

"And yet I think Fanny would start and draw her finger away very suddenly," continued he.

"Yes, papa, perhaps I would; but that would be because it would *freeze* my finger."

"Then the silver must be regarded as a good conductor of cold, as well as of heat. What say you, Alice?"

"So it would seem," she replied with some hesitancy.

"Did Mrs. Marcet teach you that, my daughter?"

"I do not clearly recollect, papa; but I think that it is wrong to say that either heat or cold is conducted."

"Why not heat, Alice?"

"Because," she replied, after a few moments' thoughtfulness, "heat and cold are two opposite conditions of bodies, and not substances themselves."

"Thank you, Alice," said her father. "I see you are well informed upon this interesting subject. I must, however, tell our young friend Herbert that you have studied chemistry and philosophy, both, with Miss Maurice—so that he need not be quite astonished out of his own thoughts, by your correct knowledge of what I presume he has never studied."

Alice blushed violently, and Herbert looked a little confused—effects which Dr. Sinclair did not intend to produce; so he hastened to relieve them both by saying:

"But if heat and cold are conditions merely, what is the cause of these conditions? Tell us that, my daughter, and then we shall be able to set the matter right before Fanny's sparkling eyes."

"The cause is a principle called *Caloric*," said Alice. "When there is more than a natural share of this principle in any thing, it is said to be hot; and when there is less than a natural share, it is said to be cold."

"Then," continued Dr. Sinclair, "it is the caloric which is conducted by the metallic urn—whether it be filled with hot coffee or with iced water—is it?"

"How can that be?" said Harry, always eager, and often jumping at wrong conclusions. "If the urn is filled with ice, there must be less—less—what did Ally call it?"

"Caloric, Harry."

"Yes, caloric—less caloric there than there ought to be; and how could the silver conduct any away to the hand?"

"Harry is in a sad dilemma, truly," said his father; "help him out, Herbert."

"I don't think I can, sir. I am in just the same fix myself."

"Then there's a pair of you—*par nobile fratrum*, as my friend, Mr. Oldbuckle, would say, if he were here."

"Who is Mr. Oldbuckle, papa?" said Harry. "As to his Latin, I can translate that myself— 'a noble pair of brothers.' That's you and I, Herbert!"

"You shall have the pleasure of making Mr. Oldbuckle's acquaintance at dinner-time, if you will contrive to get out of your dilemma by any means."

"Oh! who will help me?" said Harry, in mock tones of distress. "Can't you, my dear, darling sister, by the aid of Mrs. Marquette?"

"Mrs. Marcet," said Alice, laughing, "condescends to have compassion on you, Harry, and bids me tell you that when the urn is full of ice, the caloric does not go from the urn to the hand, but from the hand to the urn."

"Then the hand burns the urn—is that it?"

Alice did not seem quite ready to reply to this puzzling question.

"It would be so, if the urn could feel," said her father. "As it is, the caloric passes to the cold urn, and makes that warmer in the degree in which the hand becomes cold. Did you never hear of any body's being burned by frost?"

"No," said Harry, "that I'm sure I never did!"

"Oh! Dr. Sinclair," said Herbert, "I think I know what you mean. I knew a boy, in the city, who put his tongue against a brass door-knob, one very cold morning, and it blistered his tongue white, and the skin peeled off. The doctor dressed it just as he would have dressed a burn."

"It was a burn, Herbert—a frost-burn, to be sure, but as much a burn as if it had been made by his attempting to bite an inch off a red-hot poker—that difficult feat so often proposed in the game of forfeits."

The young people all laughed merrily, and Harry exclaimed:

"Well, that beats me."

"Yes," said his father; "let me play Mr. Oldbuckle's part once more, and say to you, as he would probably have done:

"'There are more things in heaven and earth, Horatio,
    Than are dreamt of in thy philosophy!'

But to clear up this philosophy of heat and cold a

little more," he resumed: "when the hand is burned by contact with heated metal, it is by receiving an excess of caloric; and when it is burned by contact with a piece of exceedingly cold metal, it is by suddenly losing a large quantity of caloric. Do you understand the subject, Harry?"

"I think I do, sir," he replied; "though it seems to me exceedingly queer that heat and cold should both burn alike!"

"You should not forget," said his father, "what Alice said just now—that heat and cold are only conditions, of which caloric is the cause. But this is quite too extensive a subject to be exhausted at the breakfast-table."

With this remark he rose, and all the party followed his example.

CHAPTER III.

The Microscope—Frost-work—Stars and Diamonds—A Fluid Globe—Why the Frost-Crystals Disappeared—The Ice-Bottle Arraigned—Its Defence—A Wonderful Exception—The Lead Tree—Affinity Illustrated.

FROM the breakfast-room our young philosophers proceeded to the library, reminding Dr. Sinclair of his proposal to explain to them the nature of the frozen breath upon the window-panes. He expressed his willingness to do so at once, and took, from a very neat mahogany box, a beautiful brass instrument, which, he told them, was a microscope, and asked Herbert if he knew the meaning of the word.

I rather think our young friend was a little proud as he replied, immediately, that he did. Herbert was a good scholar, and he had recently studied etymology—the science which teaches the origin of words. Without any difficulty, therefore, he replied to Dr. Sinclair's question:

"It means an instrument with which to see very small objects; and is from two Greek words—*mikros*, small; and *skopeo*, to see."

"Quite correct," said the Doctor. "And now, Harry, do you go and scrape from the window-panes some of the frost-work which we were talking about before breakfast, so that we may look at it through the microscope."

"Why, papa," said Harry, "it has nearly all disappeared while we were at breakfast!"

"True enough; so you must go up into one of the chambers where there is no fire to warm the room."

"Shall we see it through the mighty-scope, papa?" said Fanny.

"Not 'mighty-scope,' Fanny," said Alice, laughing merrily at her little sister's mistake; but her father immediately said:

"Fanny is not so far wrong after all, Alice; for it may well be called a '*mighty-scope*' when we consider what a vast and wonderful range of observation it affords us."

Harry now brought the frost which he had gathered from the windows of his own room; and his father, having adjusted the microscope upon a small table in the recess, which I have already described, took the crystals, and spread them out thinly upon a sheet of black glazed paper. This he placed beneath the magnifying lens of the instrument, and called upon the young people, one by one, to examine the minute particles which lay upon the paper.

"Oh!" exclaimed Alice, "how fairy-like they are! Stars and diamonds of all sizes, and glittering just like real gems! Is it possible, dear papa, that these are only particles of frost?"

"They are minute but perfect crystals of ice,"

replied Dr. Sinclair, as Mary succeeded Alice in their inspection. She, too, was delighted, and so far forgot her timidity as to ask her father if he had done nothing to them to make them so beautiful.

"Nothing, Mary, I assure you, but to magnify them."

Herbert and Harry both pronounced the sight exceedingly beautiful, and expressed their wonder that any thing so small could be of such perfect forms. Fanny, too, was delighted in her own way with what she saw through the "mighty-scope."

"Every flake of snow which falls," continued Dr. Sinclair, "is composed of scarcely perceptible crystals, each perfect in its structure as the beautiful gems of the mine, all which have been like these ice-crystals, in a fluid state at some period."

"What, papa," said Alice, "diamonds and rubies once in a fluid state!"

"Yes, my dear, the hardest flint and the most solid rock which exist, were both fluid once. Indeed, all the solid earth has cooled down, in the course of many ages, from a fiery mass of fluid."

The young people expressed their wonder, if not their incredulity, in their eyes; and Dr. Sinclair added:

"But I will not extend these lessons beyond such limits as you can easily comprehend. I was going to ask you if any of you would take another look at the fairy gems of the frost-king; but I see they have all disappeared—proving the words of the poet:

> 'The fairest things beneath the sun—
> The soonest pass away!'

"Shall I get some more, papa?" said Harry.

"No, my boy, it is not worth while; but perhaps you can tell me what caused them to disappear."

"Of course I can, sir. It was the *heat* of the room."

"True—as we are accustomed to speak; but not true, scientifically," said his father.

"It was the—the caloric, then?"

"Yes; the caloric of the air, being more abundant than that of the frost-crystals, entered into them, and raised their temperature to that of the room. Now, just the reverse of this took place when, last night, the moisture in the warm air of this room condensed first into water upon the cold glass—which took away so much caloric from the drops that they did not retain enough to remain in the fluid state, and so were changed into solid but minute crystals."

"I see, papa," said Alice; "and so the condition of bodies depends upon the amount of caloric they contain."

"Very well concluded, indeed, my daughter. And now, Harry, fetch the ice-bottle, and let us look at the wonder through the spectacles of science!"

Harry brought in the frozen contents of the

exploded bottle, and stood it in a plate upon the table, saying, with mock gravity:

"Prisoner at the bar, what have you to say in reply to the charge of breaking my bottle?"

"May it please your honour," said Dr. Sinclair, in behalf of the prisoner, "we have but a word to say. We plead guilty to the charge; but plead, in extenuation of our offence, that you confined us in such narrow bounds that when, by a law of our nature, we expanded from the loss of our natural share of caloric, there was not room within the glass walls for our increased bulk, and we were compelled to burst our prison bounds."

"Prisoner at the bar, you shall be acquitted forthwith," said the self-elected judge, "if you can show, by your attorney, how it is that you grow larger by freezing, instead of shrinking, as I should be apt to do."

"That, may it please your honour," replied the ice-bottle, by the mouth of Dr. Sinclair, instead of its own, "that is *the* exception to the law that bodies, changing from the fluid to the solid state, contract, and the only exception known. This exception is a wonderful instance of the wisdom of our Creator; for, if water were to contract in bulk by becoming solid, its density would increase, and it would be heavier when solid than when in the liquid state. The consequence of this would be, that the ice upon the top of a river or lake would sink by gravitation to the bottom; and thus, eventually, the whole lake or river would be converted into ice, and all the heat of summer would be insufficient to melt the solid mass. In this exception, therefore, to a law of nature, behold both the wisdom and the goodness of God."

The answer was considered sufficient. Mr. Bottle was therefore acquitted, and the character of Mr. Jack Frost declared to be clear as ice!

Doctor Sinclair now called the attention of the young people to a very curious and beautiful specimen of metallic crystallization. In a quart bottle of white glass, there was suspended, by a string from the stopper, a large and brilliant mass which had evidently grown in the bottle, as it was too large to go through the neck. It resembled a thick cluster of vine-foliage, with tendrils hanging down to the bottom of the vessel. When the children had admired it to their hearts' content, Dr. Sinclair described to them the process by which it had been produced, and I will repeat it here, because every little reader can easily perform the experiment for himself.

"I first filled this bottle," said Dr. Sinclair, "with pure water, and then poured into it a tea-spoonful of sugar of lead, which immediately mixed with the water and gave it the appearance of milk. I then tied to a string a piece of zinc, not too large to go through the neck of the bottle, and suspended it about half way down, forcing in the stopper so as to fasten the string. In a few hours, the milky fluid became almost clear, and the zinc was covered with thin shining crystals of lead, which multiplied until they half filled the bottle, as you see. Can any of you tell me where the lead crystals came from?"

Harry and Herbert shook their heads; but Alice modestly replied:

"From the sugar of lead—did they not, papa?"

"Yes, my child," replied her father, "the sugar of lead is a substance called by chemists, acetate of lead. It is a compound of lead and acetic acid; and all such compounds of metals with acids are called *salts*. The bond of union between substances thus united is called *affinity*, and is stronger in some instances than in others. Now, the lead and the acetic acid have not so strong a friendship for each other as zinc and acetic acid; hence, when I put the piece of zinc into the milky solution, the acid gave up the lead in the form of crystals (its native condition) and united with the zinc—forming a new salt, called acetate of zinc, which is dissolved in this limpid water. One thing more, and I shall release you from what is growing to be a lecture. I will take some of this liquid in the bottle, and spread it upon a slip of glass, which Harry may expose, for a few moments, to the fire, and meanwhile I will plant another lead-tree, that you may watch its growth during to-day and to-morrow."

When this was done, the Doctor took the slip of

glass which Harry had held to the fire, and directing the attention of the group to slight delicate crystals upon its surface—he subjected these to microscopic observation, when they appeared exceedingly beautiful—of regular form and perfectly transparent. These, the Doctor told them, were crystals of the acetate of zinc.

In this manner an hour sped away imperceptibly, and then Dr. Sinclair left them, to attend to his customary duties. Harry and Herbert sallied out for their proposed sport, while Alice and Mary and Fanny hastened to feed the squirrel and the rabbits, a duty always claiming their attention immediately after breakfast, but forgotten, that morning, in the interest of their first lesson in **natural philosophy**.

CHAPTER IV.

Mr. Oldbuckle—A Rock of Alum—Salts—A Disaster—Why the Dish Fell—Gravitation—Sir Isaac Newton's Discovery—Mutual Attraction of Bodies—An Experiment Proposed.

WHEN Dr. Sinclair returned at the usual dinner hour, he was accompanied by a very remarkable personage, of whom mention has been made in a previous chapter. His eccentricities and his excellencies were both so great, however, as to entitle him to a more particular introduction to the regard of the reader.

Mr. Oldbuckle was an English gentleman who had recently emigrated to this country, with his two sons and their families. Many years a widower, he was unwilling to be left behind when his only children resolved to leave their native land, for homes in the New World. He did not oppose their inclinations, for he was himself attracted by the accounts which he had read of the prosperity of the States, and of the admirable opportunities they afforded to young men for attaining wealth and distinction. He was quite willing to observe, for himself, an instance of national progress hitherto unexampled in the history of the world. The grand experiment of popular government which was so successfully commenced

upon our western shores interested him deeply.
Not that he was a republican in sentiment. On the
contrary, he was a warm and earnest admirer of the
English constitution and system, and passed at home
for a thorough tory. He was, however, a man of
comprehensive views. He possessed an enlightened
and iberal judgment, and he was eager to acquire information upon any and all subjects of great moment.

He had accordingly accompanied his sons to the
United States, and settled with the younger upon a
pretty farm about two miles from Beechwood. The
elder son had chosen the city, and was engaged in
extensive commercial operations.

Mr. Oldbuckle was nearly sixty years of age; but
his figure, though spare, was quite erect and elastic,
and he preserved much of the vigour of manhood.
He was a gentleman of the old school; and when
Dr. Sinclair introduced him to Harry and Herbert—
the only ones at Beechwood not already acquainted
with him—our young friends were so much surprised
by his odd appearance, that they almost forgot to
return his very friendly greeting.

He was dressed in the manner peculiar to a past
generation. His small clothes were tied at the knees
with black ribands, and below them he wore thick-
ribbed stockings of black worsted. In his shoes were
broad silver buckles, highly polished. His entire
dress was of black, which made more conspicuous a
white bushy wig that covered his head; and when

that was surmounted by a low-crowned hat, with a very wide brim, the worthy old gentleman did—as Herbert could not help whispering to Harry—" cut a queer figure!"

Mr. Oldbuckle had a very benevolent face, however; and—what told quite as well with young people—a very pleasant voice. As he was fond of talking, and related most amusing anecdotes, he was quite a favourite with the little folks of Beechwood, all of whom welcomed his arrival on this occasion with a warmth of manner quite agreeable to his feelings.

At the dinner-table, Dr. Sinclair informed his guest of the plan adopted for the amusement and instruction of the young people.

"It is a capital plan, indeed," said the worthy old gentleman, "and I am pleased to hear that my little friends show so much interest in it. You are entitled, my dear sir, to great praise for so very delightful a method of instructing your children. This is realizing the poet's idea of finding

> 'Tongues in the trees, books in the running brooks,
> Sermons in stones, and good in every thing.'

"It is a thousand times better," he continued, "than to be indulging in mere frivolous and noisy sports, though I do not object, my dear sir, to hearty play. Oh! no; I approve most cordially the words of Dr. Watts.

'In books, or work, or healthful play,
Let my first years be past;
That I may give for every day
Some good account at last.'

The Doctor was not a little gratified by the warm approbation of his excellent friend, and immediately said:

"I think our young philosophers play quite as merrily after their experiments, as if they had not been learning useful lessons. What do you think about it, Herbert?"

"Oh! sir," he replied with much eagerness, "I was never more happy in my life than I have been since I came to Beechwood, and I think your plan is perfectly delightful."

"Well, Master Russel," said Mr. Oldbuckle, now addressing him for the first time since his introduction, "so you and Harry Sinclair are such very good and dear friends, that you could not agree to be separated even for the short time of vacation?"

Herbert blushed and said:

"Harry and I have been fast friends ever since we have been to school together."

"Well, my dear boys," added Mr. Oldbuckle, "I hope you will be friends all your lives, and that both of you will live to become useful and distinguished men."

Mr. Oldbuckle had a very happy way of putting every one around him quite at ease in his company.

He was sure to find some method of securing the confidence and regard of every body. He overlooked no one, and adapted his conversation with great tact to the position and capacity of all. He now inquired of Alice what subjects they had studied in the very pleasant manner her father had described, and she told him of the experiments with the window-frost, and also of the further illustrations which they had seen of the beautiful process of crystallization.

"Your experiments in crystallization, Alice," said Mr. Oldbuckle, "remind me of the magnificent specimens of that process which I saw at the Great Exhibition in London."

"Oh! Mr. Oldbuckle," said Herbert, "were you at the Exhibition?"

"Indeed I was, my young friend, and I saw enough there to keep me busy thinking and wondering all the rest of my life, even though I should live to be 'fourscore years.'"

"What were the specimens you saw, Mr. Oldbuckle?" said Alice.

"The most remarkable one was a huge column of alum, which must have been twelve or fifteen feet high. It was twenty feet in circumference, and large sections were cut out of it to allow visitors to look inside and see the beautiful crystals of the salt, many of which were six inches long."

"Did you say 'crystals of the salt,' sir? I thought

it was a mass of alum you were speaking of," said Harry.

"So it was, Harry—alum and salt both—for alum is a salt, of which commodity, indeed, there are a great many varieties. In chemistry, every compound of an acid with a base is a *salt*. It is not every salt that has a peculiar pungent taste, for some kinds have no taste at all. Some can not be dissolved in water."

Harry was surprised to hear of any other salt than that he was accustomed to use upon his food, though he was reminded by Alice that he knew of smelling salts.

"And of *Epsom* salts, too," said Mrs. Sinclair, laughing at the wry face which Harry put on at the bare mention of them.

"But," said Alice, "how did they obtain so large a mass of alum?"

"I will tell you," said Mr. Oldbuckle, "as briefly as I can. Alum is a double salt; that is, it is sulphuric acid united to two bases—alumina and potash. These were mixed together in water, in sufficient quantity to fill a cylinder whose interior diameter was just the same as the diameter of the mass of alum. In this cylinder the liquid mass crystallized by evaporation—that is, the water passed off in the form of vapour, and the alum remained in solid and shining crystals—much like quartz. The mass was then removed from the cylinder, and the sections sawed out of its sides."

This account of the great alum rock at the London Crystal Palace interested the young people very much; and, indeed, the servant who was waiting on the table, was listening to it rather too attentively for his duties, for he suffered a dish, which he was removing to a side-table, to slip through his fingers to the floor. After the momentary confusion which was occasioned by the accident had ceased, Dr. Sinclair said:

"Here, now, is one of the incidents which we must seize and press into our service. Even accidents may be made to minister to our improvement. Can you tell me, Harry, why the dish fell when it slipped from Mark's fingers?"

"Because it was heavy, I suppose, sir," said Harry with the air of one who has settled a question.

"But if it had been light, it would still have fallen; so that does not explain it, although the observation is true in itself." Then, turning to Alice, he said:

"Have you not learned something about gravitation, my daughter?"

"Yes, papa," replied Alice, "and now I can perceive that it must be the power of gravitation which carried the dish to the floor."

"Herbert, my young friend," said Mr. Oldbuckle,

"can you tell me who it was that discovered this power of which Alice speaks?"

"No, sir," Herbert modestly replied.

"It was Sir Isaac Newton," said Mr. Oldbuckle; "and the circumstances of its discovery were very singular. That distinguished philosopher was lying under an apple-tree, and, observing an apple fall to the ground by his side, he was led to reflect upon the cause; and he came, after much pondering, to the conclusion, that the apple fell to the earth because the earth attracted it."

"Does not the earth attract all bodies?" said Alice.

"Yes," replied her father; "and at the same time they attract the earth; for gravity, or gravitation, is a reciprocal power, and belongs to every material substance in the universe."

"But," said Harry, "I do not understand that. The earth certainly did not rise to meet the apple of the great philosopher, or the unfortunate dish which slipped out of Mark's fingers."

"Not too fast, my son; you must reflect that the volume, or bulk, of the earth is millions of times larger than that of the substances upon its surface; and therefore its attraction is vastly greater than theirs, so that they move towards the earth so much faster than the earth moves towards them, that the motion of the latter is quite imperceptible. The earth attracts the sun, but the attraction of the sun for the earth is so very much greater, that the earth moves swiftly towards the sun, and the latter does not seem to move at all towards the earth, while in fact it does."

"I can understand that, papa," said Alice, "and I suppose that when an apple or a stone falls towards the earth, it must move faster and faster as it gets nearer to the surface."

"Excellent, my bird," said Mr. Oldbuckle, "you are really a philosopher, Alice, and have not studied in vain, I see."

Mr. Oldbuckle frequently called Alice his bird, because she was in the habit of singing for him, and her voice was peculiarly sweet and bird-like. She blushed very deeply at her old friend's approbation, and he continued, addressing Dr. Sinclair:

"That remark of Alice's suggests to me a very pleasing experiment, and, at the same time, a delightful excursion for this fine afternoon. You know the deep well at the village? It will illustrate our conversation, and give the young people a correct notion of the velocity of falling bodies, to measure its depth by means of a pebble."

"How can we do that?" said Harry, incredulously.

"That you will soon find out by means of your eyes. 'Seeing is believing,' you know the old adage, Harry."

Herbert and Alice expressed their interest in the

proposal, while Mary and Fanny looked theirs with their eyes.

Mrs. Sinclair also kindly yielded to their eager request that she would make one of the party.

"It will, indeed, increase the interest of this beautiful and unexpected lesson in philosophy," said Dr. Sinclair, as he rose to leave the table; "and we will therefore proceed to the well as soon as we can get ready."

CHAPTER V.

The Walk to the Well—The Yellow Leaf—Gravitation Resisted—The Guinea and Feather Experiment—Velocity of Falling Bodies—A Rule—The Deep Well—The Pebble thrown in—The Result—Preparation for the Sabbath—How the Day was Spent.

IT was somewhat more than a mile from Beechwood to a pretty village containing a few neat-looking houses. There was one house, however, which far exceeded all the others in size and importance. It stood on the hill at the entrance of the hamlet, and appeared to be unoccupied at the time of which we write. This was so nearly the case, that its only inmate was an old woman, who was employed by the owner to take care of the house, while the family was absent in Europe. Towards this our party directed its course, and the conversation upon falling bodies was naturally resumed.

"See, papa," said Harry, as a yellow leaf fluttered from a tree near them, and whirled in the air without falling at once to the ground, "all bodies do not seem to obey the power of gravitation."

"Ah, my boy, appearances are often deceitful, and this is one of the cases. The leaf reaches the ground at last."

"Yes," said Mary, "and here it is;" and she

picked up the yellow leaf, which the wind had wafted to her feet.

Harry was defeated, and he remained silent; but Alice came to his help, exclaiming

"Well, surely, Mr. Oldbuckle, gravitation does not act upon all bodies equally, since some fall faster than others."

"Right and wrong, both, my bird," replied the kind old gentleman. "Had an apple started from the branch with the leaf, the former would have reached the ground first—and yet the force of gravity is always equal, and a leaf gravitates to the earth as fast as an apple."

"True," said Dr. Sinclair to the puzzled look of his daughter, "and I think you can suggest the reason why the leaf falls slower than the apple, if you will reflect a moment."

Alice did not immediately reply, and Herbert modestly inquired if it was not owing to the force of the wind.

"The air, which, when put in motion, is called the wind, is indeed the cause of this difference," said Dr. Sinclair. "The air opposes gravity, and its resistance is proportioned to the amount of surface in a falling body. If you drop a bullet weighing one ounce and a sheet of tin-foil of the same weight, the air will resist and delay the fall of the latter on account of the greater surface it presents to its resistance."

"Would they both fall together, sir, if there was no air to resist them?"

"Certainly, Herbert, and I am sure Alice can confirm what I say."

Herbert turned to his companion, and she replied:

"Oh! I recollect, papa, your experiment with the tall glass cylinder. You put a guinea and a feather on a little platform at the top of the cylinder, and exhausted the air that was in it. Then you made the guinea and feather drop, and I could not discern any difference at all in the time each one occupied in falling."

"Correctly stated, my daughter, and I am glad you remember it so well. It is exactly what I was going to tell you, to explain the fluttering of the leaf, while the apple falls directly to the ground. Do you all understand it?"

Even little Fanny looked wise, as the others replied in the affirmative to Dr. Sinclair's question.

"We have seen, then, that all bodies are acted upon equally by gravitation. Can you tell me, Alice, how far a pebble, or any solid body, falls in the first second?"

"Sixteen feet, sir, Mrs. Marcet teaches me."

"That is right; and, of course, sixteen more in the next—"

"Oh! no, papa," she said eagerly, "velocity increases every second!"

"I acknowledge my error," replied her father:

"and now I will ask for the rate at which the velocity increases."

No one seemed quite ready with an answer until Mr. Oldbuckle volunteered to give one, and said:

"The spaces described by a falling body increase as the squares of the time increase; but," he added, "lest this definition should puzzle my little friends, I will explain it more simply. The square of a number is the product of that number multiplied by itself, as 2 multiplied by 2 gives 4, the square of 2. Now, then, let us suppose that we find a pebble four seconds in reaching the bottom of a well, we must first find the square of the time. What is that, my bird?"

"Sixteen seconds, sir."

"To find the space through which the pebble falls, we must multiply the space of the first second, which is sixteen feet, by the square of the time, which is sixteen seconds. What is the product?"

"Two hundred and fifty-six feet, sir," said Herbert.

"That's exactly right, but I doubt if our well will prove as deep as that. We shall see, however."

By this time the party had reached the old well in the park, before the dwelling we have already spoken of. The old housekeeper had readily granted their request to visit it, and even put on her bonnet and shawl to go with them. The well was covered with an antique pentice, and was built up of solid masonry

It was very deep to the eye, and Fanny looked in somewhat timidly. To her mother's question if she would like to go down in the bucket, she bravely replied:

"I will go with you, dear mamma!"

Dr. Sinclair now directed Harry to find a pebble, and Mr. Oldbuckle took out his watch to count the time. The whole party pressed eagerly around the well as Herbert prepared to drop the pebble, and to watch for the ripple it would make on the surface of the water.

"Now," said Mr. Oldbuckle, and he counted, "one, two, three."

"There," said Herbert, "it touched the water."

"Three seconds—now who will first tell the depth?" said Mr. Oldbuckle.

"One hundred and forty-four feet," said two or three voices in unison, and a merry laugh ensued.

"Very good," said Dr. Sinclair; "that is nine times sixteen."

Mr. Oldbuckle praised the young philosophers very much for their readiness, and promised frequently to take part in their "philosophical pastime," as he termed it, sorely to Fanny's confusion, for she did not at all comprehend his words. He then bade the party good-bye, proposing to reach his own home by a short cut from the old well. Dr. Sinclair urged him to return with them, but he declined the invitation. It was quite dusk when the family arrived at

Beechwood with good appetites for tea, which was only waiting their return to be served.

Saturday night at Beechwood was always devoted to preparation for the duties of the next day. Dr. Sinclair made it a point to interest his children in the study of the Bible, by regular Sunday morning lessons, which preceded the hour for the customary visit to the sanctuary in the adjacent village. In these lessons, which were chiefly drawn from the narrative portions of the Old and New Testaments, it was his aim to delight as well as to instruct his children, and he encouraged them to seek from him, and from other sources, all such information as would serve, in any way, to illustrate and improve the subject of study. It is not to be wondered at, therefore, that the young people felt this exercise to be a privilege rather than a task; and when Alice reminded Harry, after tea, of the manner in which he used to spend Saturday evening, and asked him if he did not wish to renew his Bible lessons, he said, with eagerness:

"If Herbert wishes to do so, I shall be very glad to unite with you, Alice."

Herbert needed no persuasion. He was a faithful Bible-class scholar at home, and he therefore cheerfully seated himself with his young friends around the great table, upon which Alice had laid Bibles, question-books, and a map of Palestine. The lesson for the next day was "The Flight into Egypt," and the young students spent some moments in discussing the merits of a picture—a fine steel engraving—representing that event in the life of our Saviour.

By the time the lesson was learned, the clock struck the hour for family worship. Mrs. Sinclair took her seat at the piano, and played an accompaniment, while all united in singing the well-known hymn—

> "Safely through another week
> God has brought us on our way;
> Let us now a blessing seek,
> For the coming Sabbath day—
> Day of all the week the best—
> Emblem of eternal rest."

Of the manner in which the next day was spent by the family at Beechwood, I am happy to say, with truth, that it was worthy of the Christian character professed by Dr. Sinclair and his excellent wife. There was a visible difference between it and the other days of the week, not only in the morning worship, at the village—whither nearly all of them went, in the carriage—but in all the deportment of the household—which, without being sanctimonious, was subdued and reverent. Loud talking, laughter, light reading and the ordinary amusements of the week, were not indulged in upon that day. The morning was fully occupied with the Bible lesson and the public services of God's house. In the afternoon, Dr. Sinclair read aloud from some instructive, religious book, and the evening was pleasantly occupied with sacred music. This latter service was regarded as both a duty and a delight, and there was skill enough in the home-circle to render the employment a source of great pleasure to Herbert, although he was not able to take part in it.

When Dr. Sinclair offered "the evening sacrifice," he devoutly thanked God "for the gift of singing, by which our praises are both sweetly prompted and expressed here below, and by which we shall express more glorious praises in the courts of the New Jerusalem."

It was in this manner and with this spirit, that the Lord's day was passed at Beechwood, and the young people did not complain that it was tedious and irksome.

CHAPTER VI.

A Surprise—William Sinclair—His Welcome—Mary—A Mother's Joy—Table-Talk—Evening Amusement—Music—A Charade-Play Proposed.

ONE of the arguments which Harry Sinclair employed, when urging Herbert to go with him to Beechwood, was that "brother Willie would be home at Christmas." William Sinclair was in his eighteenth year, and had been three years at college. His return for the Christmas holidays had been counted on by all the family, but he was not expected until Christmas Eve, and it wanted yet two full days to that time.

It was, therefore, with no small degree of surprise that, when the family entered the sitting room, upon their return from a pleasant walk on Monday afternoon, they saw little Fanny suddenly lifted off her feet, and folded in the arms of "brother Willie." The little girl herself was at first half frightened, but her unuttered exclamation of alarm was changed, in time, into one of delight, as she threw her arms about her brother's neck, and said, very eagerly:

"Brother Willie's come! Oh! I'm so happy—so very happy!"

Harry was scarcely less eager in his expressions of

delight at seeing his elder brother. Alice and Mary both repaid his affectionate caresses with looks and words of love, while the parents of the youth received him with mingled pride and pleasure. Herbert's eyes involuntarily filled with bright tears as he saw the fond mother rest her head upon the shoulder of her first-born, and heard her low, sweet words of welcome to him. He was thinking of his own mother's tenderness, and how fond her greeting would be when he went back to his own happy home, which even the rare charms of Beechwood did not long keep out of his thoughts, and *never* might exclude from his love.

"Well, William," said his father, after the salutations were over, "you have stolen a march upon us. What fortunate event has brought you home so soon?"

"The kind permission of the President, dear father," replied his son, "who asked me, yesterday, in what way he should testify his approbation of my conduct during the term. I replied that I should dearly like to take you all by surprise, by returning home to-day, instead of waiting until Wednesday; and, although I little expected that he would grant my wish, he immediately said with a smile—'Ah! William, I used to love to surprise them all at home, and you shall have the coveted opportunity.' It was but a brief task to get ready for my journey, and I left R—— this morning, with the dawn. The sequel of the story you know."

"But how did you get from the railway station to Beechwood?" said his mother.

"I walked," he replied; "it was a pleasant walk, too, dear mother, for I was occupied all the while with thoughts of the great surprise I should give you all. I believe I could have walked twice the distance without feeling at all fatigued at the time."

"I guess it would have tired you *some* to have walked sixteen, instead of eight miles," said Harry. "Now, *I* didn't surprise them by getting home two days before my time; but then, you see, I had a carriage to come those eight miles in."

"Ah! brother Willie," said Alice, as he threw his arm affectionately about her, "this is not the first time you have taken us unawares, and hereafter I shall *expect* you before the day you appoint for returning."

"Am I the less welcome, Ally, that I come unexpectedly?"

"Suppose I should say yes, Willie; you know you wouldn't believe me; so, I may as well claim to be perfectly happy, even as Fan seems to be."

"And you, Mary dear," said William, turning to the still half invalid sister, whose pale cheek was positively flushed with the delight she felt, "are you perfectly happy to have brother Willie back?"

"Perfectly," said the young girl, with an earnest tone; for she loved her eldest brother with a fondness which no one had excited in her gentle heart, save only her mother. William had always petted her, and manifested the warmest sympathy for her. He had read stories to her by the hour, as she used to lie upon her low couch, when too feeble to sit up for several months. It was William who carried her up and down stairs, when she grew enough better to be removed. It was he who half led and half carried her into the garden, in the sweet flush of summer time, and strove in every way to interest and amuse her. A rare and beautiful tenderness had grown up in his heart for her, and she repaid it with the purest affection of her young and strong heart. William, therefore, did not doubt that Mary's whole soul was in the single word with which she replied to his question.

Herbert was listening and looking on with deep attention. He had not succeeded in drawing many words out of Mary, and he was now a little surprised to see her usually quiet nature evidently aroused into a great emotion. She became in a moment an object of more interest to him, and he felt, perhaps, a little self-reproach that he should have thought her so uninteresting before. He had yet to learn that the hearts of young and old alike, are often sealed caskets which can only be unlocked by a spell!

William Sinclair has been left too long without an introduction to the reader. He was rather tall of his age, and withal somewhat slender. His countenance was extremely frank and pleasing, with strongly marked features. His hair was thick, and clustered in rich curls over his brow. His eyes were blue, and full of the alternating lights of tenderness and intelligence. His voice was musical, and his utterance quick but distinct. Altogether, he made a most favourable impression upon Herbert Russel, who was, by this time, quite prepared to take his part in the family admiration and love of " our eldest."

In the brief interval which remained before the hour for tea, William went out to look at the familiar objects he had left behind him six months ago, and to shake hands with Jacob Fletcher and his son Mark. The old gardener was very fond of William, and when he took the warmly-extended hand of the young man, there came a sudden moisture into his old eyes, and there was a perceptible tremour in his tones as he said:

"I thank God, Mr. William, that you have come back."

Herbert was delighted to see that William's interest in the pony, the pet deer, and the rabbits was not a bit less than that he, himself, had felt in them, as perfect novelties; and he thought how much more delighted he should be to see his own favourite dog, when he returned, than he had ever been before.

Mrs. Sinclair allowed her maternal delight in her first-born, to manifest itself in various ways. Even the tea-table seemed to testify her fresh-awakened joy, for its wonted profusion was surpassed upon this occasion; and delicacies were multiplied with a bounty which seemed to recognize this as the crowning opportunity for their bestowal.

The conversation at the table turned upon William's progress at college, and the chief incidents in his last term's experience there. His father listened, with great interest, to his account of his studies and exercises. Besides his early liberation from college duties, he had brought from the President of the college, a letter in further token of his excellent deportment and scholarship. He had returned laden with honours, to a home and to hearts, that would now overlay them with the brighter and purer gold of unselfish love. There was pleasure in every eye that beamed, and delight in every bosom that beat around the pleasant tea-table that evening.

"I am glad you have been studying natural philosophy, during the past term, William," said his father.

"Why so, sir?"

"Because we have all turned philosophers, at Beechwood—Alice, and Harry, and Herbert, and even Mary and little Fan, are all experimental philosophers."

"How is this, Alice?" said her brother.

"Oh!" she replied gaily, "we have charming times, brother Willie, in seeking instruction from our sports, and from every thing that happens."

"If you do that," said her brother, "you are philosophers, indeed. But explain to me exactly what you mean."

"Papa will tell you, as he is our president," was Alice's reply.

Dr. Sinclair informed his son of the plan he had suggested for making the amusements of the young people minister to their instruction. William Sinclair entered with great eagerness into the plan, and promised that he would do all in his power to add to the common stock of pleasure during his visit, which was to last until New Year's, and it lacked, now, two days of Christmas.

"Brother Willie," said Alice, "I hope you will like Mr. Oldbuckle as much as I do."

"Who is Mr. Oldbuckle, and how much do you like him, Ally?" was her brother's laughing reply.

"Oh! I forgot that we had not told you about him. Well, then, he is a neighbour of ours, recently from England; and he is such a delightful old gentleman, you can't think. He looks very queer, but he is very kind-hearted, and takes as much interest in all our amusements as we do. I like him very, very much, and you must like him too."

"I think it likely I shall, if all you say of him is true. When shall I have the pleasure of seeing him?"

"To-morrow; he comes almost every afternoon to have a chat with papa, who thinks a great deal of him."

Dr. Sinclair acknowledged the truth of his daughter's testimony, and gave William some further information about their agreeable friend.

"What shall we do to-night?" said Harry, as the family adjourned from the dining-room to the library.

"You shall have the ordering of the 'exercises,' to-night, brother Willie, in honour of your return," said Alice, laughing.

"Well," said her brother, "if the rest are agreed with Alice, I will accept the appointment of master of ceremonies."

"All agreed, I know, without counting noses," said Harry.

"First, then," said the newly-elected master of ceremonies, "we will have music on the piano-forte, by Miss Alice Sinclair."

"Now, brother Willie," said Alice, laughing, "that is a poor return for the honour I had conferred upon you."

"How so, sister mine? have I, or have I not a right to gratify my own wishes, in ordering the 'exercises' of the evening? If yea, then do I declare that it will afford me real pleasure to listen to the proposed musical inauguration."

"If my poor performance can give you the least pleasure, dear brother," replied Alice, "I will play without a word of apology."

"Spoken like my own Alice," he returned, ' who I hope will never hesitate to play, when she is asked in sincerity to do so."

Alice went immediately to the instrument, which

her brother opened for her, and played such pieces as were called for by him, if she knew them well enough to play without mistakes. Her musical education had not been severe, but still, she had been well taught, and had formed a very correct and spirited style. Her manner at the instrument was self-possessed and quiet, and her fingering full of grace. Her brother complimented her highly upon her progress in the instrumental part of music, and then challenged her to a specimen of her skill in vocal music. Alice was a good singer; to a really sweet voice of moderate compass, she added a careful articulation of her words, a due regard to emphasis, and a nice taste in the adaptation of her voice to the sentiment of the words she sung. All these excellencies were due, in part, to the careful training she had received from Miss Maurice; but even that would have been fruitless, had not Alice possessed both the power and the disposition to excel in every study which she pursued.

After Alice had gratified her brother, and our young friend Herbert no less, by her performances at the piano-forte, the former turned to his mother, who was very quietly employed in embroidering a little cap for the baby, and said:

"I must call upon you, my dear mother, to aid me in the discharge of the duty which I shall impose upon myself, as my contribution to the evening's amusement."

"I hope it is nothing very formidable that you expect of me, William," she replied, laughingly. "Is it to sing for you?"

"Precisely, dear mother, that will be a *part* of your task, and one for which I know you to be eminently qualified; but there is more than that for you to do. I have thought of a capital charade which I wish to act, and I know you used to be very clever at such things."

"I am very much obliged to you, William, for your double compliment to my singing and acting talents; but I am afraid that, whatever I may have been in both these parts, I shall be of little assistance to you now, in either."

"Oh! never fear, dear mother, I am satisfied that you will be all I wish you to be."

"Your confidence, my boy, shall be my talisman. Command me as you will."

"Well, then, I announce for the second and closing part of the evening's entertainment, a charade-play, in three acts!"

"Oh! a play! that will be delightful," said Alice.

"A *real* play, Ally," said her brother.

"One," added Dr. Sinclair, "which we may all witness with pleasure."

"And one in which you, dear sir," said William, addressing his father, "must oblige us by consenting to be an actor. I shall not assign to you a very laborious part."

"I shall willingly do all I can, Mr. Manager," replied his father, with a smile.

The preparations for the play were immediately commenced with great eagerness, while Harry and his young friend listened to Alice's account of some charades which had been performed at Beechwood by Dr. Sinclair, Miss Maurice, and a young lady who had visited them during the last summer.

CHAPTER VII.

The Charade in Three Acts—Mew—Sick—Music—Old Hundred.

THE work of preparation was not a tedious one. In fifteen minutes the actors were all ready, and William Sinclair thus addressed the audience, which was composed of the two school-fellows and the three girls:

"Young ladies and gentlemen, you must guess, for yourselves, the word which we have chosen for our charade, from the representation we shall give you of its parts. It is a word of two syllables, to each of which we devote an act, and a third to the complete word, which if you fail to guess, we shall be at liberty to consider you very dull of comprehension."

"May we not, in that case, have the privilege of supposing that you are very bad actors?" inquired Alice, with a merry laugh lurking in the depths of her dark eyes.

"Oh! certainly," said her brother, "you can think what you please, as this is a free country, they tell us; but then you know, my sharp little sister, that your *thinking* us bad actors won't *make* us so!"

"I hope not, indeed," she retorted; "and if our

thinking you *good* ones *will* make you so, you will be really wonderful!"

"But," said Harry, "are we to ask no questions about it?"

"Not a question, my boy."

"Please then to be very clear in your representations."

"We will try," said the obliging manager; "and now suppose the curtain to rise for Act the first."

William Sinclair now took his hat and cane and approached his mother, who had entered the room, arrayed in a pretty bonnet and a light mantilla, as if for a walk. She was to act the part of a young lady, and did not appear altogether out of character in the costume she had put on.

"Have I the pleasure of finding you ready, Miss Rosamond?" said William, bowing gracefully.

"I am quite ready, Mr. Sinclair," she replied.

"And where shall we walk this charming afternoon, my dear Miss Rosamond?"

"Oh! I have no choice; to the village, or to the chapel, or the grove, whichever you please."

"Well, to the latter then, with your favour," replied the gentleman.

"Oh! stay," said Miss Rosamond as she rose to set out, "I have forgotten my vinaigrette," and she took from the what-not a delicate little bottle of cut glass, with a gold chain attached.

They now walked about the room, discoursing as

they went, of the scenes which were supposed to surround them.

"How charming is nature!" said the lady. "How exquisite her sights which refresh the eye, and her sounds which delight the ear! I love all natural sounds—the singing of birds—the lowing of cattle—the bay of the hounds—the chirp of the squirrel—the hum of the bee—"

Here she started with a sudden scream, and seized the arm of her companion with convulsive energy.

"My dear Miss Rosamond, what ails you? Are you ill?" he asked with tones of alarm.

Miss Rosamond screamed again, in concert with the piteous wail of a cat which was now heard, and replied in great trepidation—

"Oh! no—yes—oh!—the cat!—oh the horrid thing!"

"A cat! my dear Miss Rosamond—the voice of a cat alarm you! I thought you admired all natural voices," said her companion with a slight tone of irony.

"Oh! dear!" she exclaimed, as again the crying of the cat was distinctly heard—and so loudly repeated, that all the audience discovered that this was Dr. Sinclair's part of the performance. Alice looked at Herbert, who had been previously looking at her, and their eyes met with a very puzzled look, which seemed to say, "What a very funny scene!" Harry even whispered to Herbert that he thought the word must be *cat*astrophe! But they turned again to the actors.

William Sinclair was recommending the vinaigrette to his fair friend, and after using it she was a little recovered from her alarm, but begged him to drive away the cat, which he proceeded to do with mock gravity, exclaiming to Dr. Sinclair,

"S-shue, cat!—s-shue, pussy!"

The cat departed with a prolonged and melancholy wail, which so increased the alarm of Miss Rosamond that she declared herself incapable of continuing her walk, and consequently the pair returned home, which they were supposed to do by retiring from the library, and the first act was over.

Amid the general and hearty laughter which followed this amusing scene, there were sundry speculations as to the word which was intended, though the young people were quite agreed that the first part of it must be *cat*, for as Harry very sagaciously observed,

"The cat is so far the most prominent character in the play."

After a few moments' interval the actors returned They were all dressed in travelling costume, and the lady carried a basket, while one of the gentlemen bore a carpet-bag and the other a portmanteau in his hands.

"Have you ever been to sea, Mr. Brown?" said the lady with a simpering smile.

"No, Miss Green," replied Mr. Brown, (*alias* Dr. Sinclair,) "I have never been outside the Hook."

"Oh! dear me, William, I hope we shall have a storm. I have so much longed to see a storm on the ocean."

"Nonsense, Amarintha, you won't want to see a second one, I fancy."

"Oh! you think I shall not enjoy it, William? What do you think, Mr. Brown?"

"My dear Miss Green I am sure I hope you will."

"Is this the steamer we are to go in, Mr. Brown?"

"Yes, Miss Green; allow me to conduct you on board."

"Oh! what a singular odour, Mr. Brown," she exclaimed as they passed to the stair-way which led to the upper deck.

"Delicious, Miss Green."

"Oh! I declare I don't think so," she added, resorting to her essence bottle.

"Villainous then, if you like the term better," said the accommodating Mr. Green.

"How fast she sails, doesn't she, William?"

"She doesn't *sail*, Amarintha; she goes by steam," said her brother, which was the evident relationship the younger gentleman bore to her.

"Oh! it is charming—charming, Mr. Brown. I have had such exquisite fancies of the ocean—of its vast expanse—of its colour, which Byron says is

'So deeply, darkly, beautifully blue.'

But dear me, it doesn't look *blue* now; what is the reason, Mr. Brown?"

"This isn't the ocean yet, Miss Green. We have not passed the Hook."

"Shall we see the Hook, and what do they hang on it, Mr. Brown?"

"Why, Amarintha, don't you know that the Hook is only a point of land around which we have to go to get out to sea?" said her brother.

"No, indeed, I didn't; though now I recollect it is called Sandy Hook. I wish we were already beyond it. I do so long to see the beautiful sea—

'The blue, the fresh, the ever free.' "

"Hold on, Mr. Brown," said William, as the former clutched his straw hat, with which the fresh breeze seemed to be making free, "see, I have got mine fast to my button-hole."

"The wind blows very hard," said the lady, "and now I feel the motion of the ship, like a delightful lullaby. How sweet it must be to be rocked to— Oh! dear!" she exclaimed, "how very queer I felt just then."

"Will you go below?" said her brother.

"Oh! no, indeed; I want to see the boundless ocean, to— oh! my head—what can it be?"

"Are you not well, Miss Green?" inquired Mr. Brown, with a pale face—"are you—heugh—I'm"—

"Oh! dear!" said the lady, "I must—heugh—I

must"—and her head bent over the chair on which she sat.

"I will go below and get you some water," said Mr. Brown, "but—heugh"—and he rushed out of the room, followed by William, who was half carrying the form of the fair Amarintha.

"Sick—sick—sick," said all the young people in chorus.

"Even *sic*," said Harry, venturing a little Latin pun, perhaps because his father was not at hand to hear it.

"I think it must be *sick*," said Alice, "but then what are we to do with *cat?*"

"And a cat sick—especially," said Herbert.

"It can't be *cat*, or it can't be *sick*, one," returned Harry, quite discouraged by the difficulty of the combination.

While they were discussing the matter, the actors reäppeared. William Sinclair entered with Mrs. Sinclair leaning on his arm, and he led her toward Dr. Sinclair, who immediately put on a very important air.

"I have the happiness, Mr. Blarneum, of introducing to you Signorina Phillipina Tamborina Squallina, a member of the Conservatoire Musicale of Paris."

The lady bowed, and Mr. Blarneum bowed, and the latter said—

"I am happy, Mr. Trombon, to see the lady, and

shall be glad to have a specimen of her vocal powers before we talk about terms."

"Certainly, Mr. Blarneum; I am sure she will delight you, and prove a great card for a concert tour. Her voice is wonderful, sir, in its range, its register, and its reed-like tone."

"Ah! well, let us see, or rather let us *hear*," and the speaker smiled and hemmed, as he drew a white cambric from his pocket and hid his face in it.

Signorina Squallina hemmed and cleared her throat, and hemmed again, while Mr. Trombon seated himself at the piano, and began running his fingers furiously over the keys.

The Signorina unrolled a sheet of music, and opened her mouth to sing, which she did in the most approved opera style, uttering an incredible number of notes, with incredible rapidity, leaping up a scale and then down again, warbling, and quavering, and bravuraing to the uncontrollable delight of the audience, who did not wait for the conclusion of the piece to manifest their applause. The lady sung on, however, bowing and smirking prodigiously, and surpassing herself in her renewed efforts to fling her voice off of precipices into deep caverns, and then to reach the top again by surprising vocal flights. Mr. Blarneum was evidently impressed with the lady's performances, for no sooner had she subsided, after a most amazing ecstasy of vocalization, into a corner of the sofa, than he extended his hand to Mr. Trombon and said:

"Really, my dear sir, she is an angel! and I have no doubt she will create a *furore* of wonder and admiration. I should like to make an engagement for at least one hundred nights."

Mr. Trombon was delighted in his turn, and interpreted Mr. Blarneum's flattering words to the fair singer, who blushed, and immediately rising, courtesied low to the manager.

"And how much will you give, Mr. Blarneum?" said Mr. Trombon, in a modest tone.

"Rather let me ask how much you demand?" was the reply.

"Will two hundred dollars a night, and a benefit in every important town, be out of the way, Mr. Blarneum?"

"I should be unwilling to accept those terms," said the manager, blandly, "though I do not think them beyond the merits of the Signorina. I will give one hundred and fifty dollars a night, and make no promise about benefits."

"The offer is accepted," said Mr. Trombon, "and we will be ready, sir, to commence at your pleasure."

"I will arrange matters speedily," was the reply.

"Good night, sir."

'Good night, sir."

Mr. Blarneum shook hands with the Signorina without speaking, and so the party retired from the room.

They returned immediately, however, no longer in

character, but eager to know if their play had been correctly interpreted. They were instantly assailed by Harry, with the very luminous question—

"What have sick cats to do with concerts?"

"Ah! my boy," said his father, "you don't *burn*."

"Oh! dear," said Alice, "what can it be—the first word *isn't* cat, I'm sure, now!"

"Is it not *music?*" said Herbert, rather timidly.

"Bravo, Herbert! you deserve a fiddle-stick," said Dr. Sinclair.

"Music!" said Harry; "how do you make that out?"

"Why, didn't the cat *mew*—and were not the travellers *sick*—and—"

"Oh! I see now," interposed Harry, "and the whole word was represented by Messrs. Trombon and Blarneum, and the Signorina Philomena something."

Alice was perfectly satisfied not to have guessed it herself, as was evident from the pleased smile with which she said:

"Why, Herbert, I thought you were not trying to guess it; you didn't say any thing at either of the first two acts."

"I did not guess it at all," he answered, "until Harry put cats and concerts together, and then I thought of music!"

"You thought my singing a sort of *caterwauling* I suppose, Herbert?" said Mrs. Sinclair, laughing at the idea.

"Oh! no, mamma, I'm sure he thought it wonderful," was Alice's reply.

"Well, we have had music of different kinds, to night," said Dr. Sinclair, "but I hope they have not unfitted us for still another kind—that of devotion. It is now time for prayers, and we will sing the evening hymn to Old Hundred, that grand air of Martin Luther's. My dear," he added, turning to Mrs. Sinclair, "you will play it for us, I hope?"

Mrs. Sinclair now approached the piano, no longer n the character of an opera singer, but in a character more congenial to her cultivated mind and to her domestic nature—that of a loving and grateful mother. She played and led the air, Alice sung treble, William the tenor, and Dr. Sinclair the bass, and this quartette of voices made delightful melody of the words of the evening hymn.

CHAPTER VIII.

Snow—Congratulations—Snow in the City—Snow-Crystals—Uses of Snow—The Snow-Blanket—Travellers in the Alps—Harry's Wise Resolution—Why Snow-Crystals are Opaque—Why Lofty Mountain Tops are Covered with Snow—Sledding—An Upset.

THE next morning dawned upon a scene still more wintry than that which presented itself to the view of our young friends when they arrived at Beechwood. During the night, snow had fallen to the depth of five or six inches, and the fleecy covering lay lightly upon all the face of nature. There had been no wind, and the light feathery crystals rested where they fell, whether upon the ground or upon the trees. The light branches of the latter were bent by the weight of the snow, which presented a brilliant contrast to the dark glossy foliage of the evergreens which adorned the grounds.

There was something exhilarating—indeed, almost fascinating—in the scene. The white robe concealed the barrenness of winter, even while it proclaimed the dominion of that ungenial season. It was such a type of purity and innocence, that no one could regard it without a pleasurable feeling. The sight was hailed with positive enthusiasm by all the young people. It was the first snow of the season, and they had been talking of sleigh-rides and other snow frolics, with so much eagerness of anticipation, that they could scarcely restrain their impatience to enjoy the reality.

After morning prayers in the library, they gathered in the recess of the tower-window, and discussed the out-of-door aspect of things.

"Oh! how glad I am the snow has come," said Alice.

"And I, too, am real glad," said Herbert, "for I think I shall enjoy the snow in the country, which we can't do in the city."

"Why not, Herbert?" inquired Alice.

"Because it don't stay long, or if it does lie on the ground, it is only in our narrow little yards, where it is all thrown into heaps. It is not long clean and pure, as it is here."

"Don't you have snow-men and snow-balling in the city, Herbert?" said Mary, who had learned by this time to take part in the conversation.

"Snow-men very seldom, Mary; there is plenty of snow-balling; but then that is not much fun in the little yards, and the street is not a proper place to indulge in such sport."

"Oh! we will have rare fun here, though," said Harry; and he added, turning to his brother William, who was looking over the pages of Blackwood's Magazine, " Will you join us in a snow-balling frolic, after breakfast?"

"You are reckoning too fast, Harry," said his brother. "The snow is not in a proper condition for snow-balling; when it is, I shall be very happy to engage in the sport with you."

"Won't the snow make balls now, brother Willie?" was Fanny's question.

"Not very easily, Fan; it is light and dry, now, and had there been any wind in the night, it would have been drifted into great heaps, and the ground in many places would be bare."

"Why is it light and dry, brother Willie?" asked Alice.

"Can't you think of the reason, Ally?"

"Only because it is frozen too hard—is that it?"

"That explains it. The temperature of the air is low enough to keep the crystals or flakes in the solid condition. If it were a little higher, they would melt, at least partially, and become damp, so that they would cling together."

"Then it must thaw a little before we can make snow-balls to advantage," was Alice's correct conclusion.

"Probably the heat of the sun will effect all we want, in that respect, in the course of the morning," said William Sinclair.

The breakfast-bell now summoned the family to the table, and there the subject of the snow was resumed.

"Are the snow-flakes shaped like the particles of

frost which we saw in the microscope, the other day?" inquired Alice of her father.

"Certainly," was Dr. Sinclair's reply. "I think I told you, did I not, that water crystallizes in definite forms? Snow-flakes are crystals of watery vapour, condensed in the upper regions of the atmosphere, when the temperature sinks below the freezing point."

"Well," said Harry, "the snow makes capital sport for boys—and girls, too, as for that," he added, giving a quizzical look to his sisters; "but that's most all it's good for, I guess."

"Oh! no, Harry, you are widely mistaken, there; isn't he, papa?" Alice quickly responded.

"Widely mistaken, indeed, my child; and I am a little astonished that your brother should make such a mistake. The snow of no other use than to make sport for boys and girls!"

"Oh! it looks pretty, I know," said Harry, "and it's good for sleighing; but then we could get along without either seeing it, or riding over it."

"So we could, Master Sage; but it has other very important offices and uses. Alice will tell you some of them, at least."

"One, papa, which I remember Miss Maurice told me of, is to protect vegetation from the extreme cold of winter."

"Protect vegetation!" said Harry; "over the left, you mean, I suppose? Why that's Jacob Fletcher's notion. He said, yesterday, that he hoped there would be plenty of snow this winter; and when I asked him what for, he said to keep the ground warm! I laughed at him, but he insisted that it would do so."

"Jacob Fletcher could better afford to laugh at you, my boy," was his father's reply, "for he was right; and you should learn at once that snow is one of the greatest blessings which our kind Benefactor sends with the winter. It lies upon the ground, in cold countries, just like warm blankets."

"I shouldn't like to sleep under a snow-blanket, papa," said Mary.

"Perhaps not, my daughter, but you might sleep less safely, I can assure you."

"I can not understand how, papa," said the young girl, ingenuously.

"Can you tell us, Alice?"

"I suppose, papa, you are thinking of the poor lost travellers in the Bernese Alps, in Switzerland, of whom such sad stories are related."

"I am, indeed, thinking of them, Alice. They are sometimes overtaken, in the passes of the Alps, by terrible snow drifts, which so obstruct the way that they can not reach the usual shelters, and are sometimes buried up beneath piles of snow-blankets."

"Yes, papa; but they perish if they are not soon rescued."

"They would live longer if actually covered up in

the snow, than if they were to lie upon its surface," was Dr. Sinclair's reply.

Fanny's eyes expressed great wonder, and the lips of Harry did precisely the same.

"Travellers have been rescued alive by the monks and the noble dogs, which they keep and train for the purpose, from drifts of snow in which they must have lain buried for some hours; while at the same time some of their ill-fated companions have been found dead and frozen stiff, outside of the drift."

"Oh! how terrible!" exclaimed Mary, shuddering at the scene her quick fancy conjured up.

"Terrible indeed," said William; "but had not the rescued travellers great reason to be thankful to a wise Providence for the snow-blanket which shielded them from death?"

"Alice only mentioned one benefit of snow," said William; "but there is another of importance. It not only shields plants and animals from the rigours of cold climates, but it gathers upon the mountain-tops, and then, gradually melting beneath the summer heat, flows down in streams to water the valleys and plains. If the snows of winter fell in the form of rain, these streams would swell into destructive torrents, which would deluge the low regions."

"But, brother William," said Harry, "the snow sometimes melts so fast in the spring, as to make freshets which do much damage."

"That is true, Harry; but these are exceptions

and snow freshets are not half so common as rain freshets."

"Snow, then, you see, my young philosopher," said Dr. Sinclair, "is not only ornamental, but useful in a very high degree. It is said that Alpine plants perish in the mild winters of England, for want of the snow-blankets under which, in their native clime, they sleep all the winter long."

"I will never again say that snow is of no use, except for sport," said Harry eagerly, as he listened to these evidences of the importance of snow.

"That is a good resolution, my son; only let me recommend you to extend it to every thing that God has made, however insignificant or useless it appears to be."

"I will, papa," was Harry's answer, "for I am beginning to see that my ignorance makes things seem to be of little use."

"Brother Willie," said Alice, who had been apparently deep in thought for a few moments, "I can not understand one thing about the snow."

"If there is only one thing about it, Ally," said her brother, "that you don't understand, you may count yourself wise."

"Now, brother Willie, you are laughing at me," she replied; "but be kind enough, if you please, to tell me why the snow is not transparent like ice, if the crystals of both are precisely the same?"

"Well done, Alice," said her father, as William

hesitated a moment at the question thus suddenly proposed to him, as a just penalty for his banter to his sister; "you have posed your brother, I verily believe."

William smiled quietly as he quickly replied—

"Not exactly; for although I do not recollect to have thought, or read of the reason, I imagine that it is owing to the imperfection of structure in the crystals of the snow. Am I correct, sir?"

"You approach the true reason, my son. The snow-crystals of low latitudes are seldom perfect, and the air which they contain makes them opaque or cloudy. You have, doubtless, seen ice of considerable thickness exhibiting a cloudy appearance, as if the interior was filled with snow. This is ice frozen when the temperature is not very low, and when also the air is not exceedingly calm—two conditions opposed to a perfect crystallization of water."

"What is the reason, sir," said Herbert, "that the tops of very high mountains are perpetually covered with snow?"

"Can you not think of a reason, Herbert?"

"I know it is said, sir, that it is very cold there; but if the sun is the source of heat to our globe, why are not the mountain-tops hotter than the valleys or the plains?"

"Your question is not an idle one, Herbert. It seems very proper to suppose that the tops of mountains should catch the heat first, as we know they do the light. But the rays of the sun afford little heat until they combine with our atmosphere, and this is so rare around the mountain-peaks, that the sun's rays are not as freely absorbed by it, as they are by the denser or lower portions of the air."

"I think I can understand that," replied Herbert, delighted to obtain a new idea.

"Some philosophers have supposed that heat is not contained in the solar ray until it enters our atmosphere, and acquires it in passing through it. Without adopting this hypothesis, we may be sure that the atmosphere has a great deal to do with the diffusion and action of that very subtle agent which we called caloric, in our first conversation on this subject."

Breakfast was now finished, and the whole party rose up from the table. Alice and Mary engaged their brother William to go with them in their usual morning rounds to feed the pets and the fowls, while Harry urged Herbert to go with him into the tool house and put their coasting sleds in order, for some sport. Alice found her pet deer bounding and racing about in the snow, as if he enjoyed it quite as much as the boys might do. The rabbits were in their hutch, but came out promptly at Fanny's well-known call, to receive their food from her little hands. The boys had no sooner put their sleds into good order than they came back to the house, to entreat the others to go with them to the hill and witness the sport.

"You shall ride down, and we will drag you up the hill, Alice," said Harry by way of inducement.

"That would be making you pay dearly for our company," replied Alice, laughing. "No! no! my good brother, if we ride down, we must walk up; and I confess that I shall at least enjoy seeing the sport very much."

So they all agreed to go to the hill. Mrs. Sinclair saw that the girls were well wrapped up, and that they had on their rubber-shoes, nicely trimmed with fur. Herbert and Harry had both equipped themselves in boots of the same material, and so were well prepared for any sort of frolic in the snow. The morning passed rapidly away in out-of-door amusement. The sun warmed the snow just enough to make it pack beneath the feet and beneath the runners of the sleds, which at first moved down the hill somewhat slowly. Very soon, however, the track became hard and smooth, and then they shot down with their burdens like arrows. It was some time before the boys could persuade either Alice or Mary to descend with them; and indeed, had not Fanny agreed to go down with her brother William, the girls might have enjoyed the sport as spectators only. She made so successful a descent in her brother's arms, though she screamed a very little as the sled rushed down, that both Alice and Mary agreed to follow her example, Alice with Harry, and Mary with Herbert. The boys behaved very gallantly upon the occasion, and exerted their best skill to make a safe descent, which was in both cases triumphantly achieved amid the laughter of all. I suppose that if Herbert had been entrusted with the care of Alice, he would have been more delighted, but he could not have been more careful. Harry proved himself treacherous upon a second descent, for when the sled was well nigh at the bottom of the hill, he managed to upset it, spilling both himself and Alice into the fresh soft snow, much to the amusement of the rest, and not at all to Alice's discomfiture, for she had quite too much amiability not to take the "accident," as Harry called it, very good humouredly.

CHAPTER IX.

An Accession to the Party—Mr. Oldbuckle Declines an Adventure—A Sleigh-Ride Proposed—Early Dinner—The Sleigh—The Start—Ten Miles an Hour—Viviandale—The Vivians—William Sinclair's Desertion—A Pardon and its Conditions—Gertrude Vivian—The Return Home.

WHEN Alice had picked herself up from the soft white bed into which her playful brother had upset her, and while the shouts of the whole party were yet echoing on the still wintry air, Dr. Sinclair and Mr. Oldbuckle appeared among the group.

"What!" said the latter gentleman, "my bird taking a snow-bath? I hope it will not affect her voice!"

"Oh! no!" she replied gaily, "the snow is not wet enough to cling to one's clothes. I shook it all off, almost like dust."

Harry was irreverent enough to urge his father and Mr. Oldbuckle to make a descent of the hill upon their sleds. But they, laughingly, declined the adventure.

"No! no! my boy," said Mr. Oldbuckle, "I have no solicitude to furnish additional proof in my own person of the classic sentiment—

'Facilis descensus Averni:'

even though you should offer to excuse me from
preving further—

> 'Sed revocare gradum,
> Hic labor, hoc opus est.'"

Harry was quite abashed by this learned negation
to his proposition, and, indeed, it was lost upon all
the party except Dr. Sinclair and William, who
laughed so heartily, that Mr. Oldbuckle was quite
delighted with the effect of his classical pleasantry.

When Mr. Oldbuckle heard that they had held a
philosophical discussion upon the snow, at the breakfast-table, he expressed his regret that he was not
present. Dr. Sinclair begged him to become their
guest for the period of the vacation, an invitation
which he declined, but not without a warm expression
of thanks for the hospitality and kindness which
prompted it.

He now informed Alice and the rest of the young
people, that he had made arrangements for a sleigh-ride that very afternoon, and begged them to be in
readiness to start immediately after dinner. There
was no demurring on the part of any. The sport
was just what every one of them most fancied.

Mrs. Sinclair had kindly promised Mr. Oldbuckle
that dinner should be served earlier than usual, to
give them the longer afternoon. By one o'clock,
therefore, they were all ready for the excursion. A
very large sleigh stood at the front door of Beech-

wood Hall. It was a substantial rather than ornamental vehicle. The body of it was an oblong box nine feet long by four feet in width, which was fastened to two stout frames, called runners. These were shod with flat bars of iron about the thickness of a tire for carriage wheels. These runners were curved in front and served to support a light dash-board to protect those in the sleigh from the snow which would be thrown up by the horses' feet. Four seats were arranged in the body of the sleigh. These were nicely cushioned, and covered besides with large buffalo robes. The bottom of the sleigh had been filled with fresh straw, and the whole establishment looked comfortable and inviting. Two fine horses were attached to the sleigh, and were evidently impatient to be off with it. So, without delay, our whole party, not excepting Mrs. Sinclair, who had consented to leave her domestic duties at the earnest solicitation of all, bestowed themselves with alacrity in the seats. Herbert had the extreme happiness of finding himself seated with Alice—just behind Mr. Oldbuckle and William Sinclair, and just in front of Harry and Mary. The last seat was occupied by Dr. and Mrs. Sinclair, with little Fan between them. The sun was shining bright and warm, and at first our party treated the buffalos with a little disregard; but no sooner were they on the road, the sleigh literally flying behind the fleet horses, than they found it desirable to shut out the keen air, which now me them full in their faces, by folding the fur robes close about them. Herbert wrapped up the light form of Alice with a vast deal of care, glad, I am sure, to be enveloped in the same capacious robe with his fair companion. She was in high spirits. The fresh cold air brought an unwonted glow to her cheek, which Herbert was really too blind to see extended also to a more prominent member of her face. The horses fairly flew as William Sinclair cracked the whip, in the air, over their glossy coats. The snow, also, flew bravely, and miles were passed over with a rapidity and smoothness of motion which could in no other way be achieved by horses. The sleighing was found to be excellent, for although the snow had fallen very dry, the ground was hard beneath, and the frozen road had been worn smooth by travel. The heat of the sun was sufficient, therefore, to give the snow a proper temperature for becoming firm under pressure.

Ten miles were done in considerably less than an hour, and William Sinclair reined up his smoking steeds in front of a large and beautiful mansion where a college-mate of his resided, and upon whom he now proposed to make an unceremonious call.

Edward Vivian made his appearance at the gate before William had entered it, after putting the reins into Mr. Oldbuckle's hands. The young men greeted each other cordially, and Mr. Vivian, who already knew Dr. Sinclair, having been introduced to the rest of the party, so earnestly pressed them to partake of the hospitalities of Viviandale, that they could not well refuse.

So they alighted from the sleigh; the horses were given into the care of a waiting man, and they all proceeded, under the escort of their young host, toward the house. They were met at the porch by the elder Mr. Vivian, who made them feel at ease immediately by his unaffected politeness. Edward Vivian now introduced them to his mother and his only sister, Gertrude Vivian, who was two or three years Alice's senior. The back parlour was all aglow with the radiance of a huge wood fire, and unpremeditated as the visit was, there was speedily established between all the parties a most charming accord. Gertrude Vivian played for her new friends, and played charmingly; and I am glad to have it in my power to say that Alice Sinclair made no objection when Mrs. Vivian asked her to succeed her daughter at the piano-forte. She could not play as well as Gertrude, she knew; but she cheerfully did her best, and her best elicited very cordial praise.

Dr. Sinclair was slightly acquainted with Mr. Vivian, having met him at an agricultural convention, held in the county town the previous summer. The sons of these gentlemen were warm friends and classmates, and so the family friendship grew fast. Even an hour sufficed to make them all think much of each other; and when Mr. Oldbuckle held up his watch significantly to his young friend William Sinclair, he said gaily—

"It is my intention, sir, to resign the ribands into your hands—in other words, to abdicate the box."

"What treason is this, William?" said his mother. "You are surely not going to desert us?"

"Pardon, my dear mother, I cry your pardon if I plead guilty. But hear me before you judge."

"What can you say, brother William, in self-defence, if the charge be not false?" said Alice.

"Mother—sister—all—hear me and decide! Edward Vivian begs me to spend the night at Viviandale, and I have consented to do so—"

"Oh! you traitor!" said his mother, and Alice repeated her words.

"Upon the condition"—he resumed, smiling as he spoke—"that to-morrow, Edward Vivian accompanies me to Beechwood, to spend Christmas with us."

"Oh! well," said Mrs. Sinclair, "in that case, I think your plea must be admitted."

"I shall not so easily forgive you, however," said Alice. "I must insist upon a second condition."

"Which is—?"

"That Miss Gertrude Vivian shall accompany her brother and yourself to Beechwood."

"Yes," said Dr. Sinclair, "I approve Alice's amendment, most cordially."

"And I accept the amendment with all my heart," said Mrs. Sinclair; "the proposition delights me."

Gertrude Vivian's face flushed with pleasure at these tokens of her new friends' interest in her, and her eyes turned inquiringly towards her mother.

"Would you like to go with your brother, my daughter?" said Mrs. Vivian.

"Indeed, mamma, it would give me great happiness."

"I shall accept your very kind invitation for Gertrude, then, Mrs. Sinclair and Miss Alice," replied Mrs. Vivian, "and will send her, to-morrow, with your recreant son," and she smiled archly at William.

"Not recreant," said his mother, "if he makes such noble compensation for his slight defection."

The travelling party now bade their hospitable friends good bye, and were soon comfortably settled once more in their sleigh. Dr. Sinclair insisted upon exchanging seats with Mr. Oldbuckle, and taking the reins in his hands, he suffered the eager horses to start in the direction of home. William Sinclair and Edward Vivian stood watching the rapidly vanishing sleigh, and waved their handkerchiefs just as a bend in the road carried it out of their sight.

The ride home was not less enjoyable than the ride out. Mr. Oldbuckle entertained Mrs. Sinclair with reminiscences of English Christmas festivities—a subject which was suggested by her cordial invitation that he would eat Christmas dinner with them the day after next, which he promised to do.

Alice and Herbert discussed the personal appearance and the apparent temper of Gertrude Vivian, appealing ever and anon to Harry and Mary for their verdict upon such points of the case, as afforded any opportunity for variance of opinion. They all agreed that she was beautiful, and that her manners were graceful. Herbert was perverse enough to dispute the opinion of Alice, that Gertrude sung better than she did. I wonder at Herbert's boldness in this dispute, but candour obliges me to say that he was right. How, indeed, should Alice know—as he said somewhat triumphantly—how well she could sing? This discussion was not settled by a verdict from the next bench, for Herbert refused to make an appeal.

Little Fanny had crept into the buffalo robe, between her brother and sister, and there the darling little girl actually fell asleep, and did not awake till the sleigh brought up somewhat abruptly, at the great gate of Beechwood park. Harry jumped out to fling it wide open, and so disturbed the little sleeper, who rubbed her eyes and said, very innocently—

"Is it morning, mamma?"

The merry laughter awoke her completely, so that she was ready among the first to be lifted out of the sleigh by old Jacob Fletcher, who was waiting at the great steps which led up to the front door, and close to which the sleigh was stopped.

It was quite sunset when they reached home, and the air was keen with frost. Harry congratulated his school-fellow that the pond would certainly freeze over during the night, and by the day after Christmas, they might count upon capital skating.

"I am glad," said Harry, "that the pond wasn't frozen when the snow fell, because now we shall have clear ice."

"If it don't snow again to-night," said Dr. Sinclair, looking up at the sky, which was lowering.

There were none of the party who did not welcome the sound of the tea-bell, which rung out its silvery tones very soon after they had divested themselves of their wrappers, and gathered around the fireside.

They had entreated Mr. Oldbuckle to stay all night; but he declared it to be impossible, as he intended, he said, to be with them nearly all of the next day, and he must go home to attend to some little matters of business. They had, therefore, bidden him adieu, with earnest injunctions to "come early to-morrow."

CHAPTER X.

Tea-table Chat—Alliteration—Herbert's Acknowledgment—Fanny's Wish—Papa's Consent—The Laboratory—The Magic Lantern—Its History—Lenses—The Darkened Room—A Mistake which was not a Mistake—Optical Illusions—Fanny Frightened at her Shadow—Spectral Images—Fanny's Gratitude.

"WE have had a delightful day, thanks to the snow;" said Alice, and her words chimed in musically with the clicking of knives, forks, and spoons, as they did justice to the substantial viands with which Mrs. Sinclair had bountifully furnished the tea-table.

"Thanks to Him who sends the snow, my dear Alice," said her mother.

"Yes, mamma, that was in my heart, though my tongue employed lighter words."

"How much pleasure we can derive, if we will, from the commonest gifts of a kind Providence," said Dr. Sinclair, who never missed a suitable opportunity of directing his children's thoughts to the goodness of their Creator.

"We have had both science and sport out of the snow," said Harry.

"Two S's out of one—eh, my boys?" said his father, noticing Harry's alliteration.

"And how has my young guest enjoyed himself to-day?" said Mrs. Sinclair, addressing Herbert Russel, whose happy looks were, however, a very plain index of the pleasure he felt in his heart.

"More than I can tell you, Mrs. Sinclair," was Herbert's immediate reply. "I ought to be very happy, with such kind friends and so many sources of enjoyment."

"Much of your happiness is in your own frank and ingenuous nature, my young friend," rejoined Mrs. Sinclair; "you intend to be happy, and that gives zest to every pleasure, and takes away the edge from pain."

"Yes," said Dr. Sinclair, "our happiness or unhappiness depends very much upon ourselves. If we resolve and try to be happy, there are comparatively few conditions of life which are proof against such a purpose; while, on the contrary, the most joyous and delightful circumstances fail to yield satisfaction to the discontented and fretful spirit. Cultivate, my children, a cheerful and buoyant disposition. Shut your eyes to the dark side of every picture, if it is sometimes placed before you; but be sure and keep them wide open when the bright side is in view—just as if looking at it eagerly would keep it always visible."

After a brief silence, Fanny looked up into her papa's face, as if she would very much like to ask a question.

"Well, Fan, what is it, my little daughter?" said her father, by way of encouragement.

"Papa, I want to ask a great favour!"

"A great favour, eh? I think I must grant it, then."

"Oh! if you will, papa, I shall be so glad."

"But what is it, Fanny?"

"To let us see the 'Magic London' to-night."

"The magic what, Fan?" said Harry, with a loud laugh at the little girl's mistake.

"Papa called it the magic *London*—didn't you, papa?" said Fanny, a little discomfited by the laughter.

"Not magic *London*, my child; I called it a magic *lantern*, which I probably told you came from London."

"Well, papa, the magic *lantern*, then; will you show it to us to-night?"

"Fanny," said Dr. Sinclair, "has more than once asked me to let her see some beautiful pictures which I have lately received, and I think I must gratify her to-night."

"Yes, papa," said the now delighted child, "and you promised me that when brother Harry came home from school, you would show them to me. Oh! I am so glad," and she jumped about in childish glee.

The little girl was quite impatient until the hour came for this new pleasure to be enjoyed, and perhaps the older children shared her impatience, though they did not give it expression.

As soon as tea was over, they all repaired to the library, which was to be the scene of the promised amusement. Beneath the library, and accessible by a stair-case opening from it, was Dr. Sinclair's laboratory. Lest any of my little readers should not know what the word laboratory means, I will tell them that it is a place where chemists keep their instruments and perform their experiments. Into this room, Dr. Sinclair and Harry descended, and in a few moments returned with their hands full. The former bore what resembled a large black tea-canister, only that a sort of spout extended from one side, and a bent funnel from the top. This was placed upon a small table, and beside it, Harry laid a box which he carried very carefully.

Herbert did not need that Alice should tell him that the black canister was a magic lantern. He had seen it several times before, and had witnessed an exhibition of it in the city, but of its construction and principles, as also of its origin, he knew nothing at all.

Dr. Sinclair then asked Mary to fetch him a clean white table-cloth, which, with Harry's aid, he fastened against the book-shelves, so as to make a large, smooth surface. He now placed the table upon which the lantern stood in front of the cloth, at a distance of about ten feet, while the children pressed eagerly around to watch his proceedings. From the interior of the lantern, he took a handsome brass lamp with a glass chimney over its round wick. Filling the lamp with oil, he lighted it and replaced it in the lantern, where it soon burned brilliantly. Having done all this, he said to Harry:

"Well, my son, do you know who invented the magic lantern, and at what period?"

"No, papa, I do not," was Harry's frank confession; "but I wish you would tell me, if you please."

"Your sister will do that, I am sure," he said; and looking at Alice, he added, "will you not answer my question for your brother, my daughter?"

"That I will, with pleasure," said the blushing girl, "for you told me yourself, some time ago, that it was invented by a learned monk, called Father Kircher, about the year 1656."

"Very true, my daughter; and to what purpose was it applied for many years?"

"To deceive the people, who were ignorant enough to believe that the apparitions and spectres produced by it were supernatural; and that, undoubtedly, was the reason that it came to be called the magic lantern."

Herbert looked with undisguised interest upon the beautiful girl who, scarcely one year his senior, was thus teaching him things he had never heard of until now. His attention was next arrested by Dr. Sinclair's removing from the inside of the lantern a broad ring of brass, on which was fastened a piece of thick glass, round on one side and flat on the other. This he called a *lens*, and asked Alice if she knew why it bore that name. I think Herbert was more than half pleased to hear her confess that she could not tell; for although he admired her superior intelligence and knowledge, he could not help feeling a little ashamed by the consciousness of it. It is just to our young friend to say, however, that his ignorance of many things which were familiar to Alice Sinclair, was no real reproach to him. His studies had been different from Alice's, and in some branches of knowledge he had the advantage of her.

Dr. Sinclair enlightened the group by telling them that the lens took its name from the *lentil*, a sort of bean which it resembled in shape.

"What is the use of a lens?" asked the Doctor.

"To collect or to scatter the rays of light," replied Alice.

"Well answered, Alice," said her father; "and now let us look at *two lenses* in this tube."

As he spoke he drew out from the tube at the side of the lantern a cylinder of brass, on the end of which he showed the young people two lenses not so large as the one they had already seen, and both of them round on both sides. These he described to them as double convex glasses. He next took from the box, which Harry had deposited so carefully upon the table, a number of long and slender frames made of wood, in which were placed at intervals circular pieces, or discs, of glass, upon some of which were painted very curious and beautiful pictures, while upon others there were representations of the planets and of the stars.

Harry, by his father's direction, now turned down the lamp, and placed a screen before the fire which glowed in the chimney, so as to make the library as dark as possible. Fanny thought these proceedings of Harry's were very strange, but the others were quick enough to see the need of them.

The hush of expectation succeeded these busy and interesting preparations. Mrs. Sinclair took a chair, and Fanny nestled closely to her mamma's side. The others stood by the table to observe all that Dr. Sinclair did. As he was putting one of the slender frames into the lantern, Harry stopped him with an eager exclamation—

"Why, papa, what a mistake! You are putting in that man upside down!"

"So I am, my young philosopher—thank you for your attention."

So saying, he turned the figure right side up, and putting it into a narrow space between the lenses already described, he closed the door of the lantern, and the library was immediately shrouded in complete darkness, so that Fanny clung still closer to her mamma. In a moment, however, Dr. Sinclair removed a cap from the end of the tube, and a shout of wonder was raised, as there appeared upon the

Dr. Sinclair confessed that it was so, and changing quickly the position of the slide, there appeared a vivid representation of a sailor dancing.—p. 109.

white screen, the figure of a sailor dancing a hornpipe upon his head.

"Why, Harry, the man would'nt stay on his feet, it seems. See, he is upside down, still," said his father in a laughing tone.

Harry looked exceedingly puzzled, and was silent; but Alice immediately said—

"Oh! papa, I remember that Mrs. Marcet taught me that the images of objects seen through convex glasses are turned upside down, and, therefore, you put in the slide right side up just to give Harry a lesson. Ha! ha! papa, wasn't that it?"

Dr. Sinclair confessed that it was so, and changing quickly the position of the slide, there appeared a vivid representation of a sailor dancing, just as my little readers may see in the accompanying picture.

Many curious subjects were then shown in succession, and the house rung with glee as a little girl danced with a wreath of flowers for a skipping-rope, which alternately passed over her head and under her feet, or at least *appeared* to do so. The Doctor showed them that this was an optical illusion. There were two figures and two wreaths in different postures on different pieces of glass, and by sliding first one and then the other backward and forward, the wreath seemed to pass completely round the girl. By the same plan a rose-bud was made to expand into a full-blown rose, and a caterpillar to change, first into a chrysalis, and then into a butterfly, which fluttered its wings and then vanished. Another very charming picture was the interior of a cave, partially illuminated by the light of a full moon. It was the hiding-place of a band of smugglers, who were dragging a boat, laden with their illicit goods, into the mouth of the cavern which opened from the water.

After many such representations, Dr. Sinclair proposed to show them a portrait of Fanny, and several voices exclaimed:

" Oh! that will be charming indeed!" while little Fanny, herself, looked not a little incredulous, and said:

" But, dear papa, you can't put me into that black tube!"

While the merry group was laughing at Fanny's naïveté, Dr. Sinclair pushed the table nearer the wall, and, after a moment's darkness, there appeared on the screen a very beautiful and striking portrait of Fanny—so like, that all were startled by it and gazed in silence—until its sweet blue eyes began to move, when a shout of delight burst from every lip. Then immediately the little hand was raised and a finger laid on the red lips, when in spite of the injunction to silence which it seemed to make, there was such a peal of merriment that Jacob Fletcher came running in, and when the old man saw the speaking, moving likeness of his little favourite, he said, in some alarm—

"Why, bless us, dear master, that must be Fanny's angel!"

At that moment Dr. Sinclair took the lantern in his hands, and withdrawing from the screen some paces, the image suddenly increased in size and appeared to rush upon the beholders, some of whom were frightened; so much that they were heartily laughed at for being afraid of little Fanny—and Fanny, herself, was actually frightened by her own shadow!

Her father then explained to the young people that as convex lenses make rays of light spread, those which proceeded from the face upon the slide, through the two lenses in the tube, would cover a space on the screen proportional to the distance of the lantern from it; and he illustrated it again by carrying the lantern close up to the wall and making a very small bright image; and then, by going to the other side of the room, the face covered not only the screen but the whole wall.

Alice asked her father how the monks used to produce spectral appearances by means of the magic lantern, and he replied that one method was to cast the image of a spectre, from a concealed lantern, upon the semi-transparent vapour or smoke ascending from burning incense. The shifting motions of the smoke gave a fearfully real appearance to the image which it reflected to the terrified, and, of course, not very critical eyes of the beholder. Much more curious information was imparted than I have space to record, during that pleasant evening with the Magic Lantern, which was terminated, like all the evenings at Beechwood, with family worship.

As little Fanny that night knelt at her mother's knee to repeat the Lord's Prayer, she looked up into the loving face which beamed so kindly upon her, and said, in her simple manner,

"Isn't God good, dear mamma, to make your little Fanny so happy to-night?"

CHAPTER XI.

The Arrival—Gertrude Vivian's Welcome—Her Dilemma—Mr. Oldbuckle—Fire-works—The Relations of Pyrotechny to Science—History of Fire-works—A Sad Story—Memorable Displays—Ixion's Wheel—Mr. Oldbuckle's Apology.

ABOUT eleven o'clock the next morning, the young people, who were amusing themselves with books in the library, heard a musical jingling of bells upon the lawn, and before they could reach the front steps, the expected party from Viviandale had alighted from the cutter and were just entering the door under William Sinclair's escort. Gertrude Vivian and her brother Edward received the cordial greetings of all the family, and were very soon as much at home in the charming library, as if, in Gertrude's own words, "it was the twentieth instead of the *first* time they had been there."

"You can scarcely be more welcome when you do enter it for the twentieth time, my dear Miss Vivian," was Dr. Sinclair's kind remark.

"I hope, sir," she added naïvely, "you intend to like me better when you know me better, for they can not be very worthy people who do not improve upon acquaintance."

"I have no doubt," he replied, with a pleasant

smile, "that I shall know more of your loveable qualities, my dear Miss Gertrude; but even now I give you credit for possessing them, and welcome you as if I had already more than realized my expectations."

"You are too generous, sir, I fear. I may disappoint you sadly."

"Don't tell her, Dr. Sinclair," interposed Edward Vivian, "that you can not believe it possible, or you will make her altogether too vain," and turning to his sister, whom he loved with a warm and deep affection, he added—

"I fear I shall have to disenchant our kind host, Gerty!"

"Oh! no, Edward; let time and circumstances alone break the spell. Give me all the respite you can," was her laughing reply.

"Well," said Dr. Sinclair, "the day must be very far off when Gertrude Vivian will not be welcomed to Beechwood, with quite as much cordiality as she is now."

Gertrude blushed her thanks, and a deeper flush suddenly overspread her face, as she caught the eye of William Sinclair gazing upon her with eloquent tokens of his unaffected though unspoken sympathy with the general and unlooked-for welcome she had received.

Alice was at her side, prompt to show the gentle and affectionate courtesies which so much delight a guest. Gertrude exerted herself to respond to all the tokens of interest manifested toward her. Nor was the task a difficult one. She soon discovered the interior loveliness of Beechwood, and gave herself up, with a delightful abandonment, to the happy and demonstrative humour of its inmates.

She listened with real interest to Alice's account of their various amusements and studies, and said that nothing could give her more pleasure than to take part in just such scenes and sports. She had enjoyed the best advantages of education. I say enjoyed, not meaning simply that they had been provided for her to enjoy, but that with rare good sense she had so improved them, as to have found them an ample and still abundant source of delight. She had studied diligently, and had not only two years' advantage of our favourite Alice in years, but had acquired habits of reflection and of independent thought, from generous rivalry with many others of her own age with whom she had been associated at school. Alice had never been away from home for the purpose of study, and although her mind was active and healthful, it had developed as yet, more of grace than vigour, under the delicate preceptorship of Miss Maurice. These lessons with the boys, gathered from the daily walks and events of life, were doing a good work for her. They were unfolding the yet embryo powers of her judgment, and were bringing into vigorous exercise, the very gifts which her secluded education had suffered to lie dormant.

Gertrude Vivian manifested no assumed delight when she exclaimed, after a full inspection of the treasures of the library,

"Oh! what a little paradise this must be. If I were an angel even, I could be content to have my wings clipped, so that this might be my abiding place;" and then, catching William Sinclair's eye a second time, she added, with slight confusion, "and I would shut myself up all alone with my priceless treasures."

"Surely not alone, Gerty?" said her brother.

"Oh! you might come, occasionally, if you would promise not to disturb me."

"And no one else?" said Dr. Sinclair. "You wouldn't repay my care and toil in furnishing it by excluding me, I am sure!"

Gertrude found herself in a little dilemma. Her remark, which was designed to cover a slight consciousness of William Sinclair's eager interest in her words, was an unfortunate one. It seemed selfish, and as soon as she perceived it she hastened to disclaim the sentiment, and replied gaily to her host's question,

"Certainly not, sir. I should want you to be sitting always in your arm-chair, the real *genius loci*."

"Thank you for the pretty compliment," said Dr. Sinclair, bowing low.

"Then you wouldn't be *alone*, Miss Vivian," said William.

"Oh! I didn't mean that, I couldn't mean it," was her eager reply. "I should want you all here, just as you are now. My rhapsody was certainly a very foolish one, and I am punished for it by having to retract it."

The morning was beguiled by such like pleasant conversation, among the many delightful accessories of the library. Just before the dinner hour, the merry sound of sleigh-bells again drew some of the party to the window, and Herbert exclaimed,

"Alice! Alice, here comes Mr. Oldbuckle."

Alice hastened to greet him, scarcely stopping to notice, with any thing more than a gratified smile, Gertrude's remark as she heard his name,

"Oh! Alice, I was quite delighted with your quaint old friend."

Mr. Oldbuckle was followed up the steps by a waiting-man who carried a box, which he was instructed to set down just within the hall.

"I have brought" said the old gentleman to Dr. Sinclair, as he approached to greet him, "a Christmas contribution in the shape of fire-works, which I thought would afford the young people some amusement, and perhaps some instruction for Christmas Eve."

"Oh! thank you, thank you, dear Mr. Oldbuckle," said two or three eager voices, and more than twice that number of sparkling eyes, while Dr. Sinclair replied,

"Really my dear sir, I know not how to thank you for your kindness to my little flock. I never thought until this morning of these indispensable accompaniments of Christmas Eve festivity, and I was even now reproaching myself with not having thought of them in season to have made provision. Your forethought and your goodness are equal upon this occasion, and I welcome this plethoric box with a cordial pleasure."

Mr. Oldbuckle seemed highly gratified that his present was so acceptable to all, and he said triumphantly,

"I am glad that it was my good fortune to think of what you forgot."

The young people were exceedingly pleased with the prospect of amusement for the night, and Harry could scarcely refrain from letting his exuberant feelings and anticipations vent themselves in boisterous shouts.

At the dinner-table the conversation naturally turned upon the subject of fire-works. Mr. Oldbuckle asked Alice if she knew any thing of the origin of these ingenious and beautiful contrivances. Alice was obliged to acknowledge that she did not, so her questioner supplied the information that they were probably invented by the Chinese, who have certainly known and used them, in some forms, for many centuries.

"I believe," said Edward Vivian, "that the first public display of fire-works recorded in authentic annals, was made at Florence, five hundred years ago."

"Yes," said Dr. Sinclair, "and almost from that time to the present, they have constituted a very important part of the pageantry of royal or popular celebrations."

"The Florentine show to which you alluded, Mr. Vivian," said Mr. Oldbuckle, "must have been very insignificant, in comparison with those which are got up on great occasions, now-a-days."

"Doubtless it was, for they had then comparatively few forms of fire-works; and for two or three centuries subsequently they made no great advances in the art of pyrotechny."

"Herbert," said Dr. Sinclair, "you can probably give us the etymology of the term Mr. Vivian has just employed."

"It is a Greek compound, sir, of *pur* meaning fire, and *techné* signifying art."

"Precisely, and pyrotechny means the art of fire, that is, of producing and managing fire, but the term is now generally confined to the art of making fireworks."

"I have heard pyrotechny called a *science*, sir," said Herbert.

"Yes, and it is properly so called, for it investigates the laws and properties of artificial fire, and contrives combinations according to them."

"It is sometimes claimed as a mathematical science, is it not, sir?" said William Sinclair.

"It is, but belongs rather to chemistry, I think," replied his father.

"Its relations to mathematics, however, are very clear and important," said Mr. Oldbuckle. "It has to do with measures and proportions."

"We may claim it then for mechanics," said Edward Vivian, "upon the plea that it involves forces, directions of motion, etc."

"And for optics," said William Sinclair, "because it has a great deal to do with the organs of vision, at least in its effect; so that it may be said of it, in vulgar parlance, 'It is all in my eye.'"

This humorous claim for the relationship of Pyrotechny, was acknowledged by all with hearty laughter; and then Dr. Sinclair turned to Miss Vivian, and asked her which of the sciences she would connect it with.

"Oh! with Astronomy, by all means," was her quick reply; "for does it not reveal to us suns and stars, and fiery comets, and all sorts of blazing portents?"

"Your claim is very well made out, indeed, Miss Vivian," said Dr. Sinclair, "and between us all, it does not seem likely that the art—or science, rather—of Pyrotechny, is in any danger of being disowned of the philosophic family."

"Do you recollect," said Mr. Oldbuckle, "the

terrible catastrophe which terminated the grand display of fire-works that was contrived at Paris, in honour of the nuptials of Louis the Sixteenth?"

"Now that you mention it, I recall the nature of the calamity," replied Dr. Sinclair.

"What was it, papa?" said Alice.

"He was married in the sixteenth year of his age, to the unfortunate but beautiful Marie Antoinette. The event occurred on the 16th of May, 1770, and was celebrated with the most magnificent pomp and festivities. During the exhibition of the fire-works, a vast quantity of prepared pieces, intended to take the places of others previously put up, were ignited by a misdirected rocket, and exploded with fearful violence, scattering death in every direction. A very great number of the spectators—some say a thousand—were either instantly killed, or so badly burned and crushed that they died."

"Oh! how terrible!" said Miss Vivian. "It must have clouded not only the marriage, but the whole life of the royal pair."

"I have no doubt that it would have been always a shadow upon the heart of the fair queen, had not personal sorrows pressed upon her with a deeper and darker sense of wo," replied Dr. Sinclair.

"Who of us can remember other great occasions upon which memorable displays of fire-works were made?"

"At the peace of Aix la Chapelle, concluded

between France and England, in 1745," said Miss Vivian.

"At the general peace of England and her allies with France, which was made in 1814," said William Sinclair.

"At the passage of the Reform Bill in London, in 1832," said Mr. Oldbuckle.

"At the reception of Lafayette in New-York, in 1824," said Alice.

"At the celebration of the battle of Buena Vista, in the same city, in 1847," said Herbert.

"And now for your instance, Harry," said his father.

"I shall make mine prophetic, sir, with your permission and say—

"At Beechwood on Christmas Eve, 1852, upon the occasion of a visit from Mr. Oldbuckle, Miss Vivian, and other illustrious guests."

"The defection of your memory shall be forgiven, my boy, on account of your well-timed wit."

The whole company applauded Harry's instance, and he declared that he could hardly have felt prouder, had he been Lafayette or General Taylor himself.

"It is noticeable," said Edward Vivian, "that the names of the two most famous places for the display of fire-works at the present day, in England and in France, begin with V; the French Versailles and the English Vauxhall."

"I was present," said Mr. Oldbuckle, "at a fête, given two or three years since, at Campden Hill, Kensington, upon the birth-day of the Earl of Rosse, whose great telescope has made his name famous in both hemispheres. The fire-works upon that occasion were exceedingly magnificent, both in the variety and novelty of the designs; but nothing pleased me so much as a representation of the beautiful myth of Ixion's wheel."

"I can readily imagine," said Dr. Sinclair, "that such a striking subject might be most effectively displayed."

"The body of Ixion was represented in pale fire, upon a revolving wheel of deep crimson light, while fiery and hissing serpents enveloped him in their snaky folds."

"I think it must have been a sight rather terrible than pleasing," said Mrs. Sinclair; an opinion in which Gertrude and Alice coïncided, while the boys thought it must have been "very grand," and expressed their impatience for the advent of the friendly darkness.

"You must not expect too much of my poor contribution, Master Harry," said Mr. Oldbuckle. "I shall not frighten the ladies with the Ixion of Campden, nor amaze them with the grand allegorical tableau of peace, at the celebration in 1814. I have but a modest collection of rockets, and wheels, and courantines, and candles, with something," he added, looking significantly at Alice, "which shall find a name from your own lips, my bird, when it comes off."

"Do not be too impatient for night to come, Harry," said his brother, "for it will take us some time to make suitable arrangements to display the fire-works to advantage."

"Yes, and we shall find something for you and Herbert to do in our service this afternoon," said Mr. Oldbuckle.

The boys both declared themselves ready to do any thing in their power, and begged that they might have a full share in the preparations. Mrs. Sinclair now rose, and the whole party left the table and returned to the library.

The gentlemen did not, however, spare much time from the important work they had before them, and were soon busily occupied out of doors.

CHAPTER XII.

Preparations for the Fire-works—Waiting for the Darkness—
Amusement for the Interval—Playing Proverbs—Nine o'clock.

THE spot chosen for the exhibition of the fire-works was upon the lawn, almost beneath the great tower-window of the library. It was selected to afford the ladies a good view, without exposing them to the cold air and the snow-covered ground. A light frame-work was erected for the wheels, candles, and some other pieces. From this, also, to an adjacent tree, were stretched light ropes, on which the courantines or running-rockets were to move. The preparations were not very elaborate, but they were made with care to ensure, as far as possible, the perfect discharge of the fireworks.

As the moon was near the end of her first quarter, her light, especially with the bright reflection of the snow, was too great in the early part of the night, not to have impaired the effect of the fireworks. It was therefore resolved to delay the exhibition until nine o'clock, by which time the fair queen of night would be about retiring from the scene, and as Mr. Oldbuckle said, would

"Leave the world to darkness and to—us."

As there was a long interval between tea-time and the hour named, various parlour amusements were proposed. Miss Vivian pleaded for another charade-play, Alice having told her of the one which was performed a few evenings before. Mrs. Sinclair, nowever, having laboured all day under a slight indisposition, declared herself unequal to the task of acting, and suggested that Miss Vivian herself would be an admirable substitute; the latter declined, and it was finally arranged that a charade-play should be the order for the next night, and that the broken evening before them should be devoted to the play of Proverbs. This amusing and instructive game was not familiar to the circle at Beechwood. Miss Vivian and her brother were the only ones who had participated in the play, but they very soon made the method clear to the perception of all.

Edward Vivian was named by his sister as the first to guess a proverb, and he cheerfully assented, pleading only, as he left the comfortable library, that they would not consign him long to the cold and his own miserable companionship.

"Oh! as for the cold, Mr. Vivian, you can go into the dining-room, where you will find a comfortable fire," said Mrs. Sinclair.

"Thank you," he replied, "but I will stay near the door of the library, that I may not happen to be out of call."

"Ah! you rogue," said his sister; "take care, however, that you do keep out of hearing until you are called."

He retired, laughing, and the selection of a proverb was now the immediate concern of the party.

"We must choose a somewhat rare one to puzzle Edward," said Miss Vivian, "for he is quite an adept."

Several were proposed and rejected as too easy, and Gertrude's high standard seemed little likely to be reached, when Dr. Sinclair suggested an old proverb: "The tongue is not steel, but it cuts."

"That sounds less familiar to me than most of those named; let us try it," said Gertrude, as her brother's rap on the door indicated his readiness, if not his impatience, to be put to the trial provided for him.

"The proverb," she continued, "contains eight words, and we are just eight in number, not including Fanny, who can hardly take part in this amusement, I fancy, though her eyes do sparkle with intelligence." Mary had taken her mamma's counsel—to try and sleep off a headache. "A word for each of us, and now Edward will come in and propose a question to each, in order, and in the answer to the question—which should be as brief as possible without actually endangering the secret—the word assigned must be introduced."

The explanation was understood by all, and Edward Vivian was summoned into the room. He was directed to begin with Harry, who sat nearest to the door, and to continue around the group.

"Well, Master Harry," he began, "are you impatient for the hour of nine to arrive?"

"Yes, sir, though I think I shall like the present play very much," replied Harry.

"And how is it with you, Mr. Oldbuckle?" said Edward.

"Your tongue is ready with questions, I find, Mr. Vivian."

"Tongue—ready," murmured Edward to himself; and then aloud to his sister,

"Well, sis, what is the third word in this hidden proverb?"

"That is for you to guess, sir," was the answer.

"Very little in that oracle—don't you think so, Dr. Sinclair?" was his next question.

"Not much, I must acknowledge," said the host of Beechwood.

"Will my dear madam,"—to Mrs. Sinclair—"have pity on me, and aid me in my quest?"

"My heart must be steel to refuse such a petition," was the reply.

"It is'nt *steel*—her heart, I mean—do you think it is, Alice?"

"I should say no; but then I'm a partial judge, Mr. Vivian."

"Will your word afford me much help, Master Russel?"

" I don't think it will, sir," was Herbert's prompt answer.

"So, so, chum, prove yourself my friend, now, won't you?" said Edward to William Sinclair.

"Certainly I will; no true junior ever cuts his classmate."

"There, Mr. Proverbialist, you have all the words of our riddle," said his sister.

"And now I will put them together for you," was his response. "It was from my excellent hostess I first discovered that 'The tongue is not steel, but it cuts.'"

"And the proverb is verified," said Dr. Sinclair, "for it was the tongue that cut the knot of this riddle—was it *not?*" he added, playfully emphasizing the negative.

"And now, Mrs. Sinclair," said Edward Vivian, "I shall resign my office and my guessing-cap to you by the laws of the game."

"I am afraid," said that lady, as she rose to go out of the room, "I shall not be fortunate enough to designate my successor to the honour. Let me, therefore, pray your clemency in the choice of an enigma for me."

"What shall it be?" said Alice, as her mother retired; "don't let us choose a very difficult one, if you please."

"Well, Alice, the choice be yours," said Miss Vivian.

"Oh! Miss Gertrude, not mine, I can't think of any proverbs, but—but—"

"But what, Ally?" said her father.

"'All is not gold that glitters,' papa."

"Excellent, my bird," and Alice looked pleased at the approval of her old friend.

"The proverb is not long enough to go round," said Harry.

"Never mind that," was Miss Vivian's answer; "there are words for six of us—beginning this time with Mr. Sinclair."

Mrs. Sinclair was called in and directed to her eldest son for the first clue to the labyrinth prepared for her.

"Are you glad to get home again, William?" was her query.

"I wish I could answer all questions as easily as I can say 'Yes' to that, my dear mother."

"Is the first word in his answer, Herbert?"

"Indeed it is, ma'am."

"Alice, my child, you will help your mother, I know?"

"I should not be worthy to be her child if I would not," was the dutiful reply.

"Mr. Vivian, you took the successful clue from me; can I not possibly bribe you to return the favour?"

"Let me answer you in the words of the song, Mrs. Sinclair—

> Seek not with gold to bribe me,
> Thy smiles are all I ask.'"

"Shall I grant him his request, my dear?" said Mrs. Sinclair to her husband.

"That question is too late, if I may judge from your face," he replied.

"Mr. Oldbuckle—to turn the subject a little—are you fond of fire-works?"

"Listen, dear madam, to the words of the poet—

> 'I love the rocket's arrowy flight
> That glitters o'er the sea of night,
> And makes the concave glow with light.'"

"If you are not enlightened now, my dear Mrs. Sinclair," said Gertrude Vivian, "you must begin your quest again, for the proverb is all unfolded."

"I have had repeated lessons of the same sort in my experience," said Mrs. Sinclair, "and am not inclined to doubt the truth of the adage, that 'All is not gold that glitters.'"

"And who gave you the guess-word, mamma?" said Alice.

"I ought to have found it, I suppose, in Mr. Vivian's 'gold,' but my dulness was not penetrated, I confess, until Mr. Oldbuckle's rocket glittered on my sight."

"Oh! it is Mr. Oldbuckle's turn to go out then,' said Harry.

"And I yield to my fate," said that gentleman, rising as he spoke.

Miss Vivian proposed the proverb, "Cut your coat according to your cloth," and it was accordingly chosen and Mr. Oldbuckle speedily called back. He was directed to begin where the previous proverb ended, and he, therefore, addressed himself to Mrs. Sinclair, who had taken the chair which he vacated.

"Well, my dear madam, is it a very hard knot which I have to untie?"

"You may have to do as Alexander did with the Gordian knot—cut it, Mr. Oldbuckle."

"Harry, will you lend me your knife for the operation?"

"Your scissors, mamma, will suit Mr. Oldbuckle better."

"What do you think of Alexander, William?"

"I think so great a man would have required a very great coat, especially in winter."

"A Mackintosh probably, eh, Herbert?"

"That would hardly have been according to the fashion of Babylon, Mr. Oldbuckle."

"Are you going to sing for me to-night, my bird?"

"Not to-night, Mr. Oldbuckle," said Alice.

"Mr. Vivian, the proverb is a difficult one."

"Hardly, to your acumen, sir," replied Edward.

"Well, then, do you think, Dr. Sinclair, that I shall be apt to make a mistake in cutting my coat to-night?"

"Not," said that gentleman, laughing, "if you measure the cloth I shall now furnish you."

And Mr. Oldbuckle was rewarded for his penetration, by the approval of all the company.

"The coat will fit William this time, I think," said Dr. Sinclair.

"Yes, it belongs to him, for I borrowed it from him," said Mr. Oldbuckle, taking the chair from which William now rose and immediately retired. After two or three proverbs had been pronounced too simple it was agreed to choose "Faint heart never won fair lady," and he was recalled.

"Miss Vivian," he began, "I depend upon your courtesy to put me on the right track in this difficult quest."

"You will get but a faint idea of the proverb from my answer, Mr. Sinclair."

"Well, my dear mother, do you wish me well out of this labyrinth?"

"With all my heart, William."

"Harry, had I better give it up at once, do you think?"

"It will never do to give it up so, Mr. Brown," a response, which was rewarded with a general burst of merriment.

"Mr. Oldbuckle, can you tell me why the Duke of Wellington was a great gamester?"

"Because he won the day at Water-*loo*, I suppose."

"Well, Herbert, which was the word in Mr. Oldbuckle's reply?"

"That's not a fair question, I think," said Herbert

"How old are you, Alice?"

"That's a question you should never ask a lady, brother William."

"Never mind, without your answer I know that 'Faint heart never won fair lady;' and I must be ungallant enough to send Miss Vivian into the other room."

"What," said that lady, "did you guess it upon my *faint* hint?"

"Indeed I did; it was any thing but a faint hint to me, many thanks;" and he took the chair which she resigned.

The proverb now selected was, "Strike while the iron is hot."

Miss Vivian was very soon called in again, and addressing her brother, who, in due turn, had the first word, she said—

"What o'clock is it, Edward?"

"The clock will very soon strike nine."

"You are apparently in a brown study, Dr. Sinclair?"

"Not while you are addressing me, certainly, Miss Vivian."

"More gallant than intelligible, isn't he, Mr. Sinclair?"

"You will recollect, Miss Vivian, that I know the word."

"Will you tell me, my dear Mrs. Sinclair, which is the most useful of all the metals?"

"I think I detect a little iron-y in your tones, Miss Vivian?"

"And I discover something stronger in yours, Mrs. Sinclair, so without waiting for further hints, I will 'Strike while the iron is hot.'"

"Ah! Miss Gertrude," said Dr. Sinclair, "we dealt too gently with you."

"On the contrary, sir, you began from the first to *strike* too hard."

"Ah! then, Mr. Vivian betrayed us, did he?"

"If that be the case," said Edward, "I must plead with Miss Alice to relieve me from double duty. Will she not stand for me this time?"

Alice was persuaded to take her turn upon the promise of a short and easy proverb, for the hour of nine was now close at hand. Miss Vivian named the familiar proverb, "One good turn deserves another," and Alice have been called in, began her questioning with Harry—

"Have they really chosen an easy proverb, Harry?"

"Yes, Alice, a very easy one."

"Now, Mr. Oldbuckle, give me a lift," said Alice.

"That I will, my bird, and a good one too."

"Herbert, I want some help from you."

"And I give it to you in my turn," was his reply.

"Mr. Vivian," said Alice, "it was to oblige you I went out this time."

"And such generosity deserves much praise, I am sure."

"I am not quite through the proverb yet, I believe, papa."

"You need another word only, I believe," was the reply.

"And I am indebted to you for not only that, dear papa, but for the ability to declare the proverb to be, 'One good turn deserves another.'"

"Very well indeed, my daughter; I am quite proud of you. Another time Harry and Herbert shall both have a chance to acquit themselves as well; but now we must set off our fire-works."

"Hurrah," said Harry, "not that I love proverbs less, but fire-works more."

CHAPTER XIII.

A Compromise—The Signal—Flight of Rockets—The Rocket's Path—Why the Rocket rises—Its Rudder—Roman Candles—Sea Signals—A Catharine Wheel—Courantines—A Dragon—A Spiral Rocket—Serpents—Loaded Rockets—The Daft Boy—Chinese Fire—A Mock Sun—Alice—Thanks.

WHILE the gentlemen were making the final arrangements to set off the fire-works, the ladies gathered in the window to witness the scene, congratulating themselves that they had so warm and pleasant a point of observation.

"But, mamma," said Alice, "I never thought that by staying in here, we shall completely lose all the explanations which Mr. Oldbuckle and papa will make to Harry and Herbert."

"That is a drawback, certainly, to our cosy corner," said Gertrude Vivian, "and I would rather feel a little cold air than miss the conversation."

"Let us then," said Mrs. Sinclair, "put on our shawls and bonnets and throw open the window. The gentlemen can then join us without leaving the ground, and we can join in the conversation."

This plan was immediately adopted, and all the group, including Mary, who had stipulated to be called in time, was presently gathered in the recess

As usual in all pyrotechnic displays, the discharge of a rocket announced the beginning of the exhibition.

"Oh! how beautiful," said Alice, as the brilliant herald sprang swiftly upward, with a rushing noise, leaving behind it a path of light.

"And look, Alice," said Herbert, "there is a shower of white stars falling from it."

While they were yet speaking, a number of rockets rose in quick succession, some of them almost perpendicularly, and others in an oblique direction.

"Do you notice, Herbert," said Mr. Oldbuckle, "that there is no curve in the path of the rocket until it is nearly spent, and then it bends over and falls."

"Yes, sir, but what makes it rise at all?"

"Did you observe that the rocket was kindled at the bottom?"

"I have always wondered at that, sir."

"The burning of the combustible material in the lower part of the cylinder, generates a vast quantity of gas, which rushes out of the orifice in all directions. Its escape is opposed by the air, with a force which so greatly exceeds the weight of the rocket, that the latter is driven upwards, and this motion continues until the force is quite spent."

"What is the use of the stick, sir?" inquired Alice.

"It is the rudder of the rocket, my bird."

"Its rudder, sir?" said Harry, "is a rocket steered like a ship?"

"Not exactly like a ship, my boy, but it moves in

the line of its rudder, so that when the stick is perfectly straight, the rocket must move in a perfectly straight line."

Dr. Sinclair now approached the window, bearing in each hand a white narrow cylinder, both of them already pouring out showers of bright sparks.

"Oh! see, mamma, what a beautiful blue ball," exclaimed Fanny, and as she spoke a second ball followed the first, and then a succession of different coloured balls shot out from the blazing cylinders, six from each of them, and fell; some of them so near the window, that Fanny shrunk behind mamma.

"Those are Roman candles, are they not, papa?" said Alice.

"Yes, my daughter; they are very simple but pleasing fire-works, consisting of cylinders filled, in sections, with a composition that burns slowly. The balls are made of various ingredients according to the colour they exhibit."

"Are not rockets and Roman candles made use of at sea as signals?" asked Herbert.

"Very commonly. When a ship is approaching a coast in a fog, she throws rockets, which, if seen, are answered from the shore; or when one ship is on the look-out for another in the night, she throws rockets or burns Roman candles at intervals, until she discovers a similar signal. In a hundred ways, these and other fire-works, are useful at sea, and especially upon the coast."

Mr. Oldbuckle now called attention to a large Catharine wheel, to which he applied his burning match. It began to emit sparks, and then revolved with great velocity, so that there was a brilliant disc of fire, six or eight feet in diameter, in which the rays seemed all the while streaming from a central point. In a few moments, it changed suddenly into a score of brilliant circles, one within the other, which was again succeeded by a torrent of sparks bordered by a fringe of purple flame, which resembled a broad and brilliant riband. A fourth and fifth section exhibited still more brilliant effects, and the young people gazed with unfeigned delight.

"Is the Catharine wheel propelled like the rocket, Mr. Oldbuckle?" asked Harry.

"Precisely, only its motion is circular because it is confined by a rod, or pin, passing through the centre of gravity to the whole piece."

"Oh! what a very beautiful sight," said Mary, who had been gazing, hitherto, without a word. The exclamation was elicited by the flight of a courantine, or flying rocket. It ran swiftly from the frame-work along a cord which passed to a tree, and having reached the end of its route appeared to return. This curious effect was produced by having two rockets tied together in opposite directions, and both fastened to an empty cartridge which moved upon the cord. The exhausted rocket set fire to the remaining one, which produced the retrograde motion.

"These courantines," said Dr. Sinclair, "are much employed to communicate fire to set-pieces, in grand exhibitions."

"At the exhibition at Campden Hill," said Mr. Oldbuckle, "I saw one in the shape of a dragon, which glowed with a fiery red colour and emitted jets of flame, as it rushed on its ærial way."

"This," said Dr. Sinclair, as he now drew near the group "is a spiral rocket. You observe that it is fastened to a bent rod, which, when it is ignited, will so shift its course, that the path described will be spiral."

He now placed it almost erect against a small stand which stood by, and kindled the match at its lower extremity. A shower of sparks succeeded, and the rocket whizzed off and wound its way rapidly into the air.

"Oh! papa," said Alice, "it did not rise very high."

"No, my child, because of the tortuous nature of its path. The whole line of its flight was quite as long, perhaps, as it would have been had its rod been straight instead of curved."

William Sinclair now threw a lighted serpent into the air. It sprang upward with a rocket-like motion and a shower of sparks, but at the height of the neighbouring trees, it suddenly turned and came, with a zigzag course, toward the ground close to the tower window, when it exploded with such a report as to make quite a commotion among the ladies. A second serpent was then discharged, which pursued a course equally erratic with the first, though in an opposite direction. Mr. Oldbuckle explained to Harry that the serpent is a rocket without a rod, divided into two parts, the one filled with composition, and the other with grained or mealed powder. It is the latter which explodes. Mr. Oldbuckle now produced a large rocket, to an empty cartridge on the head of which, were attached several smaller rockets, so arranged that they would ignite during the ascent. He placed the rocket on the stand provided for the purpose, so that the long stick was perpendicular to the ground, and in this position the igniting match was applied. The rocket rose in the air with a tremendous hissing, and in a few seconds the little rockets kindled, and threw out several streams of fire, which bore some resemblance to the branches of a tree, the path of the large rocket being the trunk.

This piece was so successful, that Edward Vivian took pains to prepare something still more complicated. To another large rocket, containing a petard, he affixed three serpents and some bearded rockets charged with golden rain. As the whole ascended with a mighty rush, the serpents took fire and performed some very strange antics. Presently the bearded rockets discharged their golden showers, and when the rocket reached its extreme height, the petard exploded with a very loud report.

While the group at the window was discussing the

probable effect of these blazing meteors, and startling reports, upon the people of the neighbourhood, a loud shouting was heard at the front gate, and William Sinclair proceeded in that direction. He found there a daft boy who lived about a mile off and had been attracted by the unusual sights in the sky. The boy, when he saw some one near him, made numerous violent gesticulations toward the sky and renewed his shouts. William Sinclair motioned to him to go round upon the other side of the garden, where he could see the proceedings, and during the rest of the exhibition he manifested the wildest delight. It was once changed into a sort of terror, as a serpent, after turning in the air, fell in the direction of his position and exploded almost in his ears.

Without premonition to the spectators, Edward Vivian now ignited a mass of red Chinese fire, which was placed in a crucible, just behind the trunk of a large tree. The effect was exceedingly beautiful, and vastly heightened by the snow. A deep crimson glow was diffused throughout the air, and every object, animate and inanimate, reflected the strong light. The snow seemed to be suddenly steeped in blood, and, for an instant, fear rather than pleasure seized the spectators, who could not see the burning mass itself.

This was followed by a very beautiful piece which Mr. Oldbuckle called a sun. It was formed by disposing several jets, or fixed rockets. upon a wooden disc, so nicely balanced upon a steel rod, that it turned with the least motion. A dozen of these jets were fastened on the disc with their mouths toward its outer edge. Fire was then communicated to all the rockets at once, and the disc was made to revolve with great velocity by their reäction. The result was a magnificent radiation of streams of fire filling a large circumference, and not inaptly likened to a glorious sun. This exhibition elicited the warmest admiration of every one of the spectators. Even the daft boy was seen clapping his hands with delight.

Dr. Sinclair now gave notice that the last scene of the pageant was to be presented, and Alice was reminded by Mr. Oldbuckle that the piece was to receive its name from her. Expectation was at its height, and Alice almost trembled with excitement.

The piece was arranged upon the top of the frame already mentioned. A small courantine, blazing with red fire, now darted up from behind a neighbouring tree, and ignited a group of jets which threw out sparks of various colours, and resembled a vast plume. As this died away, a number of pin-wheels were successively ignited and revolved with ever-varying splendour. In the very midst of these whirling rays there suddenly appeared, in bright red letters, which glowed for some moments after the wheels were still, the name of

Alice.

It was hailed with the most enthusiastic shouts and plaudits, and Herbert took the occasion of the excitement to press the hand of our young favourite, and to whisper, "This is the most beautiful thing of all, dear Alice." Thus ended the exhibition of fire-works at Beechwood, and Harry triumphantly declared that his prophecy of the morning had been justified to the very letter. Every one, as if by a common impulse, pressed around the worthy Mr. Oldbuckle to thank him, again and again, for the delight he had afforded them, and he, in his turn, declared that it had been one of the happiest evenings he had ever spent in the New World.

The festivities of Christmas Eve were then appropriately followed by grateful praise, and humble prayer, to Him who giveth every innocent pleasure.

CHAPTER XIV.

Fanny's "Merry Christmas"—Old Jacob Fletcher—Alice's Greetings—Mr. Oldbuckle's Memories—Morning Worship—A Christmas Hymn—Christmas in America—Why Not Generally Observed—Chronology at Fault—Wishes—Christmas at the South—Negro Festivals—The Southern "Yule Log"—Christmas-greens—Mr. Oldbuckle's Proposition—Its General Acceptance.

"MERRY Christmas!" was Fanny's eager and repeated exclamation, as one after another of the family and guests, at Beechwood, entered the library on the morning of Christmas day. The little girl had anticipated every one in rising, except the domestics of the establishment, and had resolved to be first to offer every one the beautiful salutation of the season. "Merry Christmas, Mr. O'buckle," (for so Fanny always called him,) she said, as that gentleman made his appearance, first of the guests, excepting, indeed, Herbert, who had been there with Harry for a moment, but was now off, with him, to the pond to try the ice.

"The same to you, my dear little girl," said the kind-hearted old gentleman, and he lifted Fanny in his arms and pressed a kiss right upon her rosy lips, a tribute of affection which she received from every one, I believe, who entered the library that morning. I am sure that old Jacob Fletcher paid it, for he went on purpose, and his eyes glistened with emotion as the little girl ran eagerly toward him, exclaiming, "Merry Christmas, Uncle Jacob." The old man did as Mr. Oldbuckle had done before him—took the child in his arms and said fervently,

"God bless you, dear little Fanny, and give you many a merry Christmas!"

Alice had scarcely fewer Christmas kisses than her little sister, and I can answer for one of those who forbore to offer her that testimony of love, that it was not from disinclination. Herbert Russel was charmed with her grace, as much as with her beauty, and cherished for her a very warm, but boyish admiration, which Alice was too ingenuous to observe with any other consciousness than that of pleasure.

Mr. Oldbuckle greeted Alice with more than usual tenderness, and his eyes filled with tears as he held her a willing prisoner, at his side, for a few moments. This Alice observed and looked a sympathy so gentle and anxious, that he said in low tones—

"You wonder at my emotion, my child? I once had a daughter who bore your name, and whom you resemble so much in many things, that I have often longed to tell you of it, and so have more than one excuse for making a pet of you."

Alice's eyes grew suddenly bright with tears, which were not shed, however, and she said,

"You must tell me about *your* Alice, Mr. Oldbuckle."

"She died when she was almost a year younger than you are, and sleeps within the evening shadow of an ivy-wreathed church, in an English grave-yard. She was my only daughter, and it is thirty years since I buried her; but I have not forgotten one tone of her voice, nor one smile of her beautiful face."

The entrance of Gertrude Vivian, with warm greetings, put an end to Mr. Oldbuckle's low-voiced conversation with Alice. She was immediately succeeded by her brother and William Sinclair, and a few moments, afterward, the host of Beechwood made his appearance, followed by Mrs. Sinclair and Mary. While they were still exchanging the compliments of the morning and of the season, the boys returned from their visit to the pond, and reported the ice firm and almost strong enough for skating.

The customary routine of family worship was slightly varied, this morning, by the addition of a Christmas hymn, to the usual reading of a portion of the Scriptures. All the family united in singing the well-known words—

>"Hark, the herald angels sing
> Glory to our new-born king,
> Peace on earth and mercy mild,
> God and sinners reconciled."

Dr. Sinclair offered up fervent thanksgiving to God for the gift of his beloved Son, Jesus Christ, and prayed that the rich blessings of his grace and salvation might be bestowed upon them and upon all men.

At the breakfast-table, after due attention had been paid to the delicacies which Mrs. Sinclair's care had provided, a very general conversation ensued.

"You have observed, Mr. Oldbuckle," said Mrs. Sinclair, "that Christmas is a season more observed in England, than it is in this country."

"I should say, Mrs. Sinclair," was Mr. Oldbuckle's reply, "that it is not observed at all here, except by the church. It certainly can not be called a *popular* festival."

"And 'the church,' in the sense in which I suppose you use the term, Mr. Oldbuckle, embraces so small a part of the Christian community, throughout the United States, that Christmas obtains but a sorry recognition, even in an ecclesiastical sense," said Dr. Sinclair.

"In New-England," said William Sinclair, "I believe Christmas is quite overlooked."

"Yes," replied Gertrude Vivian, "overshadowed in the superior glories of thanksgiving."

"Roast beef and plum pudding, eclipsed by roast turkey and pumpkin pies," was Edward Vivian's amplification of his sister's remark.

"I have wondered," resumed Mr. Oldbuckle, "at the popular indifference, in this country, to this famous festival of the Old World. The event which it commemorates should be as dear to the American heart as it is to the English."

"And so perhaps it is," said Dr. Sinclair, "but there are two great reasons why Christmas is not such a festival, in this land, as it is in the mother country."

"What are they, sir?" said Mr. Oldbuckle, with interest."

"The first," replied Dr. Sinclair, "is a lack of reverence for the institutions of antiquity, which marks our national character. It is, very probably, a defect, and is akin to that lack of the home-love which is alleged against us, with too much justice, by English and German writers. We are a new people, with new tastes, new 'notions,' new aims, and new manners."

"I see," said Mr. Oldbuckle, "a great deal of meaning in your words, and can understand their application to the immemorial festival of Christmas; but still I can not imagine how it is, that the birth-day of our Saviour can be so generally disregarded in this Christian, and I may say, eminently evangelical land."

"My second reason," said Dr. Sinclair, with a slight smile, "will answer your question, although it may greatly excite your surprise."

"I am indeed eager to hear it, then."

"It is a question of chronology, Mr. Oldbuckle. There is a very prevalent doubt among us, that the 25th of December is, with any propriety, fixed upon as the day upon which Christ was born in Bethlehem of Judea.'

"The fact you state surprises me less than this—that the identity of the day should be considered of absolute importance."

"It may well seem strange, I grant," said Dr. Sinclair, "to those of us who grew up into a reverence for the event, as connected with a day made imposing by all manner of ceremonies and festivities. It is otherwise, however, with a fresh and new-moulded people."

"For my part," said Mrs. Sinclair, "I wish Christmas was celebrated here as it is in England—barring the superstitions, on the one hand, and the unseemly revels on the other, which formerly blemished the festival in some parts of the land."

"I echo your wish, my dear mother," said William Sinclair, "though I do so, simply, from the high opinion which I entertain of the conservative influence of such time-honoured festivals as this upon the popular mind."

"An important consideration, certainly," said his father; "but I would add to what I said just now, that the religious sentiment of this land is so hostile to all Popish ceremonies, that it is quite impossible that one so conspicuous, in the Romish Church as Christmas, should not be looked upon with jealousy, to say the least."

"You present the matter to me in a new aspect,' said Mr. Oldbuckle, "though my heart clings warmly to the 'Merry Christmas' of 'Merry England.'"

"And so does mine," returned Dr. Sinclair, "though I am free to confess, that I can not make it a sacred or an ecclesiastical obligation, without doing violence to chronology. We keep Christmas at Beechwood, because we love occasions for the reünion of the separated, and for thanksgiving to the Author of all good. And this," he added, "is just as fitting a day upon which to be grateful for the advent of Christ, as any other in the whole year."

"We are agreed, then," said Mr. Oldbuckle, "in spirit, though we differ somewhat in the letter."

"Christmas is a great holiday at the South," said Edward Vivian. "I had the happiness of spending a December month there, with a college friend. He resided in Charleston, but his father owned a large plantation on the sea-board, and my time was passed almost equally in the city and the country home. I never saw such genial, hearty enjoyment, as that which marked Christmas week at Roseland. The hall was crowded with guests, and most bountiful cheer was provided for the company. Much as I enjoyed the festivities in the hall, however, I felt a much greater interest in witnessing the sports and frolics which prevailed among the servants, of whom there were nearly two hundred, great and small. The whole week was given up to mirth, and visiting, and feasting. Dancing was the most popular amusement of the night; and I have seen a much less animated and pleasing sight, than a large company of gaily-dressed negroes, moving to the sound of the violin and banjo."

"Do the slaves at the South generally have the Christmas holidays to themselves?" said Mr. Oldbuckle.

"Everywhere, sir, I believe," was Edward Vivian's reply. "I was told that the general rule is to exempt them from any but voluntary service as long as the yule log smoulders."

"Do they have a yule log in the South?" asked Mr. Oldbuckle.

"Oh! yes; and the servants are cunning enough to protract their holiday by selecting the largest and toughest log of black gum which they can find, and by soaking it in the creek, for a week beforehand, to make it burn slowly. If the master wants the service of a negro during the Christmas holidays, he must make a bargain with him."

"Are you aware," said Mr. Oldbuckle, addressing Dr. Sinclair, "that, in the northern counties of England, the servants were formerly entitled to ale at their meals, so long as the yule log lasted?"

"I do not think I should have remembered," he replied, "if I ever knew the fact, which certainly finds a curious coincidence in what Mr. Vivian says of the southern yule log."

"Do they decorate the halls with Christmas greens in the South, Mr. Vivian?"

"I do not know, sir, that it is universally done; but

at Roseland there was a profusion of the bright holly of the cedar, and of the mistleto about the rooms."

"I should like very much to spend a Christmas in the South, from the account you give me of it."

"Let me atone, sir, for my very meagre description of it, by referring you to a nouvelette, entitled, "The Golden Christmas," from the pen of South Carolina's great novelist, Mr. Simms. That is a picture, sir, which will make you laugh with delight!"

"I suppose your young people," said Mr. Oldbuckle to Dr. Sinclair, "are not ignorant of the Christmas sports of Old England."

"Oh! no, sir," said Alice, "both papa and mamma are eloquent, at times, with stories of Christmas in England. I have got a 'Christmas piece,' which I will show you, after breakfast, executed by papa in his juvenile days."

"I shall be happy to gaze upon the eloquent memorial," said Mr. Oldbuckle; "it will carry me back to other times; but before we leave the breakfast table," he added, as he observed the indications of a finished meal, "I wish to ask who will accompany me to St. James's Church, to attend the Christmas-morning services there?"

Alice's eyes seemed to intimate a desire to do so, and the old gentleman resumed:

"It is only a pleasant ride, and I have ordered a sleigh to be here at half past nine o'clock, which will carry as many of you as are inclined to go. I may count you one, Alice?"

"And me another," said Gertrude Vivian, "if you will accept so prompt a volunteer."

"With all my heart," was his cordial reply.

"I presume," said William Sinclair, "that it will be pleasant to all of us to go. I can answer for myself that it will."

"It would delight me to go," said Mrs. Sinclair, "but I must, of necessity, be left behind; or my Christmas hospitality may suffer, in our friend Mr. Oldbuckle's estimation, and that I could not endure. I do not think it best for Mary to go either, but for the rest of the young people, I commend to them the ride and the pleasant service, too."

"I cordially approve the idea," said Dr. Sinclair, "and if Mr. Oldbuckle will pledge himself for the pews of St. James', as liberally as he does for the capacity of his sleigh, there is no reason why we may not all go; and if one sleigh is not sufficient we can have two."

"St. James' will bid you all welcome, I am sure, and I shall be delighted to introduce you there."

St. James' Church was situated in a country parish about ten miles from Beechwood. Mr. Oldbuckle was a pew-holder there, there being no other Episcopal Church so near to his abode. The long conversasation had protracted the breakfast sitting until it was now nine o'clock, and there remained barely time enough to get ready before Mr. Oldbuckle's sleigh was to arrive.

Edward Vivian went out to order his cutter, proposing either to drive his sister himself, or to resign the reins of it to his friend William Sinclair, if, as he fancied it would, the arangement should be agreeable to him.

CHAPTER XV.

Christmas Dinner — Church Decoration — Wordsworth — Snap-Dragon — Evening Amusement — Charade Plays — Infirm — Wedlock.

ABOUT two o'clock in the afternoon the party returned from St. James', all of them exceedingly delighted with their excursion. They were none too soon for Mrs. Sinclair, who had begun to feel apprehensive that they might keep back her Christmas dinner. After a sufficient interval for the purposes of the toilet, the dinner was served; and it was evident that there were grateful reminiscences of "merrie England," in the heart of the hostess, as well as in the heart of one of her guests. When the covers were removed, there was displayed before Dr. Sinclair, a noble sirloin of roast beef, with a garland of holly leaves around the edge of the dish. At the other extremity there was a roast turkey, and this, like all the intermediate dishes, was prettily decorated with the "Christmas greens," for which it was very evident our excellent friend Mr. Oldbuckle had an amiable weakness.

The legitimate boar's head and peacock pie of the old *régime* were not, it is true, included in the bill of fare, but there was a substantial English look and odour about the dishes which could not be mistaken. Dr. Sinclair called on his old friend to say grace, which he did in good old English fashion. It was not couched in hurried and unintelligible words; but was said with deliberate enunciation and with reverent manner; very soon after which there was a rivalry between the tongues and the forks of the company, as to which of the two should do the most effectual service.

Mrs. Sinclair asked Gertrude if she had enjoyed the ride and the services at St. James', to which question she received a very cordial answer in the affirmative. William Sinclair's eyes were upon her, for he felt no little interest in the reply she made, as he had been her sole companion both going and returning, and he had found for her the lessons in the Prayer-Book. He was quite satisfied with the tone of Miss Vivian's answer, and forthwith flattered himself that he had been a most agreeable companion.

"How did you like the decorations of the church, Miss Vivian?" said Mr. Oldbuckle.

"I thought them very chaste and appropriate," she answered.

"What were they?" asked Mrs. Sinclair.

"The walls were hung with festoons of cedar and holly, and the chancel railing was dressed with wreaths of the same material. There were two or three mottoes, in letters done with small sprigs of cedar upon white cloth, which had a very pretty appearance.

That over the chancel was the verse from the evangelist Luke—'For unto you is born this day, in the city of David, a Saviour which is Christ the Lord.' There was another motto over the organ which I thought exceedingly appropriate. It was, 'Oh! Lord our Lord, how excellent is thy name in all the earth!'"

"You do not object to the Christmas decoration of churches, I hope," said Mr. Oldbuckle, addressing Dr. Sinclair.

"Not at all, my dear sir, I think it one of the most pleasing features of the festival."

"I am glad to hear you say so, for now I may venture to quote the beautiful words of one of England's noblest bards. I will venture to repeat the whole sonnet:

> 'Would that our scrupulous sires had dared to leave
>   Less scanty measure of those graceful rites
>   And usages, whose due return invites
> A stir of mind too natural to deceive,
> Giving the memory help when she could weave
>   A crown for Hope! I dread the boasted lights
>   That all too often are but fiery flights,
> Killing the bud o'er which in vain we grieve.
> Go seek, when Christmas snows discomfort bring,
>   The counter spirit found in some gay church,
>   Green with fresh holly, every pew a porch
> In which the linnet or the thrush might sing,
>   Merry and loud, and safe from prying search,
> Strains offered only to the genial spring.'"

"I am delighted to find that you and I do not

disagree in our estimate of Wordsworth, Mr. Oldbuckle. He was Nature's 'high priest' and ministered sublimely at her altars."

"How exquisite," said Gertrude Vivian, "are his minor pieces, his lyrics let me call them. That, for example, commencing

> 'She dwelt among the untrodden ways,
> Beside the springs of Dove.'

and that other inimitable ballad, the Cottage Girl,

> 'A simple child, dear brother Jem,
> That lightly draws its breath.'"

"Wordsworth," said Mr. Oldbuckle, "will grow more and more into the hearts of the people, as time hallows his genius and his song."

Much more genial discourse made the admirable dinner

> "A feast of reason, and a flow of soul."

The plum-pudding was brought in all blazing with the blue flame of the spirit of wine, and Mr. Oldbuckle said it reminded him of the game of snapdragon, which was quite common in England upon Christmas Eve. Harry begged to know what it was, and Mr. Oldbuckle thus described it:

"A quantity of plums, raisins as they are always called in this country, picked and washed clean, was spread upon a very large dish. A quantity of spirit of wine, or perhaps brandy, was then poured over them, and when the guests or the family were all gathered around it, the spirit was set on fire, filling the dish with a hot blue flame. Every one was now to 'put in his thumb (and finger too) and pull out a plum,' which was to be eaten immediately, and no one could make a second draft until he had eaten the first. It was quite a common thing for the young folks to make a desperate plunge into the burning mass and having seized their prize, to drop it upon the edge of the dish."

Mr. Oldbuckle's reminiscence of "snap-dragon" was quite amusing, and Harry insisted that he would nave had his full share of the plums, in spite of the "blue blazes."

After dinner the boys went down to the pond, promising not to venture far upon the ice, and they forebore to take their skates, lest they might be tempted to do so. William and Edward went out for a walk; Mr. Oldbuckle and Dr. Sinclair betook themselves to the library to indulge in a tête-à-tête over some choice cigars, while the ladies all resorted to their own rooms.

After tea the whole company repaired to the library, to take part, either as performers or spectators, in the charade-plays which had been agreed upon as the entertainment of the evening. William Sinclair was unanimously appointed manager, and cheerfully entered upon the duties of his office. He took a slip of paper from his pocket-book, and then announced a charade in three acts, at the same time calling upon Miss Vivian, Mr. Oldbuckle, Dr. Sinclair and Harry to withdraw with him from the room to prepare for the first act. Alice, by his direction, took her seat at the piano-forte to occupy the interval. They were not absent more than five minutes, when Dr. Sinclair reëntered the library, and seating himself at his writing-desk, appeared to be occupied with some accounts. Presently a loud knock was heard at the door and he arose to open it.

"Walk in, madam—walk in, sir;" was his courteous salutation to a lady and gentleman, both of them arrayed in travelling costume.

"Will you see to our horses, sir?" said the gentleman.

"Certainly, sir.—Hostler, here, take these horses and take good care of them."

"Yes, sir," responded a voice from the outside.

The travellers entered the room and were followed by William and Harry Sinclair, bringing in a large trunk, a carpet-bag, and a lady's hat-box.

Jacob Fletcher now put his head inside the door, and with a broad grin upon his honest face, said with a scrape of his foot:

"Please, sir, what shall I give the horses?"

"Oats—hay and oats—not a bit of corn!" was the reply of the gentleman who was divesting himself of his wrapper—an example which the lady followed.

"It is cold weather, sir," he said, addressing Dr.

Sinclair; "my daughter will need a fire in her room."

"She shall have one, sir, and yourself also," was the response.

"And when will you have supper served?" said William Sinclair, who had a white apron tied around him.

"As soon as possible," said the lady, to whom the gentleman referred the question, by look, at least.

"Coffee or tea, ma'am?" said William.

"Tea—green tea—by all means."

"Certainly, ma'am," and the waiter disappeared.

"We have travelled from B—— to-day," said the gentleman, "and I think that is fifty miles distant, is it not?"

"Fifty-two, sir," was Dr. Sinclair's reply; "you must feel a little fatigued."

"Yes, sir, and after supper we will be glad to retire, as we must resume our journey early in the morning."

Here the actors paused for a moment, and the words—"Travel—host—waiter—hotel—night," and others suggested by the scene, were uttered by the group who were playing the part of spectators; they could not quite agree which of these it was, however, that was intended; and the first act was closed upon their doubts by the withdrawal of the travellers from the room preceded by William and Harry with lighted candles.

"It must be 'hotel,'" said Alice; "papa was host—William waiter."

"And Harry was boots,' I suppose," said Herbert, laughing.

"Mr. Oldbuckle has found a daughter, it seems, in our fair Gertrude—though he does not claim you for a son," said Mrs. Sinclair to Edward Vivian.

"No, there is a mistake somewhere," was the playful reply.

While they were still discussing the word implied in the first act, the door of the library again opened and the whole party reäppeared, all of them in winter dress, and evidently bent on some out-of-door employment. The lady seated herself in a chair, and gathered her dress about her feet, while the gentlemen began to step cautiously as if they were afraid of their footing. They moved on and stamped with their feet, at first slightly and then more energetically, exchanging, meanwhile, satisfactory glances with the lady.

"That will do, I think," said one of them, as he made diligent effort apparently to shake the floor with his feet.

"Oh! yes, no danger—it will bear a loaded wagon, I'll engage," said another.

"It must be a foot thick at least," said the third.

"Hurrah! then we'll have fine sport."

"Are you quite sure it is safe, papa?" said the young lady.

"Oh! yes, Sue, we have tried it thoroughly."

"Oh! I wish I could skate," she returned.

"You must be content to be 'a looker-on, here in Vienna,'" said one of the young men, while they all stooped as if to fasten on their skates; after which they went through the motions of a skating scene, and abruptly glided out of the room.

"Ice," said Edward Vivian, "but that does not match with either of the words of the first scene!"

"Neither does 'skate,'" said Mrs. Sinclair.

"No," said Alice, "and moreover the word 'skate' was used, and William said that *the* word would not be introduced."

"Very true, Alice, then what can it be?"

No one was quite sure, but *ice* seemed to be the general choice, though it was difficult to find any thing to agree with it. They all waited impatiently for the third act, which they hoped would explain both the former ones. They did not wait long. The party reäppeared, and a shout of merriment greeted their entrance, for they all came in the character of invalids, some old and others young. Mr. Oldbuckle personated a beggar-man, with tattered clothes and a long staff; and he advanced slowly, repeating, as he moved, the well-known words—

"Pity the sorrows of a poor old man,
Whose trembling steps have borne him to your door."

Dr. Sinclair was on crutches, and Miss Vivian was

seated in Fanny's wicker-wagon, in which William Sinclair drew her along the room. Harry limped at a furious rate, and it seemed as if the whole party might be a detachment from a hospital.

"Well," said Mrs. Sinclair, "I confess myself puzzled, and shall have to give it up. I really can not make hotels, and ice, and crutches compound reasonably."

"Call the first by a more plebeian name, my dear Mrs. Sinclair," said Edward Vivian, with a knowing smile; and he added, "think of some quality of the second important to a skating party, and then put the two together, and see if there will not be probable need of the third."

"And so by your most indispensable and timely aid, Mr. Vivian, I am able, in behalf of the audience, to dismiss these INN-FIRM characters with a most hearty eulogium upon their by no means infirm acting. I hope," she added, bowing to her son, who, as manager, was waiting for the guess, "I have done the charade and the performers equal justice in this matter?"

"Certainly, my dear mother, we have no reason to complain, and are only too happy in having entertained you at our 'inn'—proved to you that the ice was 'firm,' and that we were successful though '*in-firm*' actors."

With a new set of performers, William Sinclair produced another charade in three acts, the first of which represented a bridal party, the second, the closet scene from Blue Beard, and the whole, WED-LOCK, was shown up in a pretty matrimonial squabble—a consummation against which Mrs. Sinclair protested as utterly libellous.

It was quite late when the happy party closed their Christmas festivities, and after the customary worship, bade each other "good-night," and sought

"Tired nature's sweet restorer—balmy sleep."

CHAPTER XVI.

Adieus—Departures—More Snow—Fanny's Balls—Science in
Soap-bubbles—Elasticity—Form—Inertia—Variable Colours.

THE next morning, immediately after breakfast,
Edward Vivian and his sister bade their friends
at Beechwood farewell, and took with them to Vivian
dale, not only delightful memories of their visit, but
the warm regard and affection of those whom they
left behind. Mr. Oldbuckle also departed for his
own residence, and persuaded William Sinclair to
ride over with him in his sleigh, by a promise to
return with him in the afternoon, if he should find
nothing of importance to detain him at "the Grove."
All the young people expressed their hope that
nothing would occur to prevent his return.

An additional fall of snow during the night had
covered the icy bosom of the pond, so that the boys
were disappointed in their expectations of passing the
morning in skating. They went out, therefore, with
Alice to look after the pets, and to see how the pony
came on. Mary and Fanny, by their mother's
advice, did not accompany them, both of them having a slight cold. The former devoted herself to a
book in the library, and the latter persuaded Bridget,

the maid, to make her some strong soap-suds, that she might amuse herself by blowing bubbles. She was soon deeply interested in this occupation, always so fascinating to childhood, and presently ran into the sitting-room, exclaiming—

"Oh! mamma, what a beautiful bubble. See, mamma, do see!"

Mrs. Sinclair looked up from the work upon which she was engaged, just as the little girl had succeeded in detaching from the pipe-bowl a large bubble, which fell upon the hearth-rug without breaking, and for a moment reflected, from its surface, the bright glow of the fire.

"Yes, it is very beautiful, my little daughter;" and even as the mother spoke, the child threw another frail and glittering bubble upon the rug, exulting to see it bound like an India-rubber ball. This was the first time that Fanny had noticed the effect of letting the soap-bubbles fall upon the rug or carpet. She had often blown them out of doors and watched them as they were wafted about by the air. She had noticed, moreover, that whenever the frail little globes happened to strike against any thing, they were immediately destroyed, and now when she saw the perfect sphere lying upon the soft rug, and actually rolling along as she blew gently upon it, she was almost wild with delight, and not satisfied with mamma's admiration, she ran into the library and called upon her papa and Mary to come and see the wonder. Dr. Sinclair was not busy at the moment, and he did not refuse, as too many parents would thoughtlessly do, to gratify the fancy of his little girl. He went into the sitting-room, followed by Mary, and Fanny blew another bubble, which sh. detached with so much eagerness from the pipe, that it fell upon her papa's boot instead of the rug, and immediately broke. She looked disappointed, but tried again, and this time the crystal-like globe rolled gently along the rug, stopping just at her papa's foot. He waved his hand above it, and it rolled away, lightly bounding from the rug. For a few moments he moved it about at his pleasure, but suddenly it vanished.

Alice and Herbert now entered the room and seemed not a little amused to find Dr. Sinclair interested in such a childish sport as blowing bubbles, for he had really taken the pipe and blown a very large bubble, until it burst upon the pipe.

"I want you to see my new balls—my beautiful new balls, sister Ally," said the excited Fanny, as she put out her hand to her papa for the pipe. It was a little rude in her to do this, and particularly without even asking him if he had done with it; but he overlooked her impoliteness, and put the pipe into her hands.

As quick as thought she had another fairy ball upon the rug, but before it stopped rolling, it struck against the fender and disappeared.

"Rather a soft ball, little Fanny," said Herbert; "that wouldn't do to play at trap with."

"No, Mr. Herbert, but see this one;" and in a moment it was rolling and quivering along the rug and over the carpet, before the eager breath of the little girl.

"What is the reason, Alice, that the bubble does not break when it falls upon the rug?" said Dr. Sinclair.

"Because it is so light, I should think, papa," she replied.

"That will not explain it, my daughter, for it falls just as lightly upon the chair, or upon the oil-cloth of the fire-place; but as soon as it touches either it bursts. See," he added, as Fanny let a bubble fall upon the table, and it broke instantly.

"What do you think about it, Herbert?"

Herbert was almost unwilling to say what he thought, lest it should be right, when Alice's explanation had been wrong. He did say, however, quite modestly, that he supposed it was owing to the softness of the rug.

"Not to its softness alone," replied Dr. Sinclair, "but to its softness and elasticity combined. The bubble itself is exceedingly elastic, and when it falls upon some surface which possesses the same properties it is not shattered, as you see. A bubble, carefully thrown, will rebound from the surface of water, because the water is soft and somewhat elastic."

"What does that mean, papa?" said Fanny, who had stopped blowing bubbles and was now listening to the conversation.

"Oh! I forgot that one of my auditors had yet to learn the meaning of some words, and I must make Fanny understand the meaning of *elastic*. Do you see this piece of India rubber, Fanny, and this pencil?" both of which happened to lie upon the mantelpiece; "see what will happen if I drop them both upon the floor. The India rubber has actually jumped up into a chair, and the pencil tried its best to follow it, but couldn't jump so high."

Fanny laughed, but said nothing, and Dr. Sinclair resumed.

"The India rubber jumped higher than the pencil because it is more elastic; or, in other words, because it possesses more power to spring from a blow than the pencil. All bodies have this power, but not in equal degrees, and some have so little of it, that they have been called inelastic."

Fanny did not seem quite to understand her father's explanation, and he very kindly went into the laboratory and brought out a frame, upon the top cross-piece of which, were suspended, by strings, balls of ivory and balls of hard clay. Removing all but two balls of clay, he drew them apart and then let them fall so as to strike each other. They rebounded very slightly. He then substituted two ivory balls, and repeated the experiment. The balls were driven apart over almost the whole space which divided them, when they were let fall upon each other. Fanny now saw and understood better the different elasticities of bodies.

"Fanny just now called these frail bubbles 'her pretty balls,'" he went on, "and they may be tossed like balls, notwithstanding Herbert's opinion that they are too soft."

"How, papa?" said Mary, eagerly; "please show us how."

"With pleasure, my dear child," and Dr. Sinclair took the pipe again, and slowly blowing a bubble about the size of an orange, he detached it, and as it fell presented his knee to it, from which it gracefully rebounded. As it fell again, he presented his other knee with a like result, and very much to the delight of the spectators, kept the bubble rising and falling at least half a score of times before it burst.

"But let us not dismiss the bubbles without learning some more useful lessons from them," said Dr. Sinclair. He then took the cup into his hands, and blowing a few moments into the soap-suds, raised a pyramid of small, glittering bubbles. Alice, whose perceptions were now quickened by the desire to find something new in every amusement, called the attention of her father to the shape of these minute bubbles.

"See, papa," she exclaimed, "they are not round like those which escape from the pipe, but have a number of sides, like one of those wooden blocks in your geometry case."

"True, Alice, and if you will give me a reason for this difference of shape, I think Herbert and Harry will be glad."

"I can not tell, papa, unless it is because they are so close together in the cue, they have not room to be round."

"Oh! that must be it," said Herbert, "for see, Dr. Sinclair, the outer ones *are* round except when they join the ones below them."

"Well said, my young friend. Alice is right and you have demonstrated it. We are getting along finely. The bubbles press upon each other, and being very elastic, take the shape most convenient for close contact. What sort of figures do these crowded bubbles make, Alice?"

"Hexagons, I think, sir, though I am not sure."

"Yes, they are figures of six equal sides. But let us blow a bubble and see what else we can find out about it. Harry, do you try to give us a monster one."

Harry was soon blowing away earnestly but gently, for he had already spoiled one promising effort by the violence of his breathing. The bubble expanded and waved, and appeared to the eye to be whirling around as it grew in size.

"But, papa," said Alice, "that is not a *round* bubble which brother Harry is blowing. It is shaped more like an egg. What is the reason of it?"

Dr. Sinclair replied by directing Harry to throw off the bubble, and immediately it was floating buoyantly upon the elastic waves of the air, as round as the most perfect sphere.

"There, Alice," said Dr. Sinclair, "it is round enough now. What was it that drew it out of shape when it was on the pipe?"

"Was it not the force of the breath, papa?" said Harry.

"Partly, I have no doubt, my son, but not chiefly; for even when you ceased to blow, it was still a little oblong."

"Oh! I see, sir," exclaimed Herbert, "it was its weight."

"But it is just as heavy now, Herbert, and it is not oblong."

Herbert was puzzled, and none of his young friends could help him. So Dr. Sinclair relieved him from his dilemna, by saying—

"You were not altogether wrong, in fact, Herbert, though you did not quite grasp the cause. It was its weight; but if you had said its *gravity*, it would have been better. The air which the bubble contains presses equally in every direction, and so makes the film of soap which incloses it perfectly spherical when it is free, but while the bubble is fastened to the pipe, the air can not act freely, and so the bubble *gravitates* like the leaf of the forest toward the earth."

"Why did the bubble fall, papa?" said Mary, as

the one just mentioned, after tossing a moment on the air, sunk to the floor.

"Because it is heavier than the air, my daughter, by just the weight of the soap which forms its delicate covering."

"And are no bubbles lighter than the air?" asked Alice.

"Certainly not; at least none which are filled with air."

"Why then do some of them go up without being blown?"

"They never do in a quiet air. If they rise at all, it must be from some impulse of the air below them."

"I have seen them sail out of sight in the open air," said Herbert, "but I knew it was the wind which carried them."

"If our kind friend, Mr. Oldbuckle, comes over this afternoon, as he said he would, I will show you some bubbles which will rise very rapidly without any wind or motion of the air at all," said Dr. Sinclair.

"Oh! I am quite sure he will come," said Alice.

Dr. Sinclair now took the pipe and proceeded to blow a bubble, and having carefully swung it off into the air just above his head, he blew it with a quick short breath, and it separated into four or five smaller bubbles, which went dancing and whirling off in various directions.

The young people were all interested and delighted

with this pretty and somewhat delicate experiment. Fanny tried it, but in vain; she puffed the bubble out. The others had no better success, and even Dr. Sinclair failed the second time. He repeated it, however, with such success as to assure them that it was not merely "a happy accident," but a process governed by laws.

To the eager demand for an explanation, he replied that it was probably owing to a principle called *Inertia*, or the disposition of matter to remain in the condition which it had been placed in, and which he would wait for some better example to illustrate more fully. He added that the suddenness of the shock upon the bubble broke it; but such was the tenacity of the film which composed it that it enveloped the fragments immediately, and the air instantly pressed them into spheres. With this somewhat obscure explanation, the Doctor laid down the pipe, and left the children to amuse themselves with such further experiments with the bubbles as they might please to make.

They did not continue the sport long, for it lacked a charm which they had only just begun to realize— the charm of being made a medium of instruction to the mind. They saw the exquisite hues of the bubbles at certain stages of their expansion, but they could not conjecture the cause of them. They even noticed that one very large bubble, which had lasted so long as to excite their special wonder, and which had been exceedingly beautiful with variegated colours, suddenly turned almost black, and vanished instantly "into thin air." This puzzled them also, and they wisely resolved to learn more, at an early opportunity, about the philosophy of a soap-bubble, which had thus suddenly become, to some of them, at least, something more than it seemed. They had already arrived at one of the happiest results of increasing knowledge—an earnest desire to know yet more.

CHAPTER XVII.

The Return--Anecdote of the Iron Duke—Napoleon and Wellington—Sir Humphrey Davy—A Chemical Process.

NOT long after dinner, Mr. Oldbuckle and William, true to their promise, made their appearance, and were warmly welcomed by the young people, who were reckoning upon Dr. Sinclair's promise for some very delightful amusement. Of this, Harry did not fail immediately to remind him; but as Mr. Oldbuckle had brought with him the London *Times*, containing a full account of the magnificent funeral obsequies of the late Duke of Wellington, he claimed the privilege first of glancing over it, and afterwards the conversation naturally turned upon the character and career of the illustrious soldier.

"By the by, Dr. Sinclair," said Mr. Oldbuckle, "I have heard a new and characteristic anecdote of the 'Iron Duke,' which I must beg permission to relate to you."

"By all means," said the Doctor, "I feel interested in every thing that concerns the brave old hero."

"Well, then," resumed Mr. Oldbuckle, " the Duke saw, at a late exhibition of the Royal Academy, two pictures of the Battle of Waterloo, both painted by Sir William Allen. In one of these pictures the figure of Napoleon occupied a prominent place in the foreground. This picture the Duke resolved to purchase, and having agreed with the painter about the price, requested him to send it to Apsley House, the city residence of the Duke, and to call there on a given day to receive payment.

The picture was sent accordingly, and on the day named Sir William Allen waited upon the Duke. He was shown into the Duke's library, and after some conversation, Wellington went to his escritoire, and producing a bag of sovereigns, commenced counting out the price of the picture. Sir William suggested to him that it would save him trouble to draw a check upon his bankers, but the Duke went on with his counting. The artist renewed his suggestion, supposing that the Duke had not heard it, when the old soldier raised his head and exclaimed with a smile, "Do you think, Sir William, that I am willing to let them know at Coutts's, what a fool I have made of myself!"

Mr. Oldbuckle joined heartily in the laugh which his anecdote occasioned, and added—"Capital, is n't it, just like the 'Iron Duke' for all the world?"

Dr. Sinclair assented to his friend's remark.

"What is the 'Iron Duke,' papa?" said Fanny. "Is it a statute like that in the garden?"

At this question, there was such a burst of laughter that the little girl was almost overwhelmed, but papa soon came to her relief, and explained to her the difference between a statue and a statute. He then told her that the great Duke of Wellington had been called the "Iron Duke," because he had fought so many battles and had been through so many dangers without harm to his person.

"I should like to become as famous as the Duke of Wellington," said Harry.

"Would you not rather have been Napoleon?" inquired Herbert, with real enthusiasm.

"Not I," said Harry. "I think Napoleon was as selfish as he was great."

"Oh! no," rejoined Herbert, "I do not think so. Do you think so, Alice?"

Alice did think so, but she wished to spare Herbert the mortification of telling him so, and she replied with some hesitation,

"He certainly professed to do every thing for France; but then," she added, "he seemed to think that he was France."

"Bravo," said Mr. Oldbuckle, "bravo, my bird, that is just it! He loved France, because in his estimation, France was Napoleon, and Napoleon was France."

"Nay," interposed Dr. Sinclair, "I think it was almost impossible for Napoleon to separate himself from his country, when he saw how all his countrymen hung upon his word as their law."

"Well," said Mr. Oldbuckle, "we will not make another Waterloo of this pleasant library, where all around us breathes of peace. Wellington needs not a second time to conquer Napoleon, and I need not," he added with a smile, "seek to aggrandize my successful hero, by depreciating the vanquished hero of that unparalleled field of battle."

"So let us make, instead of a Waterloo, a St. Helena of this room, and bury here the great Napoleon," playfully added Dr. Sinclair.

"Requiescat in pace," said William Sinclair, who had come in just as the conversation was drawing to a close.

Mr. Oldbuckle could not help adding,

"But they wouldn't do even that, William, and must needs take his bones to Paris, the scene of his magnificent plans for conquering Europe."

William Sinclair had too great a respect for his father's friend, to appear to notice the sarcasm of his words, though he had formed, in the school of Carlyle and Hazlitt, an estimate of Napoleon's character in many respects antagonistic to that of Mr. Oldbuckle.

As soon as the war of the heroes was brought to an end, Harry again reminded his father of his promise to show them those magic soap-bubbles, which rise without compulsion.

Dr. Sinclair then told his guest of the simple amusement of the morning, how they had looked for beauty in bubbles, and found also books therein, or what was equivalent, knowledge, which forms the best material for books. Mr. Oldbuckle was delighted, and said that he had such a passion for blowing bubbles, that he must beg to have the lesson repeated, with all the explanations, for his gratification.

"I have promised the young people a different lesson for this afternoon," said Dr. Sinclair, "though it was suggested by that of the morning. I must ask your aid, my dear sir, or that of William, a little while in the laboratory."

"Most willingly shall I elect myself adjunct Professor of Natural Philosophy, in Sinclair University," said Mr. Oldbuckle, with great good humour, and he started up to enter at once upon his duties.

The whole party descended into the laboratory, and prepared to watch, with eagerness, the preparations for their amusement.

"I told you," said Dr. Sinclair, "that no bubbles filled with air would rise of themselves. You all saw that however they were driven about, they finally descended to the ground, if they did not burst beforehand."

"But," said Harry, "suppose you could make them quite empty, papa; they would rise then, would they not?"

"I will show you, by and by, my son, that bubbles could not exist without air inside."

"Now, papa, I must convict you of a contradiction," said Alice, "for you told us this morning that no bubbles filled with air can be lighter than air. Now you tell us that bubbles can not exist without air inside, and yet you are going to show us bubbles that will rise in the air, because they are lighter than the air."

"Very well reasoned, my bird, and your worthy papa stands convicted of a contradiction, from which he must now clear himself," was the laughing comment of Mr. Oldbuckle.

"That I can easily do," said Dr. Sinclair, smiling with pleasure at the prompt operation of his daughter's mind in detecting the apparent error in his premises; "but I must confess to having involved myself in this dilemma, by a too free use of words. I said that a bubble could not exist without *air* inside, when I ought to have said without an *æriform* fluid, something resembling air in some of its properties. My magic bubbles are to be filled not with air, but with an æriform fluid, called gas."

"The truth dawns upon me," said Mr. Oldbuckle, "you are about to press chemistry into the service of sport, and make toys of some of her mysterious paraphernalia. What would the spirit of the illustrious Sir Humphrey Davy say to such a profanation?"

Fanny lifted up her blue eyes in evident dismay at these long words, and Doctor Sinclair, laughingly, replied,

"Very true, Mr. Oldbuckle, I am about to make chemistry minister to our pleasure, but I need hardly remind you, my dear friend, that Sir Humphrey

Davy himself condescended to blow just such soap-bubbles for the amusement of little people like these around us."

"I did not know that interesting fact," replied Dr. Sinclair, "but I do not wonder at it; for I know that he was a kind-hearted man as well as a great philosopher."

"That he certainly was, or he wouldn't have spent so much time in inventing a safety-lamp for the use of the miners," said William Sinclair. "If he had done nothing more for the world than that, he would still be one of its great benefactors; for it saves, every year, a large number of lives, and enables the colliers to work in some mines, which without it, they would have to abandon."

Harry's eyes were now sparkling with an evident desire to say something, and his father perceiving it, said,

"Well, Harry, what is it?"

"O papa, I couldn't help thinking of the curious way in which I saw the name of the great philosopher spelled the other day."

"How was it spelled, Harry?" inquired Mr. Oldbuckle.

"Oh! Mr. Oldbuckle, so very queer. It was in the paper I saw it, and it was said to be an exact copy of the spelling upon a letter found among the philosopher's papers after his death. It was spelt thus:

'*S r u m f r e d a v.*'"

"Rather a doubtful story, Harry, but still a very amusing one," said his father, laughing, with all the rest, at this extraordinary *spell* of English.

All this while, Dr. Sinclair had been at work. He had placed a Florence flask, such as sweet oil comes in from Italy, upon a stand, and fitted to its neck a bent glass tube, the end of which he made to pass under water in a wooden cistern or tub which stood near by. Mr. Oldbuckle busied himself in preparing a bag made of India-rubber cloth and fitted, at its only orifice, with a screw and stop-cock. This he set open, and then rolled the bag closely so as to expel all the air it contained. This done, he closed the stop-cock and screwed it into another at the top of a large bell-glass, which stood upon a shelf in the cistern already mentioned. The bell-glass had no bottom, but, nevertheless, it stood there quite full of water, to Herbert's great wonder; which Alice herself could not explain to him, although she had some idea of the cause. I believe they both found out all about it during the holidays. When all these arrangements were made, Dr. Sinclair withdrew the tube from the mouth of the flask, and put in, with his fingers, quite a number of small shining pieces of zinc, till the bottom was pretty well covered. He then poured into the flask, from a glass jar, a mixture, nearly colourless, of water and what is commonly called oil of vitriol. This mixture he had made carefully some time before. As soon as he had done this, he replaced the tube, and immediately there was a violent commotion among the materials in the flask. The fluid appeared to boil vehemently, and the pieces of zinc moved about rapidly, while from the end of the tube in the water there escaped great bubbles of air. Dr. Sinclair had removed the tube, so that these bubbles did not go up into the bell-glass. In a few moments, he held a lighted splinter of wood just over the escaping bubbles, and they at first took fire and snapped loudly, but, afterward, burned with a pale flame and faint noise. He now placed the tube so that the bubbles ascended into the bell-glass, which they did with great rapidity, causing the water to descend until it was all expelled.

Meanwhile Mr. Oldbuckle had filled another bell-glass and raised it upon the shelf, and when the first was quite emptied of water, Dr. Sinclair carried the tube rapidly beneath the full bell-glass, into which the bubbles ascended as before, only a little more slowly, until, in a few minutes, they ceased altogether to rise.

Alice observed to Herbert that the boiling in the flask was quite over, and that the whole mass was somewhat swollen and quite black.

While the second bell-glass was filling, or as Fanny would have it, "getting empty," Mr. Oldbuckle and William Sinclair were doing something which arrested the attention of the little people. They had moved the bell-glass from the shelf into the deeper water of the cistern, and when Mr. Oldbuckle had opened the stop-cock of the gas-bag, which he held up above the jar, William pressed the glass down into the water. The bag swelled as the bell sunk, until in a few moments the bell was again full of water and quite at the bottom of the cistern. Mr. Oldbuckle then reclosed the stop-cock, and unscrewing the bag from the glass, he waved it with the air of a magician, exclaiming—

"Now, my bird, now for the magic bubbles which are to rise without wind to propel them!"

CHAPTER XVIII.

Hydrogen Gas—Its Levity—More Soap-bubbles—Miniature Balloons—Origin of Balloons—Dr. Sinclair's Balloon—Its Ascent—Effect of Hydrogen upon the Voice.

THE young people had watched with interest and curiosity the operations of Dr. Sinclair, and they listened attentively to his brief description of the process he had pursued.

"The bubbles," said he, "which you have seen escaping from the end of the tube, and ascending into the bell-glass, are not such as would rise in it if I were to blow through a tube. Each one of them is a small volume of hydrogen gas."

"What is the meaning of the term, hydrogen, Herbert, or did your etymological studies stop short of scientific words?"

"They included many, sir; but I am sorry that I can not answer your question," said the young boy, frankly.

"Hydrogen is a term made from two Greek words, and means *to form water*. It is the most abundant element of water, every drop of which is composed of two gases, the hydrogen, of which I am speaking, and another, called oxygen. A drop of water converted into these two gases occupies a space many times as great as before, and the hydrogen fills two thirds of it. This gas is a very extraordinary fluid, for it is highly inflammable, and exceedingly light. Perhaps Alice can tell us how many times lighter it is than the air we breathe."

"Fifteen times, sir," she replied, "according to Mrs. Marcet."

"Then, of course," continued her father, "if we can succeed in filling some of these filmy bubbles with this gas, they will be lighter than the atmosphere and ascend in it."

"But how are we to do that?" said Harry.

"Very easily indeed," said Mr. Oldbuckle, "by means of this bag, which will serve instead of lungs."

Dr. Sinclair now took the bag and fastened a tobacco-pipe to the end of the stop-cock. He then introduced the pipe into a bowl of strong soap-suds, and opening the stop-cock, he pressed the sides of the bag gently, and the soap-suds were immediately covered with minute bubbles. Upon withdrawing the pipe and again pressing the bag, he produced a bubble about the size of a small orange, which, to the great admiration of the young people, did not wait to be shook off the pipe, but detached itself, and soared away rapidly to the ceiling, against which it burst. One or two other bubbles of equal size, followed it in like manner.

"There," said Mr. Oldbuckle, "there, boys, you have *bona-fide* balloons."

"Oh! yes," exclaimed Harry, "I recollect now, Herbert, that when we went to see the great balloon go up from Castle Garden, Mr. Wiseman told us that it was filled with hydrogen gas, and that the gas in the balloon was so much lighter than the same bulk of air, that even the silk, and cords, and car, and every thing in it did not make it so heavy."

"Yes, Harry, and when I said that I should like very much to go up in the balloon, Mr. Wiseman said that I should feel very differently if I were actually in the car, after the rope was cut that held it down."

"Oh! how handsomely it shot up," said Harry, "when the rope was cut, just like one of these light bubbles, though it swayed about a good deal when it first started."

"That was owing, perhaps, to the man waving the flag," said Mr. Oldbuckle. "I saw a balloon-car nearly upset once, by the carelessness of the man in it, but he soon became more quiet."

"Can any one of you tell me when, and by whom, the balloon was invented?" asked Dr. Sinclair.

"In 1782, by Montgolfier, a Frenchman," said Alice.

"Where did you learn so much, Alice? not from Mrs. Marcet, I think."

Amid the playful laughter which this allusion to Alice's usual authority produced, the blushing girl replied—

"Not from Mrs. Marcet, I acknowledge, but from a 'Record of Interesting Events,' which I cut out of a newspaper and committed to memory."

Her father applauded her thoughtfulness, and Herbert admired her intelligence, though without saying so.

"But," said Mr. Oldbuckle, "the balloon of the Montgolfiers—for there were two of them, Joseph and Stephen—was not a gas-balloon. It was an air-balloon."

"How then could it be made to rise?" inquired Herbert, remembering the allusion to that point in the case of the bubbles.

"Ah! how, indeed?" chimed in Harry, thinking that his school-fellow had really caught their antiquated friend napping.

"By making the air of the balloon much thinner than the external air," was Mr. Oldbuckle's quiet answer.

"How could that be done, sir?" said Herbert.

"By heating it. The Montgolfier balloon consisted of a large bag of silk of a curious figure, called by a very hard name, which would puzzle Fanny too much for me to venture on it. The mouth of the bag was left open, so that they could introduce lighted paper, the heat of which so rarefied the air in the bag that it rose, first to the ceiling of the room, and afterwards, to a height of seventy-five feet in the open air. This was the first air-balloon. They made larger balloons afterwards, which succeeded very well indeed."

The young people listened with great interest to this history, and when Mr. Oldbuckle ceased, Alice eagerly inquired—

"When was gas first employed to fill the balloon, sir?"

"Not very long after the experiments of the Montgolfiers," said Mr. Oldbuckle.

"Was it M. Charles or M. Robert who made the first gas-balloon?" inquired William Sinclair. "The question seems to be somewhat debated."

"It is debated," said Mr. Oldbuckle, "but I think it was M. Charles; and his balloon, made of silk, and twelve feet in diameter, rose several thousand feet very rapidly, and descended at Gonisse, fifteen miles from Paris, where some peasants attacked it with pitchforks, supposing it to be an evil spirit."

"What a set of fools they must have been!" said Harry.

"Did no one go up in that balloon, sir?" asked Alice.

"No one, my bird; nor did any one ascend in a balloon until toward the end of 1783, when two men made an expedition in the air, starting from the Castle of Muette. They were in the air about half an hour, and in descending, the balloon, which was made of linen, collapsed and fell into the fire employed to arefy the air within it, for it was not a gas-balloon.

Soon after this adventure, M. Charles and M. Robert made a very successful ascension in a large gas-balloon, and the experiment was then frequently repeated both in France and England."

"How I should love to see a real balloon!" said Alice.

"How I should like to go up in one, notwithstanding Mr. Wiseman's opinion!" said Harry.

"So should *not* I," said his father; "I would much rather stay upon *terra-firma* with Mr. Wiseman and all other wise men; but as Alice wishes to see a *real* balloon, I think I can gratify her."

"You, papa! Surely, now you are joking!"

"No, Alice, I am in earnest; my balloon is a real one, but it is a miniature specimen;" and as he spoke he took from a drawer a little box, and from the latter he produced a folded bag, which seemed to be made of oiled-silk.

"This," said Dr. Sinclair, "is a bag made of gold beater's skin, which, besides being very light, is also air-tight. It is striped with varnish of different colours to give it a gay appearance. It will not take long to inflate this with hydrogen, and we can do it very easily in the same manner that we filled the India-rubber bag."

"And will you send it up out of doors, papa?" said Fanny.

"Yes, if you will go up to guide it, Fanny."

"No, thank you, papa," said the little girl, tossing her curls.

The preparations were soon made, and the balloon was filled with the gas, until it looked like a huge pear. It was twelve inches in diameter, and when it was released from the bell glass through which it was filled, it suddenly escaped from William Sinclair's hands and ascended rapidly to the ceiling, where it remained until a chair was brought and the truant secured.

Dr. Sinclair now asked Fanny for her little basket, which she ran to fetch, and when it was brought, he fastened it to the neck of the balloon with blue ribands, and put into it a figure made of pith, to whom he told Fanny he was going to entrust the guidance of the balloon. He next fastened a fine but strong flax-thread to the neck of the balloon, and with these preparations the party, now joined by Mrs. Sinclair, by special invitation, adjourned to the lawn to send it up in the air.

Dr. Sinclair himself took charge of the ascent, telling William that he could not trust Fanny's basket to his slippery fingers. The air was still and the sun shone out pleasantly, when the little æronaut departed on his voyage. Up shot the balloon rapidly, and Fanny again clapped her hands with delight, while Harry commemorated the event by discharging a small cannon.

Mr. Oldbuckle invoked the breezes to be propitious to their bold adventure, and Dr. Sinclair kept fast hold of the line which bound the balloon to the earth. Still it rose until he had no string remaining, having paid out upwards of five hundred feet, at which elevation the balloon looked scarcely larger than a large bubble, and the little wicker car was lost to sight.

While they were looking up with great interest, the balloon suddenly swayed in the air, and began tugging at the string with a force which betokened the danger of its breaking away, before a current of air which had evidently encountered it. But by skillful management, Dr. Sinclair brought the voyager to the earth again, to the delight of all the spectators. The travelled basket was restored to its laughing owner, who was told that she must prize it more than ever. The little man of pith received the congratulations of the merry company, of which, however, he took no notice. The balloon was moored to the table of the laboratory, where each one tried its ascending force by pulling upon the string.

While Dr. Sinclair was hesitating whether to discharge the gas from the balloon, or not, William proposed to give them a very novel experiment with the hydrogen, and one which he had successfully performed during the University course of lectures. This was to inhale the gas and exhibit its effects upon the voice. Mr. Oldbuckle was somewhat opposed to his doing this, as he had always considered hydrogen to be unfit for the lungs. Dr. Sinclair, however, knew more of its actual properties, and had more than once tried the effect of breathing it for some moments. He therefore consented that William should try the experiment.

"Do not breathe it too long, my young friend," said worthy Mr. Oldbuckle, whose old-school notions were not altogether dissipated by the doctor's testimony, that hydrogen gas is not really injurious to the lungs.

"That I can't do," said William, "for when my lungs are full of it, I can't continue the act of inspiration, as they stop of themselves."

He then threw out the air from his lungs, and immediately applied his mouth to the orifice of the gas-bag, and inhaled its contents. He breathed the gas for several moments, and then withdrawing the bag from his mouth, commenced reciting with furious gesticulations—

> "My voice is still for war, gods!
> And should a Roman Senate long debate
> Which to choose—liberty or death?"

The shouts and laughter of his auditors bore testimony to the ludicrous effect of the gas upon his voice, which, from being a full, rotund organ, was suddenly converted into a shrill treble, or half-squeak, much like that which escapes from the orifice of a penny trumpet!

The effect was speedily over, and Harry insisted upon it that his brother feigned the voice in which he had recited, nor was he satisfied until he had tried the experiment for himself, and set all his auditors into convulsive laughter, by his declamation of the famous apostrophe:

> "You'd scarce expect one of my age
> To speak in public on the stage;
> Don't view me with a critic's eye,
> But pass my imperfections by."

"How do you account for this extraordinary effect of the gas, upon the organs of the voice, my young friend?" said Mr. Oldbuckle, addressing William Sinclair.

"By the quality of the air which is employed to fill and work the organs of speech. The hydrogen is too light to perform the vocal function perfectly, and on account of its levity, it soon escapes altogether from the lungs."

"How does the gas taste?" inquired Mr. Oldbuckle.

"It is almost tasteless, sir; a little sweetness is at first perceptible, but it does not continue," replied William Sinclair.

"This," said Mr. Oldbuckle, "is quite a novel experiment to me, and I thank you greatly for the gratification you have afforded me."

"Surely, sir," said William, speaking warmly, "we are all under obligation to you, for the delightful manner in which you have entertained us this afternoon."

"I hope," added Dr. Sinclair, "that our kind friend will often join us in our philosophical pastime, and enrich it by his knowledge and observation."

"That I will certainly do with cordial pleasure; but I must now bid you all good bye until the morrow. 'Pax vobiscum, et valete;'" he added, as he disappeared from the room, leaving Herbert to translate his words for Alice.

CHAPTER XIX.

The Aurora Borealis—Mr. Oldbuckle's Appearance—Polar Phenomena—Cause of the Aurora—Dr. Sinclair's Illustration—The Electrical Theory Triumphant.

"OH! brother William," exclaimed Harry, suddenly appearing at the door of the parlour, "do come out and look at the sky! there must be a big fire somewhere!"

Not only William Sinclair, but all the family answered Harry's eager summons, and gathered upon the piazza of the house. Mrs. Sinclair alone took the precaution to wrap herself in a shawl, for the night air was cold and frosty.

The sky was glowing with a bright crimson radiance, and seemed to justify Harry's notion that it was the effect of a great conflagration. The peculiar form, however, of the luminous area, clearly indicated to Dr. Sinclair and his eldest son, that it was a display of the Aurora Borealis, or Northern Lights. The upper edge of the brilliant cloud was clearly defined into rays apparently diverging from the horizon, and becoming more faint in their hues, until they faded into the deep blue of the sky. Along the horizon line, however, the light was exceedingly bright—surpassing even the splendour of a summer sunset.

After they had all gazed upon it for a few moments, Dr. Sinclair directed Alice to go for her cloak, and recommended to the boys to follow the example he was about to set them in putting on an overcoat; for, said he—

"This is a curious scientific wonder, which is not of such frequent occurrence in this region that we may overlook it; and it will afford us some useful as well as beautiful lessons. We will watch the light for a little while."

A very few moments sufficed to bring the group back to the piazza, so well wrapped up as to bid defiance to the chill air of a bright December night. But even while they were absent, a change had taken place in the appearance of the sky. Instead of a segment of brilliant crimson light, there appeared two or three arcs, one above the other, of rose-coloured light, separated by dark intervals, while, from the outside arc, there shot up towards the zenith, a fringe of white and purple, with perpetual oscillations and faint flashes throughout its whole extent.

"Oh! how beautiful!" exclaimed Mrs. Sinclair, while Alice and Mary pressed closer to their mother's side, and gazed in silent wonder and delight upon the unusual scene.

It was indeed a scene of indescribable beauty, with its ever-shifting forms and varying hues. Gradually the rays of light which shot up from the arch, stretched even to the zenith, and there seemed to gather into a vast plume, which waved to and fro, as if swayed by a wind. The arch disappeared from the horizon, and the whole glory concentrated in mid-heavens, so that our group of eager gazers could not see it without going from beneath the shelter of the piazza into the open air, which all but Mary did. A vast canopy of radiance now overspread them, like hangings of crimson and gold tapestry, and the tremulous motion of the whole was like the moving of the royal curtains by invisible hands.

While they were yet gazing, Mr. Oldbuckle made his appearance. His attention had been called by his gardener to the singular aspect of the sky, and fearing that the spectacle would be lost to his friends at Beechwood, he immediately ordered his horse and rode over to enjoy with them the wondrous scene. His horse was soon consigned to the care of the hostler and he joined the group, expressing his satisfaction that they were not unaware of the regal beauty of the sky.

"I could not bear," said he, "to think that such a gorgeous spectacle as this, should be lost to you, as a similar one once was to me through unconsciousness of its passing glories."

"We are indebted to Harry," said Dr. Sinclair, "for our enjoyment of this unparalleled vision, though he mistook it for a great conflagration at a distance."

"Quite a natural mistake," said Mr. Oldbuckle, "and the very one which James Renton made, when he called my attention to the spectacle half an hour ago. Is it not sublime!" he continued. "See how the crest, there, at the very zenith grows brighter, until it seems like an opening into a furnace of molten glass."

"How fast the glory grows dim!" said William; "we have probably seen the grandest part of the display."

"Yes," replied Dr. Sinclair, "these exhibitions are frequently as brief as they are sublime; though in more northern latitudes, the pageant often lingers all night, fading only with the coming on of day."

"I have read," said Mr. Oldbuckle, "accounts given by travellers in the polar regions, of these displays, accompanied by noises like the explosion of crackers, and something of the same kind has been noticed even in England."

"Have you formed any conclusive opinion of the cause of these lights?" said Dr. Sinclair, addressing his friend.

"I can not say that I have. Between the reflection theory of some philosophers, the solar hypothesis of others, and the more common notions of their electrical or magnetic origin, I have suffered myself to be still in doubt."

"It is indeed a subject of mystery," said Dr. Sinclair, "though I have much inclination to the electrical theory. But," he added, "our terms are too scientific for these young auditors, who would doubtless like to know the cause of such magnificent effects. As the brilliancy is fast fading from the sky, let us retire, from this cold night air, to the more genial atmosphere of the library, where we may talk more about this phenomenon."

The party accordingly proceeded into the library where a bright wood fire glowed upon the hearth.

"I do not wonder," said Mr. Oldbuckle, "that the ignorant natives of northern latitudes, are terrified by these appearances, and regard them as supernatural. Some of them have supposed them to be occasioned by a great battle of the spirits or gods of the air, darting fiery arrows at each other!"

"There is some poetry in that notion, at all events," said William Sinclair, "and the savage philosophy which could cherish such a notion, might be exalted by true science to something noble.

"Yes," said his father, "I have always thought that the noblest creed of the heathen world is that of the Persian, which makes the sun and fire objects of adoration; though any object-worship, whatever, is too degrading to be called noble."

"I see the eyes of Alice are making eager inquiries for some more information than we have yet given her about these Northern Lights," said Mr. Oldbuckle; "pray enlighten her, my dear sir."

"Do, papa, if you please," said the young girl

"It is not I alone, who desire to know more about them."

"My opinion," said Dr. Sinclair, "is formed from the most general views of modern writers, which regard these lights as the effect of streams or currents of electricity, flowing in a rarefied region of the atmosphere, at a great distance from the earth, quite above the cloud-region. The brilliant colours of crimson and purple which they assume, are occasioned, perhaps, by the vapours of the air which they decompose into gases. This is all theory or supposition, I know, but fortunately I have it in my power to make it appear quite plausible."

"How, papa?" exclaimed Alice and Mary, in a breath.

"I will show you," he replied, "with great pleasure. To do so, however, I shall need to use the electrical machine, with which I have already so frightened Fanny, that I am afraid she will run away at the very mention of it."

"No, I won't, papa, if you will promise not to make it spit fire at me."

"Very well, Fan, I will promise;" and so saying, he opened a deep cupboard in the library, and brought out the machine, which he placed upon a table. The machine was covered with a brown linen case to keep it dry and free from dust. As the night was advancing, Dr. Sinclair lost no time in getting the machine into good working order, not a difficult task, as the air was dry and warm. The pith-balls on the machine flew wide apart, when the handle was turned, and the sparks were bright and plentiful from the prime conductor when the hand or a brass ball was presented to it.

"But how are you going to make streams of electricity flow through the air, papa?" said Harry.

"Have you any idea of the method, Alice?" inquired her father.

"I have not forgotten what I learned about it from Mrs. Marcet," she replied with a quiet laugh.

"Who is this wonderful Mrs. Marcet?" whispered Herbert to Harry; for he had not yet been told that she was the author of some very interesting "Conversations on Natural Philosophy and Chemistry," which had been for years popular school-books for girls.

"Some learned old lady, I guess," said Harry, "who takes an interest in Ally, and teaches her all manner of odd things which I have never even heard of."

Alice now laughed in earnest, and declared that she had derived both pleasure and benefit from Mrs. Marcet's "Conversations."

"Well, my bird, what does the learned old lady of Harry's fancy, say about the experiment now to be performed?" said Mr. Oldbuckle.

"I do not recollect her words, sir, but she taught me that a current of electricity will flow through rarefied air, in a tube, with great rapidity and with a purple light."

"Well, if this can be shown, we shall have something very much like an *aurora borealis*, I must confess."

Dr. Sinclair had now produced from his closet a large glass tube nearly three feet long, capped at both ends with brass. At the top there was a brass knob at either end of a stem, which descended into the tube, and at the lower end, which was screwed to a wooden stand, there were three brass stems terminating in points within the tube. He now fastened a brass chain to the prime conductor of the electrical machine, and connected it also with the knob at the top of the tube. Then he caused the room to be darkened, and upon working the machine, flashes of light were seen to play about the glass plate, and to dart spitefully from the links of the chain, while now and then a delicate brush of purplish-tinted light was projected from the knob of the prime conductor upon the near approach of William Sinclair's hand.

"What is the matter, papa?" said Alice, "not a ray of light descends the tube. Mrs. Marcet must have been wrong after all."

Harry and Herbert looked mystified, but the elder people looked wise. There was a mystery somewhere.

"Have we fulfilled all the terms of the experiment

according to the description of Mrs. Marcet, Alice?" said her father.

"I can not think of any thing that has been omitted, papa."

"What was it you said about *rarefied* air, just now?"

"Oh! how stupid I am," she said, smiling. "You must use the air-pump, papa, and then, I think, we shall see."

"Very well, my daughter. William will bring the air-pump from the laboratory, and with the aid of it, we will take away some of the air which is in the tube."

So saying, he detached the tube, turned a stop-cock at the bottom of it, and then screwed one end of it into the plate of the air-pump and re-connected it with the machine. William now worked the pump a few strokes, and Dr. Sinclair turned the machine as before.

"Oh! how beautiful!" exclaimed Alice; "what lovely tints of rose and purple!" as streams of the electric fluid now ran with lightning flashes down the long tube, making all manner of graceful configurations in their descent. At some moments, the whole tube was full of intense blue light, which quickly changed to crimson, and again to purple. Then for an instant it would cease to flow, only to flash with renewed brilliancy, and this continued while the machine was turned, and for some time afterward.

"Admirable—admirable!" said Mr. Oldbuckle. "I am a convert to the electrical theory. I shall vote for the *currency* bill. If I could only imagine a source for the electricity to come from, I should regard your opinion as absolutely demonstrated, Dr. Sinclair."

"Currents of electric fluid are constantly generated by the equatorial motion of the earth, and they may flow periodically to the poles."

"I see, I see, and I shall believe in your theory until a better one displaces it. I can not say more, my dear sir, in this age of new theories and shifting philosophies."

"No," said Dr. Sinclair, smiling; "I shall change my own opinion, I assure you, when I can get a more rational one."

"Electrical science is yet in its childhood," said William Sinclair. "Its expounders are observing facts rather than demonstrating laws."

"It is a splendid science, truly," said Mr. Oldbuckle. "I almost wish I was a youth again, that I might hope to keep pace with its extraordinary development.

"Come," said Dr. Sinclair, "let us now close this pleasant evening with our wonted acknowledgments to the Author of all science."

"Nothing," said Mr. Oldbuckle, "is more fitting, and nothing could give me more pleasure than to join with you in worshipping Him whose glory is declared in the heavens, and with whom is 'terrible majesty.'"

Dr. Sinclair read the thirty-eighth chapter of Job; the whole family united in singing the beautiful hymn,

> "I sing the mighty power of God,"
> That made the mountains rise,
> That spread the flowing seas abroad,
> And built the lofty skies!" etc.,

and then Dr. Sinclair offered fervent thanksgiving and prayer to God.

CHAPTER XX.

A Gift for Alice—Narrow Escape of the Æronaut—The Fugitive Bubble—Making a Noise in the World—A Wonderful Change—Water at Fires—Illuminating Gas—Elements—Carbon.

ABOUT the middle of the afternoon succeeding the day upon which the balloon had been sent up, Mr. Oldbuckle again made his appearance at Beechwood. Alice was the first to greet him, for she cherished a warm affection for him in return for the especial interest which he always manifested for her. Seldom, indeed, did he come without bringing to her some token of his kind remembrance, such as a book or a flower. Upon this occasion he was accompanied by a waiting lad, who bore in his hands a beautiful cage, containing a Canary bird—one of the most golden-hued, fairy-crested little sprites of the vocal tribe which Alice had ever beheld.

The cage was scarcely placed upon the table of the sitting room, and all the family summoned to behold it, when the little songster poured out his greetings to his new home in such a burst of song, as fairly created a *furore* of delight, such as the most successful *débutante* of a concert-room might envy.

Alice looked her thanks to her kind friend, who said in his usual playful manner,

"You are my bird, you know, Alice, and that is your bird. Now, I will venture to say that you do not think half so much of your prize, as I do of mine."

"Oh! Mr. Oldbuckle!" said the excited and delighted girl, "you are, indeed, too kind to me entirely."

"Nonsense—nonsense," said he, "this is your just reward for your discriminating verdict the other day upon my hereditary foe, Napoleon," and he turned the conversation at once upon the sport of the previous day, by saying,

"What do you think, Harry? our little æronaut narrowly escaped with a whole neck yesterday."

"How was that, Mr. Oldbuckle?" said a chorus of voices.

"Why, James Renton, my gardener, told me that as he was passing on the other side of your beech-grove he saw the balloon just above the trees, and taking it for a large bird, was about to shoot at it, when suddenly it began to descend, and got out of his sight."

"What a narrow escape!" said William, "supposing always that he could have hit it!"

"I am glad he did not shoot, at all events," said Dr. Sinclair, "for I did not want the balloon injured. But come," he added, "let us go into the library while day-light lasts, and see if we can find any thing to amuse and instruct us there."

"It quite escaped him, although he rose on tip-toe"—p. 218.

"Did you not say yesterday, papa, that hydrogen gas is inflammable?" asked Harry.

"I did, my boy, and I will show you a beautiful experiment to prove it, if you will light a wax taper or a candle."

The candle was speedily brought, and William Sinclair went, with his father, down into the laboratory, to obtain a fresh supply of hydrogen gas. Having filled the India-rubber bag as before, they returned, and Dr. Sinclair fixed the bubble-pipe and plunged it into the fresh soap-suds, which Harry had volunteered to prepare.

In a moment, a bubble escaped from the pipe and rose rapidly into the air. Mr. Oldbuckle pursued it with the lighted candle, but so swift was its ascent, that it quite escaped him, although he rose on tip-toe, and extended his arm above his head as far as he could possibly reach. There was the provoking little sphere just beyond him, and the whole company could not restrain a merry laugh at the expense of the kind-hearted old gentleman, who, when he had given up the chase as hopeless, joined heartily in their chorus.

"I will be up with the next one, see if I am not," he said.

He was as good as his word, and the beautiful bubble, the moment it came in contact with the burning wick, took fire, and vanished in a crest of pale yellow flame. The young people were exceedingly delighted at the result, and Fanny eagerly exclaimed,

"Blow a very large one, papa, and make a big flame."

"Yes," said Harry, "I agree with Fan; one as big as her head, papa."

"You forget, Harry," said his sister, "that the gas is so very light, that the bubbles won't get large before they rise of themselves."

"True," said her father, "I am glad to see that you observe so well, my daughter. Just as soon as the bubble is large enough to weigh less, film and all, than the surrounding air, away it goes, like the balloon with its mooring rope cut."

"How very quietly the bubbles burn!" said Herbert.

"Quietly, eh, Master Russel?" said William Sinclair; "let me see if I can't stir them up a bit, so that they will manage to make a little more noise in the world."

"That is the way!" said Mr. Oldbuckle, laughing. "There's nothing like stirring people up to bring out what is in them!"

"May I appropriate the rest of this gas, sir?" said William, addressing his father.

"It is quite at your service, my son."

William took the bag, and measuring with his eye the bulk of the gas it contained, he took off the pipe, and opening the stop-cock, inhaled fresh air into his lungs, and then blew into the bag, until he had about doubled the quantity of its contents.

"Oh! brother Willie," said Harry, "take care you don't go up like a balloon!"

"Touch him off," said Mr. Oldbuckle, approaching the lighted candle, very much to the amusement of all but Fanny, who was somewhat frightened at the idea.

William Sinclair again attached the pipe, and having blown another bubble, of somewhat larger size than the previous ones, he detached it from the pipe, and it floated gently upon the air, without rising.

"See," said Herbert, "it does not go up like the others."

"No, and it won't burn, either, I know," said Harry. "William spoiled the fun by breathing into the bag."

Before he had done speaking, Mr. Oldbuckle had touched the bubble with the lighted candle, and it exploded with a report like that of a small pistol, at which the young people all started with evident surprise.

"There, Master Harry, it wouldn't burn, eh?" said his brother, meanwhile raising in the soap-bowl a huge mass of minute bubbles into the shape of a glittering crown. In an instant, he took the candle from Mr. Oldbuckle's hand, and applying it to the sparkling mass, it went off with a tremendous report, which brought Jacob Fletcher in haste to the scene of operations, and sent Fanny, in alarm, to her mamma's side.

"You stirred them up effectually, I must say, William," said Mr. Oldbuckle; "and Harry will confess, I think, that you didn't spoil them, as he alleged you would, by blowing into the bag."

"I don't know, Mr. Oldbuckle, that I shall confess it. He certainly made them very noisy, and I have heard it said that boys when they are very noisy are *spoiled*."

"Very good, my lad, very well retorted."

"But," said Dr. Sinclair, "will any one of you tell me what made the bubbles explode so loudly, after William had blown into the bag?"

"The air, papa, of course," said Harry.

"Very true; and how did the air produce the effect?"

Harry was silent. He had made a bold answer, and exhausted his courage with his knowledge. But Alice very kindly came to his relief, under the guidance of Mrs. Marcet, as usual.

"I think, papa," said the young girl, "it is the oxygen of the air which makes the difference. It unites with the hydrogen and forms an explosive gas."

"Precisely, Alice; you have not studied Mrs. Marcet in vain, I am glad to see."

"No," said Mr. Oldbuckle, "my bird sings to some purpose;" and he drew Alice to his side, smiling on her very kindly. "But tell us," he added, "what became of the contents of the bubble when it burst with so loud a noise?"

Alice hesitated a moment, and then replied, "I think, sir, they were instantly changed into a drop of water."

"A drop of water!" said Herbert, half-admiringly and half-incredulously, "I can not imagine such a thing!"

"It is true, nevertheless, Master Herbert," said Dr. Sinclair, "and this brings us back to what I told you a little while since—that every drop of water is composed of these two gases, which occupy a space much larger than the drop itself."

"It puzzles me very much," said Herbert, half-musingly.

"What puzzles you, my boy?" asked Mr. Oldbuckle.

"How it is," said Herbert, blushing deeply, "that water should be converted into fire."

"I am delighted to hear you speak out your mind, Herbert," said Dr. Sinclair. "That is the way to learn new truths and to conquer difficulties. The problem you stumble at, is one of the phenomena of nature."

"Funny—what, papa?" said inquisitive little Fanny.

"Oh! I see I must not use big words before you, Fan, unless I stop to explain them. It is one of the wonderful things, then, of nature—and these are called '*phenomena.*'"

"From the Greek 'phaino, to show,'" whispered Herbert to Alice.

"An eclipse is a phenomenon, so is a water-spout, and so is every thing which is not of common occurrence," continued Dr. Sinclair; "does my little girl understand?"

"*Comprenez-vous, petite fille?*" said Alice, laughing; for Alice was now in her early French lessons, and like most beginners was proud of the few phrases of which she was mistress.

Fanny looked blank at her sister, but told her papa that she thought she understood him.

"Well, then," said Dr. Sinclair, "let me try to help Herbert out of his difficulty. Water, in its liquid state, is the opposite of fire, as we all know; but chemistry can convert it into two gases, one very inflammable, and the other, though not inflammable, a great supporter of combustion, or more plainly speaking, of *burning*. These two gases are combined in unvarying proportions in water, and may be separated by intense heat. When water is converted into steam, the two gases separate readily, if there be any thing present with which the oxygen can combine, as red-hot iron. I might have made hydrogen gas by passing steam through a heated gun-barrel, which would take up the oxygen and set the hydrogen at liberty."

"I should think if intense heat converts water into these gases, it would be dangerous to throw water upon burning buildings; and yet this is the way in which fires are put out," said William Sinclair, whose philosophy was now, perhaps for the first time, a little at fault.

"It is dangerous, sometimes, my son," said his father, "and indeed, generally, a little water is worse than none at all. If you can not drown the flame altogether, the water thrown on it will only serve as fuel; for, converted into steam by the great heat, the hydrogen will burn furiously, and the oxygen being, as I have said, a supporter of combustion, will help the process."

"I have often seen," said Mr. Oldbuckle, "the flames burst out with great violence, when water has been thrown upon a smouldering mass of fire; and this was owing, doubtless, to the liberation of the gases in the water."

"By and by," said Dr. Sinclair, "I may show you some experiments with this curious oxygen gas which we have been talking about. Do you think I can burn up a ten-penny nail as fast as a match commonly burns, Herbert?"

"I should think not, sir; though, if you can, I should like to see it done."

"Well," replied the Doctor, "remind me of it some day, and I will give you a proof of my skill in that line."

"Is the gas with which the streets of the city of New-York are lighted, hydrogen gas?" inquired Herbert.

"No, but it is a combination of hydrogen with a substance called *carbon*, and the gas itself is called carburetted hydrogen. Carbon is regarded as one of the elements, or simple substances of the globe, because no evidence has yet been obtained of its compound nature."

"But, papa," said Harry, "I thought there were only four elements, and that they were—air, water, earth, and fire."

"That was the mistake of the old philosophers," replied his father. "Not one of these bodies is really an element; they are all composed of two or more substances, which latter are accounted really *elements.* Instead of four, there have been discovered more than sixty first principles in matter, of which about fifty are metals, and the remainder are non-metallic; of these are hydrogen, oxygen, and carbon. The latter is found in the form of coal, from which substance much of the city gas is made, by burning the coal in large iron retorts. It forms also a great part of resin, oil, and all fatty matter which is employed for producing artificial light. The lead in cedar pencils is almost pure carbon, while in the exquisite form of the diamond we find this element absolutely pure."

The conversation was now interrupted by the teabell, and Mr. Oldbuckle gratified the young people by remaining with them at the pleasant evening repast. When it was over, he departed for his own home, leaving them to their accustomed Saturday night duties, in preparation for the next day, which was spent by the family at Beechwood in the manner previously related. William Sinclair, however, went over in the morning to accompany his friend Edward Vivian and his sister to church in the village, where pleasant greetings were exchanged between them and the Beechwood circle.

CHAPTER XXI.

The Pond—Skating—A Collision—Harry's Mysterious Departure—Sledding on the Pond—An Upset—Inertia—Dr. Sinclair on the Ice—A Surprise at Home—More Sport on the Ice—The Skating Trio—A Novel Sleigh-ride.

"COME, Herbert," said Harry, as they arose from the breakfast-table on Monday morning, "we must have some sport on the pond to-day. Here we have been at home more than a week, and I have not had my skates on yet; it is positively too bad."

Herbert was willing enough, and especially as Mrs. Sinclair told Alice that she and her sisters might go down and witness the amusement, which they were much inclined to do. Alice entreated her father to accompany them, but he excused himself upon the plea of business of immediate importance.

As soon, therefore, as the young people had taken care of their pets and dependents, and protected themselves thoroughly against the cold, which was not severe, in the pleasant brightness of the sunshine, they all set out for the pond. This was a natural lakelet of more than a mile in length, and of a variable width, reaching in the centre about a quarter of a mile. It was beautifully situated—skirted upon one side by the beech forest, which stretched beyond the hall, and upon the opposite shore by a belt of meadow-ground. In summer it was a favourite haunt of the family. A boat and bathing-house, over which was a sitting-chamber, had been erected by Dr. Sinclair, at the western end of the pond.

Very different was the winter aspect of this scene from that which it exhibited in the radiant summertime. But the hearts of the boys exulted in the wide expanse of ice which stretched out before them, and while Alice and her sisters took temporary possession of the boat-house, Harry and Herbert buckled on their skates, and the former was very soon gliding swiftly over the ice. Herbert was less accustomed to the sport than his school-fellow, and he moved cautiously, especially fearing to catch a fall—not so much for the personal discomfort of it, as for the observation of Alice and Mary.

He soon gathered courage, however, and followed Harry in his rapid flight. The ice was in good condition, the wind having first nearly cleared its surface of the light snow, and the warmth of the sun melted that which remained. Now they glided hither and thither, and once they started upon a race across the pond, in which, however, Harry gained so much upon Herbert that he generously cut it short, and satisfied himself by describing curves and figures upon the ice, where his sisters could see the sport. While he was thus occupied, it happened that he and Herbert came unexpectedly into collision, and the result was that both of them fell backwards with an uncomfortable force upon the ice, greatly to the amusement of the group who stood upon the margin of the pond, and made no attempt to restrain their merriment; especially as the boys picked themselves up with loud bursts of laughter. Harry now whispered something to Herbert, and immediately afterwards took off his skates and started eagerly homeward, leaving his young friend to explain his purpose to Alice and her sisters.

"He is gone," said Herbert, "to fetch the sleds, so that we may give you all a good ride upon the ice."

"Oh! that will be charming," said Alice; "won't it, Mary?"

Mary assented with a quickened colour in her face, and Fanny's bright eyes danced with her pleasurable emotion.

"How would you like to live in Holland, Herbert?" asked Alice.

"Why do you ask me that, Alice?" he replied.

"Because there, during the winter, they skate more than in any other country, we are told."

"I did not know that," was Herbert's ingenuous reply.

"The canals are covered with people upon skates. The women skate to market with heavy baskets upon their heads, and nearly all the population move about in this way."

While he was thus occupied, it happened that he and Herbert came unexpectedly into collision.—p. 224.

"I think I should like to live in Holland, then," said Herbert, "and I should become very expert in skating."

"It requires practice, I suppose," said Alice.

"Indeed it does; it was some time before I could even stand up on my skates, and I got many a fall, before I learned to move upon them."

Harry was not long absent, and he reäppeared, drawing after him, at a swift pace, the two sleds which they had used in the coasting frolic. Giving one of them to Herbert and again buckling on his skates, he directed Mary to seat herself upon his sleigh, and to take her younger sister in her lap. This arrangement left Alice to Herbert, who was delighted enough when she said,

"You have Hobson's choice, Herbert—in me or none."

"I am perfectly satisfied, Alice, though Harry has taken the lion's share."

"I will change with you, Herbert, if you please," said Harry; but without waiting for the answer, he seized the rope of the sled and started off so suddenly that both Mary and Fanny were immediately upset upon the ice, and a very amusing screaming and scrambling ensued.

"So, so, Master Harry, you are giving your sisters a practical lesson upon *inertia*, eh?" said Dr. Sinclair, who had this moment arrived at the edge of the pond, quite unperceived by any of the group there.

"I should call it a lesson in holding on, papa," said Harry. "Mary should have held on."

"She did *hold on*, Harry, and that was the reason she fell off."

"Now, papa," said Alice, "that is a paradox which I must ask you to explain."

"I will try and do so to your satisfaction, my daughter. Mary and Fanny were in a state of rest, together with the sleigh, when Harry so rudely disturbed that state by his sudden start. If the rope had been fastened to them, as well as to the sleigh, they would not have fallen off; but they *held on* to the state they were in, and the sleigh, alone obeying the impulse of Harry's pull, moved from beneath them. This is what philosophers mean by the *inertia* of bodies. If Mary and Fanny trust their brother after this, to draw them upon the ice, they must look out both for his starts and his stops; for if he were to bring up his sled suddenly, they would *hold on* to their motion and continue to move, if they did not meet with opposition from the ground, or rather, from the ice."

"Mary and Fanny, and indeed Herbert and Alice, too, ought to be very much obliged to me for giving papa an opportunity to teach us the philosophy of tumbling off a sled," said Harry, with a laugh, in which all the rest joined.

"It is a useful lesson, Master Magpie," said his father, "and I recollect another occasion when you afforded us the opportunity of learning it, though I did not express the philosophy of it at that time."

"When was that, papa?" asked Alice.

"Surely you remember to what I allude, Alice?"

"Oh! yes, I'm sure I do, papa. You mean the time when Harry tumbled out of the boat into the pond. He was standing up in the boat, Herbert, just as it came to the steps, and it struck so hard against them, that he was plunged head first into the water."

"That lesson was at his own expense," said his father, "but this time he made his sisters pay for it."

"Mine cost the most, any how," said Harry, "though I did not mind it at all."

"After the fright was over, you mean, my boy, for you made a terrible ado when it happened."

The laugh was decidedly against Harry, and he bore it with the grace of a generous boy. He now persuaded Mary and Alice to try again, and they showed no reluctance, notwithstanding their first fall. The sleds were freighted with their burdens, and a safe start was made. The boys exerted themselves bravely, and the light vehicles fairly flew over the smooth surface of the pond. Dr. Sinclair was soon behind them also upon skates, and he afforded the young people much amusement by his superior skill in the art. He would rush past them with the speed of the wind, and suddenly doubling on his track, describe a path completely around them. Bidding Herbert throw the rope to Alice, he laid his hand lightly upon her shoulders, and while the sled still glided along with its previous impulse, he urged it forward with increased speed, and left Harry and his sleigh far behind.

Then rejoining the group, he resigned Alice again to the care of their young guest, and proposed to Fanny to exchange her seat in Mary's lap for his arms. To this proposal the little girl joyfully consented, and her papa, apparently quite unconscious of his assumed burden, glided away again while she clung to his neck with one arm and waved the other, over his shoulder, to the party they were leaving behind.

It was a morning of rare enjoyment to all, and not one of them failed to express regret that Mr. Oldbuckle and William were not there to share in it. The latter had returned to Viviandale after the morning service of the previous day, and had found so much to interest him either in Edward or in Gertrude—no matter which—that he had not yet arrived at home when the young people started for the pond.

When they reached the Hall, however, about the dinner hour, they were exceedingly delighted to find, in the library, not only their truant brother, but both the objects of his attraction to Viviandale, whose presence saved him a little scolding, perhaps, from Alice's lips, and a gleam of reproach from the sweet soft eyes of his darling sister Mary. As it was, he was greeted with cordial, if not clamorous delight, and Edward and Gertrude Vivian had no reason to doubt that they had come where a welcome awaited them.

"Oh! brother Willie," said Alice after the salutations had ceased, "we did miss you so much upon the pond."

"We would all have come down and joined you there," was his reply, "but your mamma was quite inexorable in her plea that there was not time before dinner."

"Well then," said Harry, "let us make a day of it, by going back after dinner. Don't you vote yes, Herbert?"

Herbert certainly voted yes, and so did Gertrude Vivian, with so much earnestness in her declaration that she enjoyed sports on the ice with a keen delight, that it was immediately agreed to pass the rest of the day at the pond.

Dinner was no sooner over, than all were busy in putting on their wrappers. Dr. Sinclair left a note to be handed to Mr. Oldbuckle, in case he arrived at the Hall, inviting him to come down to the scene of amusement. William Sinclair informed the ladies that to him was delegated the honour of driving them in the cutter to the pond.

"Why, surely, brother Willie, you don't intend that we shall ride that little way, do you?" said Alice.

"No Alice, don't you hear that he intends to

'*drive*' us. I hope he won't use the whip very freely," said Gertrude Vivian, playfully.

"Pardon me, Miss Gertrude," said William Sinclair, "but how shall I better express my intention of being your coachman—"

"*Sleigh*-man," suggested Edward Vivian.

"Than by the words I used?" he continued, smiling at the parenthesis of his friend.

"I'm sure I don't know," she replied archly, "but one thing is certain, ladies don't like to be driven."

"I am at a loss for a happy substitute for the obnoxious word, unless I say, escort or conduct you," was the rejoinder.

"Either of the latter you may do," she said, with a heightening flush upon her cheek, and amid this badinage the ladies all stepped into the light cutter, in which the party from Viviandale had arrived. When they reached the pond, the horse was taken out, tied to a post, and a warm blanket thrown over him. Harry and Herbert insisted upon resigning their skates to William Sinclair and Edward Vivian, who were both well skilled in their use, and quite equalled, if they did not surpass, the morning performances of Dr. Sinclair, which had elicited the admiration of our young friends. It was a noble and exhilarating sight, as Gertrude Vivian justly remarked to Mrs. Sinclair, to see the three gentlemen striving in a race the whole length of the pond, their figures first receding swiftly into the distance, and then returning like a flight of arrows, while the sound of the steel upon the clear ice bore some resemblance to the rushing of the wind.

Harry and Herbert had brought their sleds with them, and Mary and Fanny readily consented to let them run with them on the ice, which they could do without peril, in their India-rubber boots. But the young men had nobler sport than this in view, and just as the boys were about to put their plan into execution, Dr. Sinclair called to them to bring the cutter upon the pond.

Alice divined at once the reason why they rode instead of walked to the pond, and indeed none were so dull as not to discover it.

Fanny clapped her hands with great glee, and exclaimed, "A ride! a ride, and skaters for ponies!"

The boys launched the cutter with great alacrity, and if it did not glide gracefully into the water, as another kind of *cutter* might have done upon the same pond, in the summer time, it certainly did move with great ease upon the icy bosom of the lakelet.

The ladies needed no urging to enter the sleigh, and when they were all comfortably seated, Dr. Sinclair placed himself between the light shafts, while William Sinclair and Edward Vivian stood each in advance of him upon the outside, and laid one hand upon the shaft nearest to him.

Harry and Herbert elected themselves footmen extraordinary to this novel *cortège*, which now started and soon attained such a surprising speed, that the boys were compelled to relinquish their feet and cling to the back part of the cutter. It required less than five minutes to traverse the extreme length of the pond, and all the fair riders declared that never before had they enjoyed so exciting and charming an adventure in a sleigh. The return flight was even more rapid, for the skaters were inspired by the unstinted praises bestowed upon them. Merrily rang the laughter and the light shouts of the happy revellers upon the still, cold air; and the first shadows of the brief winter twilight fell, before they left the scene of their innocent and inspiriting frolic.

CHAPTER XXII.

Better Late than Never—Christmas Gifts—Their Distribution—Fanny's White Swans—The Magic Wand—Feeding the Swans—Fanny's Wonder—Magnetism—The Mariner's Compass

MR. OLDBUCKLE did not arrive during the absence of the family, but before the twilight had quite deepened into night, the jingling of sleigh-bells was heard, and the young people bounded out of the library, quite sure of having to bid him welcome. Nor were they disappointed. It was he, and he bore in his hands a light box, which he handed to Harry, saying,

"There, Harry, 'Better late than never,' you know. That box contains some philosophical gifts which I hoped to have received in season for Christmas, but it has only just reached me. I appoint you my almoner. Open the box carefully, and see what there is for each one of you."

"Bring it into the library, my boy," said Dr. Sinclair, who had also come out to bid his friend welcome; and he added, addressing him,

"Your kindness to my children, my dear sir, lays me under many though, I am happy to add, not irksome obligations."

"Do not speak of it, I beg of you," was the reply "It is I who am laid under obligations. Your happy young people are helping me to live over again days of pure and healthful pleasure which I thought for ever gone by."

Mr. Oldbuckle was glad to meet again the young people from Viviandale, and they rejoiced in his arrival.

Harry, under his father's direction, speedily and safely removed the contents of the box, and distributed them according to the direction upon the parcels. There was one for each of the young philosophers— not excepting Herbert Russel—whose eyes certainly grew somewhat moist with the pleasure he felt at this token of regard, which was quite unexpected. The gift for Alice was first examined, and it excited not a little wonder by its appearance, which was utterly strange to nearly all the party. It consisted of a mahogany frame containing an oblong piece of glass, upon which were fixed irregular rows of little discs of tinfoil, some upon one side and some upon the other, while strips of the same substance were fixed in various positions.

Alice did not comprehend the nature of the gift, but this did not, in the least, diminish the warmth of her acknowledgments to her kind friend, who simply whispered to her,

"Your good papa will make it all clear to you, by and by, my bird."

Mary's gift was a tall glass jar, accompanied by a little box, which contained a fairy-like balloon and car all of glass of various colours.

"Your brother William will doubtless make the gift complete for you, Mary," said Mr. Oldbuckle, as she thanked him, with few words but with eloquent looks.

"That I will, presently," said her brother; "but I am curious to see the rest of these scientific souvenirs. What have you got there, Fanny?"

"Oh! see," exclaimed the delighted little girl, "two beautiful white swans and a—"

"A magic wand to feed them with when they are good, and to drive them away with when they are naughty," said her papa.

"How can that be?" said Fanny, with wonder in her eyes.

"We shall see, by and by; but you have not thanked Mr. Oldbuckle for these beautiful new pets."

"Dear Mr. O'buckle, I thank you very much," and she proffered her sweet lips for a kiss, which no one, much less a warm-hearted old friend, could have refused.

"And now for your present, Herbert," said Dr. Sinclair.

"Mine, sir, is a microscope, and I can not thank Mr. Oldbuckle, as I should for his goodness."

"Your pleasure in receiving it, my dear young friend, is all the thanks I want. I thought it would remind you of Beechwood as well as of me, after your return home."

"That it will, sir, and it will delight my dear papa very much."

Harry's gift was a singular-looking contrivance, consisting of a pane of glass set in a neat mahogany frame, with a handle attached, and with a square of tin foil pasted upon both sides of the glass. He looked at it with bewilderment in his countenance, and then he looked from one to another of the group which surrounded him, but most of their countenances appeared as blank as his own. As Mr. Oldbuckle did not give it any name, Harry forebore to ask him what it was, but concluded his curious but unsatisfactory inspection of both its sides, by exclaiming—

"Well, I declare, I can make neither head nor tail of it!"

Harry had forgotten his duty, in his perplexity, but he speedily remembered it, and added his thanks to those already lavished upon Mr. Oldbuckle, who declared that he thought so much pleasure, and so much appreciation, would be cheaply purchased at ten times the cost of his gifts.

"We can not make a better use of this evening, perhaps," said Dr. Sinclair, "than by explaining to the young people the nature and uses of these beautiful gifts—at least, of those which are not already familiar to them."

There was evident approval of this proposition in every face, and the Doctor continued:

"As for you, Fanny, you ought to provide a pond for your swans to float about in; and they must certainly want to be fed after being kept so long without food."

"Now, papa, you are making fun of me, I know; the swans can't eat, even though they can swim," said the little girl.

"I will venture to say, Fan, that if you offer them some bread, they will swim up to you immediately, and take it!"

Fanny's eyes dilated with wonder, but she shook her curly little head with incredulity. Meanwhile, however, William Sinclair had placed a glass basin full of water upon the table, and into it he put the swans, which sat gracefully upon the water, and certainly looked as natural as life.

"Here, Fanny," said her father, "here is a piece of bread upon the end of this wand; call them, and see if they won't come and take it."

"Yes, call them," said Mr. Oldbuckle; "they are named 'White-wing,' and 'Bright-eye.'"

Fanny looked puzzled, but as all were waiting in silence, she ventured timidly to call—

"Bright-eye!"

"Offer him the bread, Fanny," said her brother.

She extended the bread towards the swan which was nearest to her, and to her utter amazement, it immediately began to move towards her and actually buried its beak in the crumb which she presented to it. This was entirely a novel experiment to the little girl, and she eagerly offered the bread to the other, calling, at the same time—

"White-wing! White-wing! will you have some supper?"

White-wing was as ready as Bright-eye to be fed, and Fanny was almost wild with delight at her swans.

"Send them away, Fanny," said her father, as they both plunged their beaks into the bread.

"Go 'way, swans," said Fanny, but they did not heed her.

"Offer them the other end of the rod, and they will be offended and go away at once," said Mr. Oldbuckle.

Fanny said nothing, but her look was expressive of doubt. Still, she tried the experiment, and the moment she put the other end of the wand towards them, they both turned proudly away. The child's admiration was unbounded, and her enthusiasm created pleasure for all around her, although they knew the simple secret of these curious motions. It is not well, perhaps, to say that all of them knew this secret; all of them, except Fanny, had before seen similar toys, and knew that the rod was a magnet; but beyond this, neither Mary nor Harry had any definite idea of magnetism. Herbert had been more fully enlightened at home upon this very subject, and of course, Mrs. Marcet had not left Alice in ignorance concerning it.

"Well, Harry," said his father, "you look wise; tell Fanny why the swans wanted the bread which they could not eat, after all."

"They didn't want the bread, sir—see, they will come just as well without it, if the rod is held out to them!"

"Well, that seems to be true. What brings them to the rod, then?"

"It's a magnet, sir, and that draws them."

"We saw as much as that," said his father, laughing at Harry's rather equivocal reply. "What is a magnet, Harry?"

"A rod that will draw swans and fishes in the water, I suppose, sir," was the hasty reply.

"Ah! my boy, you're a candidate for information, I see, as well as my little Fanny and my gentle Mary. Come, Alice, give us a few words from Mrs. Marcet."

"A magnet, sir, is a piece of iron or steel which possesses the power of attracting other iron or steel," replied Alice.

"So far, so good; but what do you say of the singular effect produced upon White-wing and Bright-eye just now by the unbaited end of the rod?"

"I should have added," was her ready reply, "and of both attracting and repelling another magnet."

"That sounds like it, my daughter. Now, Fanny, you must know that each of your little swans has a magnet in its mouth, and that the rod is also a magnet. Perhaps you may not be able quite to understand me, but the power which dwells in a magnet, and which is of the same kind as that which spits at you in the electrical machine, is different at the two ends of each magnet. When two magnets are brought together, the ends which contain different powers unite, but the ends which contain the same sort of power separate from each other. Now the rod contains, at the point, a different magnetic power from that in the swan's mouth, so they are drawn together; while the other end of the rod contains the same sort of magnetism as that in the swan's beak, and they separate from each other. Look at this rod as I float it in the water upon a flat cork. It moves toward the swan almost as fast as the swan moves towards it. If I turn the rod round, see how they both move away from each other."

Even Fanny understood this simple explanation, at least so far as to have a clear idea that there was a fixed cause for the strange motions of the swans; and she no longer thought that they came after the bread, or were angry when she turned the bread away. Dr. Sinclair took this occasion to call the attention of the young people to the magnetic needle, placing one upon the table before them. He also removed the swans from the basin, and leaving the rod upon the cork, pointed out to them the fact that it lay in the same direction with the needle upon its pivot.

"Who invented the mariner's compass, sir?" inquired Herbert of Mr. Oldbuckle.

"That is a matter of profound mystery, I believe," he replied. "It was certainly in use more than six hundred years ago."

"So long as that, Mr. Oldbuckle?" said Dr. Sinclair. "I have fixed the date of its origin in my mind as 1302."

"That is the common chronology, my dear sir; but the mariner's compass is mentioned in the Cardinal de Vitri's History of Jerusalem, as being indispensable to navigators, and that history was written early in the thirteenth century, if not indeed before it commenced."

"That is an interesting fact which I did not know," returned Dr. Sinclair. "I am aware that the compass is claimed as a Chinese invention of very remote date, and that some affirm it to have been introduced into Italy in 1260, but I had held this latter point as doubtful. Your fact seems to have a good foundation, however, and I must yield to it, since facts are, proverbially, 'stubborn things.'"

"You said just now, papa," observed Alice, "that the power which dwells in the magnet is of the same kind as that which is seen in the electrical machine. Do you mean that electricity and magnetism are one and the same?"

"They differ only in quality, Alice, if modern teaching is not in error. Magnetism is nothing but a form of electrical action, and the magnetic force of the poles toward which the needle directs itself is supposed to be produced by electrical currents flowing around the Equator, just as electrical currents, flowing around an iron bar, will make it magnetic for the time."

"Will you please tell me, sir," said Harry, "how it is that this little needle can guide ships over the ocean?"

"I will try to explain it to you, my boy, with pleasure. The needle directs itself always toward the north and south; and so, if it be placed in a ship where it is free to move, it will maintain this position, no matter in what course the ship is sailing. By fixing beneath it a disc or dial with all the points of the compass in their order marked upon it, and contriving so as to keep the whole apparatus always horizontal, it must follow that the actual course of the ship will be shown by the dial. If she is sailing directly east or west, the needle lying always over the north and south line will have a direction across the line of the course. If she is sailing between any of the four great divisions, the particular direction will be shown by the line which lies in the ship's path, since the needle always lies north and south, and the dial being fixed to it, must necessarily remain in one position."

"Here, Harry," said Mr. Oldbuckle, "is a pocket compass, which will enable you, perhaps, to understand it more clearly. You see there are thirty-two points on the dial, called the points of the compass. Now, as I hold the case, the needle pointing north and south across the library, the length of the room is shown to lie exactly in the direction of east and west."

Harry had no further difficulty in comprehending the use of the compass; but while this long lecture was going on, Fanny had restored the swans to the basin, and was repeating her experiments in attraction and repulsion, beyond which principles of magnetism it is quite doubtful if she made any satisfactory advance.

CHAPTER XXIII.

The Fairy Balloon—William Sinclair's Magic—The Spell Explained—Alice's Ink-stand—The Canary's Water-bottle—Alice in Spangles—The Diamond Necklace—Electrical Light.

"SEE, dear Mary," said William Sinclair, reëntering the library after an absence of a few minutes, "your beautiful gift from Mr. Oldbuckle is now perfected," and, as he spoke, he placed it upon the table. The tall jar was nearly full of water, at the top of which floated the fairy balloon, with its car and the figure of a man, all in glass. The mouth of the jar was covered with cloth. Mary thanked her brother for his kindness, and greatly admired the little æronaut. Fanny thought it was even prettier than the balloon with her little basket for a car, but then she added—

"However, papa, that balloon could go up, and this one can't."

Harry reminded Herbert that they had seen just such a jar and balloon in the window of a store in the city, and wondered what use could be made of it, since, as Fan said, it couldn't be made to go up.

"But suppose it can be made to go up, Fanny?"

Fanny shook her head, as she was wont to do when it could not quite comprehend things, and said—

"Then, brother Willie, you will have to take the cover off, which you have tied on very tight."

"Suppose I bid it go down to the bottom of the jar, and then rise up again, will that satisfy your doubts?" said her brother.

"Do, do—oh! do, brother Willie; perhaps it is like Bright-eye, and will obey you?"

"Not like Bright-eye, Fanny, but here goes," and flourishing his hand, he suffered it to fall lightly upon the cover of the jar, exclaiming as he did so—

> "Water sprite, I bid thee go
> To the crystal depths below;
> Hasten in thy fairy car
> To the bottom of the jar!"

"He's going down—he's going down!" exclaimed Fanny, and the little girl was almost wild with excitement as the car touched the bottom and remained stationary.

"Shall he go up again, Fanny?" said her brother.

"Yes, oh! yes, let him go up now."

> "Water sprite, no longer stay!
> Up! I bid thee, haste away;
> Through the crystal ether rise,
> To the region of the skies."

To the increased delight of Fanny and, if the truth must be told, to the astonishment of Mary and of both the school-fellows, the balloon rose gracefully to its former position at the surface of the water. By an adroit but scarcely perceptible movement of his fingers upon the covering of the jar, William Sinclair made the balloon alternate between the top and bottom several times, and then suspended it about the middle of the jar, to the fresh surprise of the younger spectators.

"Your water-sprite seems to be very obedient to your will, my son," said his father.

"I can not comprehend it," said Herbert, half-musingly, and then turning to Alice, he added, "Do you know, Alice, why the balloon rises and falls?"

"I think I do," she replied; "but, perhaps, papa or brother Willie had better undertake to explain it."

"I have performed the experiment," said William Sinclair, "and, therefore, must beg to be excused from delivering the lecture."

"Do, dear papa, explain this beautiful and amusing experiment," said Mary, quite eagerly.

"That I will, with pleasure, my child; and I am glad to see you so much interested in it. It is properly called the pneumatic balloon—though a very common name for a similar contrivance is the 'bottle imp,' in which form of it, a grotesque little image is substituted for the balloon. You noticed, I presume, Mary, that your brother controlled its motions by placing his hand upon the covering of the jar?"

"I saw he kept his hand there, papa; but I can not imagine how that had any effect upon the balloon," was Mary's reply.

"What is there in the jar beside the water and the balloon, Mary?"

"Nothing, papa, that I can see."

"Nothing, Mary! What do you say about it, Harry?"

"I say just what Mary says, sir; and that is 'Nothing.'"

"And you, Fanny, can you see nothing more?"

"Nothing at all, papa."

"Well, my dear children, nothing is something now, at all events, though, to be sure, you can not *see* it."

"Oh! papa, do you mean the air above the water?" asked Mary.

"I do, indeed, mean the air, and it is that which causes the balloon to move! The cloth over the jar is made of India-rubber, and it is air-tight, so that the air beneath it is confined. If you had seen William prepare the balloon, you would have noticed that it is not only hollow, but that there is an orifice in its neck to admit water. By warming the glass-balloon, he expelled some air from the inside, and then he put it into water, and soon the fluid entered to fill up the space left when the heated air was cooled into less bulk. I presume it cost him some pains to get just enough water into the balloon to make it so heavy that it would sink almost below the surface, as you see it now does. When this was done, he put the balloon into the jar, and tied down the cover very close upon the little air remaining in the jar. Now observe, that I press lightly with my fingers upon the cloth, and the balloon begins to descend."

"But your fingers don't touch the balloon, papa," said Mary.

"No, they do not, truly, Mary; but they diminish the space above the water, in which the air is confined, do they not?"

"I can see that they do that."

"Well, then, they condense the bulk of the air by their pressure. The balloon also contains a little air over the water, and the pressure of the fingers is communicated through the water of the jar to the air of the balloon, the bulk of which it condenses, and so makes room for a little more water. That is instantly pressed in from the jar, and its weight disturbs the nice balance of the balloon, and carries it down as you see!"

Herbert was not the only one who drew a long breath, as the doctor closed this part of his explanation, which had been most eagerly and attentively listened to by all.

"There, William," said Mr. Oldbuckle, laughing, "we have still another instance of the '*facilis descensus.*'"

"Yes; but there will be no illustration of the '*hoc opus*' to follow it," was William Sinclair's rejoinder.

"Not the slightest," said Dr. Sinclair, "for lo! I remove my fingers from the cloth, every thing is restored to the state which their pressure disturbed, and the balloon is just where it was at first!"

"Really, Mr. Oldbuckle," said Miss Vivian, "I do not know how to thank you for affording me such a treat in this charming little toy—for so, I suppose, you regard it; and my thanks are equally due to Dr. Sinclair for his clear and simple explanation. Let me make the humble confession, that I did not understand the philosophy of it, at all, when Mr. Sinclair first displayed his magic control of it."

Both the gentlemen, thus repaid by Gertrude's thanks and ingenuous acknowledgment, assured her that it was a happiness to them to know that they had contributed to her pleasure.

"But, papa," said Mary, when these compliments were over, "I wish to learn every thing I can about this balloon, as I have the great delight of being its owner. Will you please tell me why every thing was restored to its former state when you lifted your fingers from the cover of the jar?"

"I commend your desire, my daughter, and I ought to have been more particular about the manner of *undoing* my first labor. I will be so now. When I removed my fingers from the cloth, the condensed air was immediately restored by its elasticity to its proper bulk. The pressure on the air in the balloon was also withdrawn, and that assumed its former bulk—which it could not do without expelling the additional water which made the balloon heavy enough to sink—and that forced out, the balloon became as light as it was at first, and, of course, rose to its first position. When William balanced the balloon midway in the jar, he did it by delicate and rapid changes of pressure upon the cover, producing corresponding changes within the jar."

"Oh! papa," said Alice, "now I can account for something that puzzled me very much indeed, only yesterday."

"Well, Alice, what was the mystery?" said her father.

"I brought my inkstand down-stairs to fill it with ink. You know, it is one of the new-fashioned sort with a spout at the side, which is the only opening. I took the bottle out on the back-step, and filling the stand as nearly as I could, I took it into the library, where I wanted to find a book to carry up stairs. When I had found it, I went to take up my inkstand, and the ink was running over, from the neck, upon the table. I could not imagine the cause of it at the time; but now I see, very clearly, that the cold air confined in the inkstand must have expanded in the warmth of the library, and so expelled the ink to make room for its increased bulk. Am I not correct?"

"Not only correct, my dear child, but, really, I must thank you for your very pretty illustration of the subject," said her father, in a gratified tone.

Every one applauded Alice's happy illustration, some with words, others with beaming looks, and Herbert among the latter, though he whispered to Harry,

"If I only knew as much philosophy as Alice does!"

"You will be likely to have another instance of the same kind, my bird," said Mr. Oldbuckle, "if you should happen to fill the Canary's water-bottle in very cold air, and then put it into its place in the cage in a warm room."

"That phenomenon has already happened," said Mrs. Sinclair, "though not within Alice's observation. Only yesterday, as I was sitting beneath the cage, just after Alice had renewed the water, several drops fell upon my work, and I looked up, thinking that Dolce was drinking or washing. But he was on the upper perch, and I perceived the water-glass to be overflowing; though I thought no more about it, except to remove my chair, until Mr. Oldbuckle's observation recalled it to my mind."

"Really," said Dr. Sinclair, "it never rains but it pours. Here are three illustrations of one principle, the elasticity of the atmosphere. I hope, my daughter," he added, turning to Mary, "you are now mistress of the pneumatic balloon in more senses than one."

"I think I am, papa; thanks to Mr. Oldbuckle in the one sense, and to you in the other. However," she added, "I must beg your pardon for desiring yet one more piece of information about it, as I should not like to be asked what its name means, and have to confess my ignorance."

"'Pneumatic' is the word which puzzles you, I suppose, Mary."

"Yes, papa, that is quite above my comprehension."

"Then I must lift your comprehension up to it. It is a technical, or scientific, term, from the Greek root *pneuma*, meaning *breath;* and it is applied to that branch of science which treats of air and its kindred fluids."

"And now, papa," said Alice, "if you are quite through with Mary's balloon, I shall be very much obliged if you will let me know in what sort of characters Mr. Oldbuckle has had my name written upon the crimson glass plate, which he has given me."

"How do you know it is your name that is written there, Alice?" said Mr. Oldbuckle.

"Oh! I have been able to trace it out among the numerous lines and spots which cover the glass," she replied.

"It is written, my bird, as it was on Christmas, in letters of light," returned Mr. Oldbuckle; "but I am sure your papa will now show it to you, for it is your turn."

"I must produce the electrical machine, then," said

Dr. Sinclair, going to a deep closet in which he kept it safe from dust and moisture.

"Oh! I know now what it is," said Alice, clapping her hands as gleefully as ever Fanny did. "It flashes upon me that this is like Mrs. Marcet's spiral tube or diamond necklace."

"It is nothing else, indeed, as far as the principle goes," said her father, "but it is a much more complicated line of light than that produced by the spiral tube."

The electrical machine did not require much care to put it in admirable order. The pith-balls flew asunder violently, and Fanny drew to a respectful distance from the prime conductor, as it began to "spit," as she called it.

"This," said Dr. Sinclair, as he took up Alice's Christmas gift, "this is Alice's name written with the pen of the lightning."

"How can that be?" said Harry; "I did not know that the lightning had a pen!"

Harry was well laughed at for being so literal, and in a few moments he understood better his father's words. The lamps were extinguished, and the firelight screened, as at the exhibition of the magic lantern, and immediately after, every one uttered an exclamation of surprise or pleasure, as there shone out, just above the prime conductor of the machine, the name of ALICE, in glittering spangles of light, while the crimson glass was also sufficiently illumin ated to increase the beauty of the effect. Suddenly the name vanished, and then flashed out again, as bright as before. Dr. Sinclair then substituted for the name, the diamond necklace of Mrs. Marcet, and a spiral line of spangles was produced, as Alice had said.

As it was now late, Dr. Sinclair did not extend his illustrations of electric illuminations; but when one of the lamps was relighted, he showed the young people the spiral tube, which was a glass tube, eighteen inches long, with a row of tin-foil discs, nearly as large as peas, pasted upon it in a spiral form. They did not touch each other, and hence at every interval, a spark was visible when a current of electricity from the machine was flowing along the metallic line.

"But why did we not see the sparks at first, one after the other, Dr. Sinclair, instead of all together?" inquired Miss Vivian.

"Because such is the velocity of the electric fluid," he replied, "that it occupies no perceptible time in traversing a vast distance. Hence it is that we see the flashes of lightning from cloud to cloud, or to the earth, all at once."

"What is the use of cutting the tin foil into little pieces, papa?" said Harry; "why not paste it on in a long strip?"

"Oh! Harry," said Alice, "then there would be no light at all; for the fluid would pass over it without interruption."

"We have not time, to-night," said Dr. Sinclair, "to investigate this wonderful subject further; but if you all wish it, we will devote to-morrow morning to it."

Every one expressed an eager desire to do so, and with this understanding, the electrical machine was restored to its closet, and the party prepared for rest, after the excitement and delights of a long and busy day.

CHAPTER XXIV.

A Cold Day—Electrical Apparatus—History of Electricity—Origin of the Term—Electrics—Conductors—Insulation—Harry Declines the Rod—William and Mary Conductors—How Franklin Caught the Lightning—Lightning Rods—The Leyden Jar—Induction—Harry's Gift.

TUESDAY was the coldest day of the winter so far, and the happy inmates of Beechwood congratulated themselves that they were not obliged to expose themselves to the keen north wind, which wailed dismally enough through the beech slope at the back of the dwelling. A larger fire than usual burned upon the hearth in the library, and the after-breakfast duties, which called some of the young people out of doors, were dispatched with more than customary haste. Fortunately the weather was dry; for otherwise the electrical amusements, which were to occupy the morning, might have been somewhat hindered.

Some especial preparations were made by Dr. Sinclair and William. The electrical apparatus was usually kept in the library-closet to protect it from moisture and from dust. It was now brought out, and placed upon a large table, upon which the machine was securely fastened by a brass clamp.

These and other arrangements the young philosophers watched with interest, and when they were completed, Dr. Sinclair sent Fanny to beg her mamma to favour them with her company. When Mrs. Sinclair entered the library, and had seated herself to her netting, the doctor gave the plate of the electrical machine a few quick turns, which excited so much of the subtle fluid that it began to snap from the prime conductor, and indicated a very satisfactory state of things. He then presented his knuckle to the brass knob on the conductor, and drew a number of loud and brilliant sparks, every one of which made little Fanny shrink, though she took good care not to be very nigh the machine.

"Before we begin our experiments," said Dr. Sinclair, "we ought to learn something of the history of electricity. Can you tell us, Herbert, whether it is an ancient or a modern science?"

"I believe it is modern, sir," was his reply.

"You are quite right, my young friend, it is modern; for, although the ancients knew something of the curious property of attraction, which amber and a few other substances possessed, when they were rubbed, they knew only the fact, and never explained it."

"What do you consider the foundation of the present science, Dr. Sinclair?" said Mr. Oldbuckle.

"The treatise of Dr. Gilbert on Electricity and Magnetism, published in 1600," was the reply.

"And yet," rejoined Mr. Oldbuckle, "Dr. Gilbert announced no general laws, nor were any definite principles discovered until the year 1730, when Mr. Grey, a pensioner of the Charter-House, made known the striking results of his long-continued experiments. I am disposed to think, after all, that this grand science is only a hundred and twenty years old."

"Perhaps that is the more philosophical conclusion," said Dr. Sinclair; "and certainly nearly all its grand developments have been made within a century."

"What is the hard name of this science derived from, papa?" said Mary.

"Ask Herbert, my dear," said her father.

She turned to Herbert, and questioned him with her gentle eyes, and he said, with a slight degree of confusion,

"I can tell you, Mary, but I am indebted to Alice for the ability to do so. It is derived from the Greek word *electron*, which means *amber*."

"That name was given to it, Mary," said her brother William, "because it was in a piece of amber that Thales, a Greek philosopher, first noticed the attractive power, which is one of the simplest exhibitions of the curious principle."

"See," said her father, as he turned the handle of the machine, dropping, at the same time, a few scraps of paper near the conductor, "see how these light substances are attracted by the electricity. A piece of amber, when it is rubbed hard, will produce the same effect."

"What is it that attracts the paper, sir?" said Harry.

"To answer you in your own off-hand way, Harry, it is the electricity; but, I suppose, you would know what electricity is."

"Yes, sir."

"Well, it is a very curious and subtle principle—which we agree to call a fluid—existing everywhere, and manifesting itself in a great variety of ways. We are only now beginning to understand its true character and relations, and yet a very large book might be filled with what is known and conjectured about it."

"Why do you not have amber, instead of glass, in your machine, papa?" said Mary.

"Because it has been found out that glass is more readily excited than amber, and it is vastly cheaper," he replied.

"I am told, sir," said Mr. Oldbuckle, "that gutta-percha is found to be even better than glass as an electric."

"What do you mean by an electric, sir?" asked Herbert.

"Any substance which is capable of being excited readily by friction," was the answer.

"Are not all substances electrics, then?"

"By no means. All the metals and the liquids

are such good conductors of the fluid, that, when they are subjected to friction, the fluid passes off, as fast as it is produced."

"Then electrics are non-conductors, I suppose, sir?"

"And conductors are non-electrics," added Mr. Oldbuckle.

"But," said Harry, "the prime conductor is of metal, and yet it holds a great deal of electricity, I should think, by the way in which it snaps at my fingers."

"Oh! that," said Alice, "is because it is insulated."

"Insulated!" said her brother; "what does that mean?"

Alice did not reply, and Dr. Sinclair took up the question, and said,

"When a body is charged with electricity, the fluid seeks to escape to the earth, but it can only do so through a conductor. If it is surrounded by non-conductors, it must remain. Now, the prime conductor, though of metal, is supported by a glass pillar, down which the fluid can not pass to reach the earth."

"Why does it not go off through the air?" said Herbert.

"It would," said Dr. Sinclair, "if the air were moist; but dry air is almost a perfect non-conductor."

Dr. Sinclair now took a glass rod, and told Harry

to hold it near the prime conductor while he turned the plate. Harry hesitated a little, but at length presented the rod. To his evident surprise, no effect was produced, even when he ventured to touch the conductor with the glass wand.

"Here, my boy," said his father, "take this brass rod, and try it."

Harry took the brass rod, which terminated in a ball, and as soon as he brought it near the conductor, a bright spark leaped to the ball, and the rod fell from Harry's hands, who jumped as though he had been struck. Every body laughed heartily, and he did the same, though he declined repeating the experiment.

"You see the difference, Harry," said his father, "between glass and brass, and these two substances represent two great classes, embracing all material things."

"Tell me, if you please, papa, what that chain, which hangs to the machine behind the plate, is made to go out of the window for," said Mary, who was growing decidedly curious.

"To keep up a good supply of the fluid in the rubber," replied her father. "The rubber soon gives all its electricity to the plate, and must have a fresh supply all the time."

William Sinclair detached the chain, and turned the plate vigorously, but the sparks from the conductor were very feeble and few. He now held his knuckle to the ball of the rubber, and bright sparks passed between them, while Dr. Sinclair obtained stronger sparks from the conductor.

"See, Mary," said William "I am now supplying the place of the chain, or, at least, of one end of of it," for he was still holding it in his other hand.

"Does the fluid really pass through you, brother Willie?" said Mary, incredulously.

"Yes, indeed, it does, and if you will take my hand, it will pass through you also."

Mary rather timidly consented to do so, and, after several faint efforts, mustered courage to bring her finger near the rubber, when a spark flew out of it and quite upset her resolution. The chain was now readjusted to the rubber, and Dr. Sinclair asked Alice if she could tell who proved that the electric fluid and the lightning were the same thing.

"Benjamin Franklin, papa, the great American philosopher," said Alice.

"Go on, Alice," said Mr. Oldbuckle; "the story is a very delightful one."

Alice begged him to narrate it, and he kindly consented.

"It is just a hundred years ago," said Mr. Oldbuckle, "since Dr. Franklin proved this remarkable fact. He had long suspected it, and in June, 1752, when he resided in Philadelphia, he went out with his son, to the common, near the city, just as a thunder cloud had come up in the sky He made a kite, by stretching a silk handkerchief over a light wooden cross frame, and fastened a hemp string to it, to sail it with. To the end of the string he tied a key, and to the latter a silk cord, which he held fast in his hand. As the cloud passed over him, he sent up his kite, and watched it till it was nearly hid in the cloud. For several minutes he observed no effect, but presently a little rain fell and moistened the string of the kite. Immediately afterward, its fibres bristled up, and putting his knuckle to the key, a bright spark, and another, and another passed to it just as they did from the electrical machine. And then the great philosopher *knew* that lightning was the same as electricity, and his delight can hardly be imagined. His little son was greatly astonished to see the tears gush from his father's eyes, but I do not wonder at it at all."

"Nor I," said Dr. Sinclair, "it was such a grand discovery, that it was worth tears of joy."

"And how did Dr. Franklin bottle the thunder and lightning, papa, as I read in some book?" inquired Harry.

"He had a Leyden jar with him, and charged it from the key, just as we may do from the conductor."

"Franklin invented the lightning-rod, sir, did he not?" asked Herbert.

"Yes, Herbert, and that was one of the noblest gifts of philosophy to man."

William Sinclair now took up the rod which Harry had dropped upon the floor, and screwing off the ball at its end, disclosed a fine point. He then approached it to the conductor, which was heavily charged. Harry looked to see him start, but, to his wonder, the pith-balls on the machine fell down, and yet there was no spark.

"A lightning-rod—a lightning-rod, brother Willie!" said Alice.

"Even so, Ally," was his reply, "and if you will present a needle to the conductor, the effect will be precisely the same as that which astonishes Harry so much."

Alice tried the experiment, and before she could venture to get her hand quite up to the conductor the needle had dispersed all the fluid, and she felt no shock.

"What sort of a jar did you say Franklin had with him, papa?" asked Mary.

"A Leyden jar, Mary, so named after a city in Germany, where it was first contrived."

"I thought you said a *leaden* jar, papa, and I wondered what it meant."

"If I had pronounced it correctly, my daughter, I should not have mis-*led* you. Spelled as it should be spoken, it would be the *Ly*-den jar. But let us look at it and see what it is like, and what it is for."

Dr. Sinclair took up a quart jar, which looked as if it might be, as Mary said, a *leaden* one; for although it was made of glass, it was coated nearly all over with tin foil, and covered with a wooden cap. Through this a brass rod passed. On the top of it was a ball, and on the other end a chain, which dropped to the bottom of the jar. He removed the top and showed the young people, that the inside was almost as much coated with tin foil as the outside. He then explained to them that when the fluid is collected anywhere, it dwells only on the surface, and that the tin foil, being a conductor, distributed it evenly over the surface of the glass beneath it, until no more could be forced in.

"But, papa," said Alice, "I do not see the use of the tin foil which is attached to the outside of the jar."

"Then, I fear, my daughter, that you have forgotten what Mrs. Marcet certainly must have taught you."

"Very likely, papa, and you will kindly remind me of it," she rejoined.

"I never fully comprehended that part of the Leyden jar," said Gertrude Vivian, who had been an eager, though hitherto generally silent listener to the discussion.

"It is an exceedingly important part, Miss Vivian," said Mr. Oldbuckle.

"Yes, and it is quite as difficult as it is important, I think," said Edward Vivian.

"Till it is thoroughly understood, I grant," said

Dr. Sinclair. "Perhaps I shall be able to make Gertrude and Alice quite comprehend, even if my younger auditors are left in the dark. It involves the induction theory. Whenever an excess of the fluid is produced upon one surface of a jar, the opposite surface immediately becomes deficient in the same degree, and the two sides are said to be positive and negative. The outer tin foil, therefore, is to aid the dispersion of the external fluid. The simple proof of this curious fact is this: If we contrive to prevent the fluid from escaping on the outside, we can not, by any means, force an excess into the interior of the jar."

Here Dr. Sinclair charged the Leyden jar, and effected its discharge in the usual manner; and then he placed it upon a stool with glass legs, and tried to charge it again. But the pith balls of the conductor fell for a moment only, and the sparks flew freely from it to his knuckle, showing that the fluid did not enter the jar. Nor did it discharge when the bent rod brought its two surfaces into contact. But when William Sinclair presented his knuckle to the outside of the jar, sparks passed freely from it, and the fluid from the conductor entered the jar and charged it as at first. Gertrude Vivian expressed herself perfectly enlightened upon the point by this beautiful demonstration, and Dr. Sinclair, turning to Harry, said—

"And now, Harry, we are quite prepared to comprehend the mystery of that gift which you received from Mr. Oldbuckle yesterday, and of which you will find no difficulty, I think, in making *both* 'head and tail.'"

Harry was eager enough to make the discovery, which my readers will find that he did in the next chapter.

CHAPTER XXV.

The Miser's Plate—Harry's Avarice Outwitted—Gertrude Vivian Shocked—William Sinclair's Stratagem Detected—The Penalty—Fanny's Hair on End—A Bright Kiss—Harry on the Stool—A Pistol Fired by his Nose—Ether set on Fire by an Icicle—The Fatal Stroke.

HARRY'S present from Mr. Oldbuckle was briefly described as "a pane of glass set in a neat mahogany frame, with a handle attached, and with tin foil pasted on both sides of the glass." He had no further information concerning it, and did not even know by what name to call it. Neither Herbert nor Alice could enlighten him, and his brother William had told him to "wait and see." He was now to be initiated into its mysteries; nor he alone, for many curious eyes were directed towards the novel contrivance.

"You want a name for the *thing*, I suppose, Harry?" said Mr. Oldbuckle.

"I think it would be quite convenient to have one, sir," replied Harry, laughing.

"Well, then call it 'The Miser's Plate!' and let me say at once, that I gave it to you with reference to its philosophical interest only, and if you find any moral significance in the name, it will only be. I am sure, by suggesting a contrast to your own generous disposition."

Harry deserved Mr. Oldbuckle's compliment, for he was generous "to a fault," as it is sometimes expressed.

"The miser's plate!" said Harry. "Do misers eat tin foil? for I can see nothing else on this plate for any one to eat."

"Let me put something on it, then, that many people eat fast enough," said Mr. Oldbuckle, and he took from his pocket and laid upon the plate a bright gold sovereign!

Harry's eyes dilated, but he was too much interested to speak, and Mr. Oldbuckle continued:

"The miser who owns this plate, (not you, Harry, but its mythological proprietor,) makes a great show of liberality, but he takes good care to offer his gifts upon such conditions that very few can accept them. Now, for instance, he has authorized me to say that whosoever can take this piece of gold from the plate, when, and in the manner he directs, may keep it and welcome!"

Looks of surprise and interest were exchanged among the group, and Harry found his tongue to say—

"I shall certainly try my luck at the gold."

"Will *you* 'make an effort,' Miss Vivian, as good Mrs. Chick suggested?" said William Sinclair.

"I am not avaricious, I assure you," was her play

ful response, "but the terms 'come and take me seem easy, and I may be tempted to a trial."

Dr. Sinclair now hung a short rod to the prime conductor of the machine, to the extremity of which he approached the plate, which he held in one hand, till it touched the piece of gold, and having given the machine one or two turns, he withdrew the plate and said to Harry—

"You are to have the first chance, by right of ownership in the plate. Give me your left hand, my boy, take the sovereign with the other, and put it quietly into your pocket."

Harry put his left hand into his father's, and scarcely suspecting the nature of the opposition he was to encounter in his effort to grasp the gold, he prepared himself boldly to make the effort.

"Only once, remember," said his father; and even these vague words intimidated him a little. But he put out his fingers, and was just about to close them upon the shining prize, when he drew back his hand with a sudden start, and at the same time uttered a loud scream.

"What is the matter, Harry?" said Mr. Oldbuckle.

"Ah! sir," said the defeated boy, "he is a regular old miser, and a coward, too, sir; for he hit me in my elbow just as I was about to pick up the money."

There was a wild and uncontrollable burst of merriment over Harry's failure, mingling with surprise at the way in which it had been brought about. Nor was this latter feeling at all diminished when Dr. Sinclair, having again put the money to the pendent wire, called Harry to witness that it only required a little nerve to obtain the prize:

"See," said he, "I can take it without difficulty;" and stretching out his hand, he lifted up the gold from the deceitful plate.

"Now, Miss Vivian, with such a successful example before you," said William Sinclair, "you will not fail, I am sure, and I shall be happy to offer you the prize."

So saying, he took the plate and brought the money into contact with the conductor for a moment only. He then offered Gertrude his hand and she accepted it with a slight hesitation. In another moment her fair fingers were upon the coin; but, alas! she did not carry away the prize; and I can not conceal the truth that she uttered a very lady-like scream, which was instantly converted into a most musical burst of laughter.

"Well punished for my avarice, I confess," she said, as soon as she ceased laughing; "but what can you say for your treachery, Mr. Sinclair?"

"Really, my dear Miss Gertrude,"—he ventured this mode of address, under cover of the general mirth—"I can only say that I was as much *shocked* as you were, at the unexpected result."

"Of that I have no doubt at all," said Dr. Sinclair.

Gertrude shook her head as her only reply to these protestations; but, turning to her brother, said—

"Come, Edward, get that glittering peril for me, like a generous knight—won't you?"

"Let me be your cavalier, Miss Vivian," pleaded William Sinclair. "I will encounter the danger alone, if you doubt that I shared it with you."

And with these words he applied the gold to the wire, and turned the machine with unusual vigour. Then grasping the plate firmly, he attempted to lift the coin, and very quietly did so, offering it to Gertrude, who exclaimed,

"Treachery! treachery! I saw you turn the plate, and I call for an explanation of the mystery."

"Let Miss Vivian examine the plate for herself," said William Sinclair, "and if she can convict me of a *ruse*, she shall decree such a penalty as she may think proper."

"Excellent—excellent," said several voices, and the magical plate was immediately proffered to the fair arbitress, who, however, hesitated to take it into her hands. This she did at length, and inspecting first one side and then the other, she discovered upon the latter a strip of tin foil, extending from the handle and connecting it with the tin foil in the centre of the plate. She immediately perceived that when the coin was laid upon this side of the plate the fluid passed through it to the hand, and none of it lingered in the gold. She saw, also, that upon the upper side of the plate, the coin was insulated, and the charge lingered in it until a connection was made between the upper and lower surfaces, by the approach of the fingers of the person holding the plate, or some one else holding his hand. Her discovery was hailed with great applause by all the party, and declared to be complete and satisfactory. Even William Sinclair acknowledged himself vanquished, and professing penitence, begged Miss Vivian to be merciful in the infliction of her penalty.

"I decree," she said, "that you shall try to take the gold, with as full a charge of the fluid on the right side, as you had before on the wrong side."

"I will not ask for any abatement of the verdict, but die nobly," was his answer, as he proceeded to charge the plate, and turned the machine, until his fair judge, laughingly, ordered him to desist.

His effort to seize the gold was a desperate one, and, in spite of a heavy shock, he actually lifted it from the plate, but it fell back with a loud and mocking ring, that was drowned in the chorus of merriment that ensued.

"Hurrah for the miser's plate," said Harry. "It is as good as an iron safe or a vault, any day, to keep gold in!"

"And now, Fan," said her father to the delighted little girl, "I want you to let me perform an experiment upon you."

"You won't let it spit at me, papa, will you?" she said pleadingly.

"I will promise not to hurt you, Fanny."

"Well then, I'm ready, papa."

The insulated stool before mentioned was now placed upon the floor, and Dr. Sinclair lifted the child upon it, and putting the brass rod into her hands, bade her place it on the prime conductor. She obeyed him with a little trepidation, but as the machine was at rest, she did so with impunity. He then worked the machine, and immediately Fanny's hair, which hung lightly on her neck, and was quite dry, began to rise, until in a few moments the whole mass was erect. She was frightened, but not hurt at the shouting of Harry and the laughter of every one else, as they beheld the phenomenon; and when Alice thrust a looking-glass before her eyes, she put her hands up to her head in dismay, and tried in vain to smooth her hair.

"Kiss me, Fanny—kiss me," said Alice, approaching the stool, and the little girl put out her red lips for her sister's caress. It was the most remarkable kiss that Fanny ever had, for a bright spark passed from her lips to Alice's, and the shock would have nearly upset her, if her sister had not clasped her in her arms. Harry required very little persuasion to mount the stool, and his hair rose till, as Mr. Oldbuckle said, with his accustomed devotion to the poets, "Lo! it makes,

'—each particular hair to stand on end
Like quills upon the fretful porcupine.'"

Our young philosopher proved himself equally a hero. He bore the sparks bravely, capering a little as William slily drew them from his toes or from some other unsuspecting quarter. He vainly besought his sisters to kiss him, and with equally poor success challenged Miss Vivian, and his mamma, to the same sort of conflict. They none of them felt inclined tc tempt the fire of his lips. While this sport was in progress, Dr. Sinclair had brought up, from the laboratory, a very neat apparatus for producing hydrogen gas at any moment, and opening the stop-cock, he allowed some of it to enter a short brass tube, about an inch in diameter, which he held in his hand, and the mouth of which he then closed with a cork. Near the other extremity of this tube there were inserted, in the opposite sides, two insulated pieces of wire, which did not quite meet in the interior, and terminated upon the outside in small brass knobs. While Harry was still standing upon the stool, his father approached him with this little instrument, and suddenly presenting one of the little knobs to Harry's nose, a spark passed from it, and coming into contact with the hydrogen gas, mixed with the air of the tube, it exploded with a loud report, driving the cork out with violence, and quite upsetting Harry's equilibrium and the gravity of even Mr. Oldbuckle, whose tall form was almost bent double by the energy of his mirth. As for Fanny, she was so frightened that she stood transfixed, and did not even run to her mamma's arms, her usual place of refuge in the hour of peril. Harry did not know what had happened to him, though when he found himself utterly unhurt, he made himself merry enough over the matter, and challenged his father to repeat the experiment.

"Will you go, Herbert," said Dr. Sinclair, "and bring me an icicle from the pump, or from the eaves of the carriage-house?"

Herbert's mission was soon accomplished, and he reäppeared, bearing in his hand a fine long icicle. Meanwhile, Dr. Sinclair had poured into a small metallic dish with a long handle, a quantity of ether, the peculiar odour of which soon diffused itself through the library. He now directed Herbert to stand upon the stool and hold the connecting rod, and as he did so, and the machine was turned, Dr. Sinclair held the ether dish out, and told him to touch the fluid with the point of the icicle.

"Do see, Alice," said Mary, "it is all on fire!"

The ether blazed up brightly, and the experiment was declared to be quite as wonderful as it was successful.

"These, I presume," said Miss Vivian, "are illustrations of the destructive power of the lightning which sets on fire combustible bodies."

"They are," said Dr. Sinclair, "and I am glad to have it in my power to show you a direct experiment in proof of the value of the lightning-rod."

He then took from the closet a small mahogany house, constructed of several pieces easily put together, and slightly held by small magnets. The gable end had a stout brass wire fastened to it, the point of which terminated above the chimney. A small square of the end, containing about an inch of the rod, could be taken out and reversed, so as to connect the rod with the wire of a gas-pistol inside the house. This was charged with hydrogen and put in its place, with the cork pointed to the roof. Dr. Sinclair then discharged a Leyden jar down the rod, which was still perfect, and no effect was produced upon the house. He then repeated the discharge, having reversed the section of the rod, so as to turn the fluid into the interior of the house. Instantly, there was an explosion, and roof and walls of the miniature edifice came tumbling down with a pretty clatter, which was much augmented by the unrestrained mirth of the spectators.

The dinner was announced at this moment, but Dr. Sinclair insisted that they should all receive a parting memento from the electrical machine. So, with a little coaxing, the hands of all were joined in a circle, which terminated at one end with Dr. Sinclair, who held the jar, and at the other, with Mr. Oldbuckle. I know not how it happened, but cer tainly, William Sinclair held the hand of Gertrude Vivian, and Herbert that of Alice. The jar was charged only partially, and at a wink from Dr. Sinclair, Mr. Oldbuckle applied his finger to the knob. The effect was decidedly electrical. There were little screams and loud screams, and some of the party thought they were certainly killed; but when they found they were not really dead, they rubbed their elbows and prepared to answer the summons of the dinner-bell.

CHAPTER XXVI.

The Afternoon—Tea-time—Music—Capping Verses—Verse *versus* Stanza—The Play—Conundrums.

MR. Oldbuckle's departure, immediately after dinner, for "the Grove," had not been effected without a promise to Alice that he would return by tea-time. His cheerful presence heightened all the pleasures of the young people, and he, himself, needed no persuasion to unite with them in their beautiful and rational amusements. Notwithstanding the cold wind, Edward Vivian and William Sinclair resolved upon having an afternoon ride; and preferring the backs of horses to the more comfortable cushions of a sleigh, they mounted, and bidding adieu, for two or three hours, to the group which assembled upon the piazza to see them off, they galloped away in the direction of the railway station. Harry and Herbert, not being able to persuade the girls to go with them to the hill, started somewhat reluctantly with their sleds; but they soon forgot their little disappointment in the excitement of their sport, and gave a glowing account, upon their return, of their "haps and mishaps" upon the snow-covered track.

The tea-table brought all our circle together once more, and those who had been facing the keen air found occasion to plead their exercise therein, as an apology for their evening appetite. Miss Vivian protested that it was ungallant in the gentlemen, to excuse their devotion to the delicacies of Mrs. Sinclair's table by such a plea, thereby leaving herself without such an excuse for a devotion no less palpable than theirs. The hostess, on her part, expressed her gratification at having been able to minister successfully to their tastes, and in this and other playful conversation, the tea-time was beguiled.

"Are we to have more philosophy, to-night?" said William Sinclair, when the party had returned to the library.

"I think not," replied his father; "the long lessons of the morning should suffice us for one day; and I have no fear that this evening will hang heavy on your hands without the aid of science."

"I hope," said Mrs. Sinclair, "that whatever direction the amusements of the evening may take, music will not be omitted altogether."

"By no means," added Dr. Sinclair; "and I am sure that Miss Vivian will gratify us by opening the performances at the piano-forte."

"I should be both rude and ungrateful to hesitate a moment to comply with your wish," said Gertrude, rising as she spoke and approaching the instrument, which William Sinclair hastened to open for her.

She played and sang with her wonted excellence, and then Mrs. Sinclair consented to sing with her the beautiful duet from "Norma," which elicited the admiration of the auditors. The music over, it was proposed by Gertrude Vivian that the whole party should unite in the play of "Capping Verses." This also, like the game of "Proverbs," was new to the young people at Beechwood; but that was no reason, certainly, why they should decline it; on the contrary, they were the more eager for it, that they might increase their sources of healthful and innocent recreation. To the question of Mrs. Sinclair, as to the manner in which the game was played, Miss Vivian replied:

"The play consists in the successive quotation, by all the party, of some verse of poetry, the only restriction of which is, that it must begin with the letter which terminates its predecessor."

"Do you use the term *verse*, my dear Miss Vivian, in its 'proper,' or in its 'common' acceptation," said Mr. Oldbuckle.

"I use it in its strict and proper sense, my dear sir," was the reply.

"What is the difference between them, Mr. Oldbuckle?" said Alice.

"A verse of poetry, in the vulgar use of the term, means a group of connected lines—it may be three, or four, or eight. Thus we hear, commonly, of the verses of a hymn; and even educated clergymen will direct the choir to omit such and such *verses*. In the strict sense of the term, a verse is a line of poetry be it long or short, and a collection of these verses is called a stanza."

"I did not know the distinction between them," said Alice, "and I am much obliged to you for the information."

"You are more than welcome, my little bird," was Mr. Oldbuckle's reply.

"Miss Vivian must introduce the play to us by the first quotation," said Dr. Sinclair.

"Mine is indeed an easy task," she replied, "since I have no verse to 'cap.' I give you, Mr. Sinclair, as the one next to me, the familiar verse of Goldsmith—

'Sweet Auburn, loveliest village of the plain.'"

"And I cap it," said William Sinclair, "with this, from the same source—

'Near yonder copse, where once the garden smiled.'"

"And I," said Mrs. Sinclair, "must draw upon Thomson, who exclaims—

'Delightful task, to rear the tender thought.'"

"How can I do better, then, my dear," said her husband, "than to carry out the thought and words of your poet—

'To teach the young idea how to shoot.'"

"Suppose I fire in the same direction," chimed in Mr. Oldbuckle, "and so contribute—

'To pour the fresh instruction o'er the mind.'"

"I can only think of one D," said Herbert, after a little pause, "so please

 'Don't view me with a critic's eye.'"

After a moment's hesitation, Alice took up her verse—

 "Each pleasure hath its poison too."

"I respond to that sentiment," said Edward Vivian, "in the exquisite words of Moore—

 'Oh! yes! oh! yes!'"

Harry and Mary both pleaded to be excused for the present, and Miss Vivian took up her brother's verse, saying:

"I will exclaim with Milton—

 'Sweet is the breath of morn—her rising, sweet.'"

"And I," responded William Sinclair, "will add—

 'Throw up the window; 'tis a morn for life.'"

"You must excuse me," said Mrs. Sinclair, "if I prefer the twilight—

 'Ere the evening lamps are lighted.'"

"Allow me, then," replied her husband, "to sing with Shakspeare, of—

 'Dark night, that from the eye its function takes.'"

"And I," said Mr. Oldbuckle, "am free to confess that my heart

 'Sits light and jocund at the day's return.'"

"What shall I do for N?" said Herbert, with a perplexed look. "Oh! I have one—

'Now's the day, and now's the hour.'"

Alice declared that she could not think of any verse beginning with R, and so Edward Vivian interposed with—

"Roll on, thou deep and dark blue ocean, roll."

This time Harry was more fortunate, and with only a moment's delay he said:

"Make way for good old Dr. Watts—

'Let dogs delight to bark and bite.'"

Miss Vivian observing that Mary was not prepared to follow up her brother's verse, continued the play by quoting the poetical adage—

"Early to bed, and early to rise."

William Sinclair, laughingly protesting that it was not fair to perpetuate the initial letter by the use of verses beginning and ending with the same, capped Miss Vivian's quotation with the verse from Wordsworth—

"Earth hath not any thing to show more fair."

Mrs. Sinclair, with her usual promptness, quoted the verse—

"Remote, unfriended, melancholy, slow."

Dr. Sinclair, with a memory of famous John Gilpin stealing over him, took up the final letter thus—

"What news? what news? your tidings tell!"

"Pardon an old man," said Mr. Oldbuckle, "if he dares to be sentimental, but L suggests love, and—

'Love is, or ought to be, our greatest bliss.'"

Herbert was obliged to pass the letter S to Alice, and she, after a little fruitless thinking, resigned it to Edward Vivian, who found speedy use for it in the line—

"Some natural tears they dropped, but wiped them soon."

Miss Vivian now observing that the letter lingered again with Harry, and fearing that the younger members of the party might not find the play as pleasing as it was to herself, proposed to devote the rest of the evening to conundrums, and the proposition was hailed with evident and eager pleasure by all the party.

"Are they to be original, only, Miss Vivian?" inquired Dr. Sinclair.

"We will make no positive rule to that effect, sir, if you please; but let all do their best to promote the general amusement; and I shall entreat of you to begin, and then whoever guesses right, to have the question."

"I suppose," replied Dr. Sinclair, with a smile,

"you will at least expect something new from me, and I must beg a moment to think."

After a moment's thought, he inquired—

"Why is the snow like a tree?"

After sundry guesses, to which Dr. Sinclair merely shook his head, Gertrude Vivian replied with eagerness—

"Because it leaves in the spring."

"You have fairly won the right of puzzling us, Miss Vivian," said Dr. Sinclair.

"I will avail myself of it, then," she replied, "to ask—

"Why is a writer on horticulture a traitor?"

One after another declared themselves ready to "give it up;" but Gertrude waited still, nor did she wait in vain, for Mrs. Sinclair solved the riddle by replying—

"Because he writes trees-on."

"Oh! Gerty," said her brother, "I did not think you would be guilty of such a perpetration as that! but we will hope for something better from Mrs. Sinclair."

"You will be disappointed, then, Mr. Vivian, for I have to ask—

"Why is a book like an organ?"

"Because it contains stops," exclaimed Edward, immediately.

"You are so far right as to insure to yourself the right of succession, Mr. Vivian," said Mrs. Sinclair, "unless some one else completes the answer which I require."

No one volunteered to improve upon Edward's reply, and Mrs. Sinclair amended it thus:

"Because it contains stops, and requires puffing to make it go."

"Capital!" said Mr. Oldbuckle; "really, my dear madam, you are an adept in the art."

"Why should a well-finished book last a long time?" asked Edward Vivian.

"Ha! ha!" said William Sinclair. "Because it is bound to do so, I suppose?"

"Exactly," said Edward, "and now you have a chance to beat that, if you can."

"As books seem to be the popular subject for our conundrums, allow me to ask, Why is a dull volume like an air-pump?"

"Oh! brother Willie, I can guess that," said Alice. "Because it exhausts the receiver!"

Alice's readiness won for her a very general expression of praise, but it won also something which she did not think of at the moment, or she might have been less prompt. It was the duty of proposing the next riddle.

"My conundrum," she said, "is not original, but it will be all the better for that. It is this, 'Why is a wafer like an inhabitant of the sea?'"

"I should think you have given us the answer in the question, Alice, or, at least, within an ell of it," said

Mr. Oldbuckle, "and so I reply, because it is a seal."

"Yes, sir, that is the answer, and I am glad you guessed it, because I want very much to hear your conundrum."

"Instead of being rewarded for acuteness, we have to pay a penalty," he replied, "and so I will inquire, Why is an antiquarian like the treasurer of the mint?"

The word coin was upon several lips, but it was some moments before any one shaped an answer. Then Dr. Sinclair replied,

"I suppose it is because he determines the amount of coin-age."

"My dear sir," said Mr. Oldbuckle, "your answer does more honour to my conundrum than to yourself."

"I wanted the opportunity to ask," said Dr. Sinclair, "Why is a newspaper like the Mosaic dispensation?"

No one offered a satisfactory answer to this question, and to the general cry of, "We give it up," Dr. Sinclair responded—

"Because it is made up of types!"

"Well," said William, "that conundrum ought to make an impression upon us, I'm sure."

"I shall resign my right to Herbert," said Dr. Sinclair.

"I can not think of any good conundrum," replied

Herbert; "but I recollect a 'curious question,' which amused papa very much when I told him of it. Shall I substitute that, sir?"

"By all means, my boy. Let us have it," replied Dr. Sinclair.

"What," said Herbert, "is a brief method of writing 'a thousand fiddles?'"

Herbert was unanimously called upon to answer his own question, which he did by saying,

"I should write it, Fiddle D D, (fiddle-dee-dee!)"

As Herbert still had the question, he resigned it to Mary, who seemed to have something which she wished to propose.

"Come, my daughter," said her mother, "do honour to Herbert's generosity."

"I will, ask then," said Mary, "Why is a game of Blind Man's Buff like sympathy?"

Mary's conundrum was one of the most successful of all, for it happened that not one in the company had heard it, and no one could make a satisfactory answer. She was obliged, therefore, to reply to it herself.

"Because it is a fellow-feeling for a fellow creature!"

It was received with hearty approbation, much to Mary's delight. She asked Harry to take her privilege, and he consented to do so, proposing the following:

"Why is a kiss like an irregular Latin noun?"

"Oh! my boy," said his mother, "because you find it difficult to decline; is that it Harry?"

Harry, laughingly, assented, and Mrs. Sinclair said that she now resigned her turn to Fanny, who, if she was not mistaken, had a little riddle to propose to the company.

"Well, Fanny, dear, what is it?" said her papa, encouragingly.

"Why can I raise a breeze?" said the little girl with eagerness.

"Oh! because you are a Fan," said her papa, laughing, and he added, "you shall have the honour, Fanny, of having proposed the last riddle; for it is now past bed-time for a little girl whom I know very well, and there may be others of our party who will not object to repose after our usual evening worship."

CHAPTER XXVII.

Why Natural Science is often a Dull Study—Harry's Experiment—The Sucker—The Atmosphere—Winds and Hurricanes—Weight of the Air—Alice Raised by the Air—The Difference.

THE morning of Wednesday brought more snow, which was still falling when the family, and their guests, gathered for prayers. As there was no inducement for them to seek out-of-door amusement, and as Edward Vivian and his sister were to depart on the morrow, Dr. Sinclair cheerfully consented to the request of Gertrude, that the morning should be devoted, like that of the previous day, to philosophy, a request which was, indeed, earnestly seconded by all the party.

Gertrude Vivian was possessed of an eager mind, which had been cultivated to a degree not usually attained by young persons of her sex. In natural science, however, she had studied books without the advantage of experimental illustration, a defect surprisingly common in the best seminaries, even where a scientific apparatus is duly paraded, in the annual catalogue or circular, as among the appliances of the school. The delightful entertainment of the previous day served to awaken in her mind, therefore, a new idea of the charms of science, which, it must be confessed, she had hitherto considered to be exceedingly mythical. She began to understand how its votaries might be fascinated in its pursuit, and she regretted that her progress, through the text-books of Philosophy and Chemistry, had not been enlightened and beautified by practical instruction.

"I have regarded," she said, addressing her host, "the time I devoted to the Natural Sciences while at school, as completely thrown away, except as an exercise for the memory, in the verbatim recitations of dull chapters full of inexplicable terms; but I now see that it might have been otherwise, had I enjoyed the advantages of experimental lessons. It is well, perhaps," she added with a smile, "that I did not, however, for I should certainly have been an enthusiast in those branches, and might have neglected others of no less importance."

"I am surprised, my dear Miss Vivian," said Dr. Sinclair, "that there can be, in this practical age, such palpable neglect of the natural sciences in all our schools—and I mean the colleges as well as the seminaries—for, with honourable exceptions in both classes of institutions, they treat the science of Nature with culpable disrespect."

"I perfectly agree with you, my dear sir," said Mr. Oldbuckle; "and if I had the dictatorship of our schools, I would decree that physical science should be taught from the lowest to the highest forms Now, I am sure that even little Fanny here has obtained more knowledge of a useful kind from your playful instructions than she could get from mere book-lessons in a month."

"The science of every-day life is sadly overlooked by all of us, and we should be wiser and better, too, if we paid more heed to the philosophy that shines in our daily paths."

"Your words remind me," said Gertrude Vivian, "of the exquisite lines of Mrs. Hemans, for whose poetry I have not, I am free to confess, outlived my girlish love—

> 'There's beauty all around our paths,
> If but our watchful eyes
> Can trace it in familiar things,
> And 'neath their lowly guise.'

I do not know," she added, "that the sweet poetess alluded to the philosophy of 'familiar things;' but if she did not, we may certainly apply her words to that, with a beautiful propriety."

"The poets are not all ignorant of the philosophy of common things," said Mr. Oldbuckle. "One of them says, if you recollect:

> 'Nature has nothing made so base, but can
> Read some instruction to the wisest man.'"

"See, papa," said Harry, entering the library with Herbert and the girls behind him, "see my philosophical experiment."

As he spoke, he swung before him a flat slab of

marble, suspended apparently to a piece of cord which he held in his hand.

"I call this 'a sucker,'" he added, "but Alice says that it is one of Mrs. Marcet's philosophical experiments. We used to do it at school, and it was great fun to lift up the flag-stones in the yard in this way."

"Suppose," said Dr. Sinclair, turning to Miss Vivian, "that we make this interruption of Harry's, the key to our morning amusement. It will introduce us to a very beautiful branch of science, and to a very wonderful, though common fluid."

"You mean by the fluid, the atmosphere, papa, do you not?" said Alice.

"I do, my daughter, and the branch of science is the very one we touched upon, while explaining Mary's balloon."

"I am delighted at the proposal," said Miss Vivian, "and much obliged to Harry for his timely interposition with his 'sucker.'"

Harry felt a little proud at the elevation of his sport into a subject for scientific discussion, a result very far from his thoughts when he found the slab in the hall, and bethought himself of a nice leather sucker which he had brought from school in his trunk. To get it, and soften the leather in water, was the work of a few moments, and immediately after he made his appearance, as already described, in the library.

Dr. Sinclair now directed him to detach the sucker from the slab, which he accomplished by putting his feet upon the stone, and pulling with considerable force. He then explained to Mary and Fanny, that the only hold the round piece of leather had upon the slab was that of contact, by being pressed closely upon it. They both wondered that the leather should cling fast enough to lift the stone, which weighed twenty or twenty-five pounds, while the leather was not larger than the palm of Fanny's hand. Harry and Herbert did not wonder at the result in the same sense that the young girls did, because they had seen it so often that it was a familiar sight; but they could not have given any better explanation of it than Mary herself, who now asked her father with a look of eager interest,

"What is it, papa, that makes the marble hold to the leather?"

"It is the air which we breathe every moment, Mary," was her father's reply.

Mary looked puzzled, and Fanny shook her head sagely, while the former said, with a little hesitation,

"I can not see how the air can lift it, papa, when it can't keep an apple from falling, or even a feather, for that."

"You *shall* see my daughter, before we dismiss the subject. I perceive that we shall find some opportunity for important lessons here. What do you think the air is, Mary?"

"You have called it a fluid, papa; but I do not know how you can tell any thing about it," was Mary's answer.

"Science teaches us all about it," said her father, "just as it does about all other material substances. It teaches us that air is a fluid which envelops the earth like a vast ocean of uniform depth, and that the depth, or perhaps I should say height, of the atmosphere is about forty miles."

"Why, papa," said Harry, "who has ever been up high enough to find that out?"

"No one, Harry, I must confess; but it is found that the higher we go up, the lighter the air becomes, and its density decreases so regularly, that it is easy to calculate at what height it must cease to exist. This ocean of air, like the ocean of water, is full of life and activity. Myriads of beings live in it, and besides this, it is subject to great agitations, and rolls and heaves with vaster billows than those of the stormiest sea."

"You are thinking of winds and hurricanes, sir, I perceive," said Gertrude Vivian.

"Yes," replied Dr. Sinclair, "they are themselves, the huge billows and surges of the atmospheric sea, set in motion by heat and electricity. These winds and hurricanes toss the waters of the ocean mountains high, and dash the largest ships to pieces, or they uproot the giant oaks of the forest, and destroy the grandest works of man. And yet Mary says that she can not see how the air can lift a little slab of marble like this!"

Mary's face flushed a little at her father's words, but she could not say that her difficulty was overcome; and Harry kindly interposed in her behalf, by saying,

"But it is not a hurricane, papa, which holds up this stone."

"You are safe in saying that, Harry; but the force which does hold it, is precisely the same as that exerted by the hurricane. It is the weight of the air which produces the effect in both cases."

"The weight of the air, sir?" said Herbert; "why I did not know that it had any weight!"

"Not when you were running home in the face of a gale, Herbert?"

"Oh! yes, sir, I suppose I must confess that; but then I did not think of that as being the weight of the air."

"Herbert's difficulty is a very common one, I fancy," said Mr. Oldbuckle. "The air is used as a symbol of lightness, and the poet speaks of 'trifles light as air.'"

"And yet, Herbert," continued Dr. Sinclair, "the air which encompasses our globe is estimated to be equal in weight to a sphere of lead sixty miles in diameter, or to more than five thousand billions of tons!"

This astonishing result startled every ear, not

withstanding it was known to several of the listeners, and the young people expressed surprise.

Dr. Sinclair asked Alice if she remembered the weight of the atmosphere upon a single square inch of surface..

"Fifteen pounds, I believe, papa," she replied.

"Alice is correct," said Dr. Sinclair; "and now, Herbert, I will suppose that there are in your body fifteen hundred square inches, or a little more than ten square feet, which is not much out of the way, I am sure. At the rate of fifteen pounds upon every square inch, there must be a continual pressure upon your body of twenty-two thousand five hundred pounds!"

"P-h-e-w!" was Harry's incredulous utterance of wonder, while Herbert said,

"Such a weight as that, sir, would crush me all to pieces."

"So it would, my boy," said Dr. Sinclair, "but for this one thing, that it is exerted upon you with equal force in every direction, internally and externally, and therefore you do not feel it all."

"How, then, can you find it out, sir?" said Herbert.

"By taking away the pressure upon one part, and leaving it to act upon another. Let us look a little at Harry's 'sucker,' which has been almost forgotten. Harry will have to moisten the leather again, for the heat of the room has shrunk it a little."

Harry soon put his apparatus into excellent order, and Dr. Sinclair resumed:

"When Harry spread the soft leather, just now, upon the stone, he excluded the air between it and the stone's surface. By pulling on the string, which passes through the centre of the leather, the latter is lifted up into a sort of cone, or cup, which must be empty, or, in other words, can have no air in it. In that space, therefore, there is no power exerted upon the upper surface of the slab, but the air below the slab still acts, and its force is sufficient to lift the stone up and keep it pressed against the leather, so long as the air is kept from entering the vacant space above."

"How large a stone would it lift, sir?" said Herbert.

"That depends upon the size of the cavity made by the leather. If it contains two square inches of surface, of course it will lift thirty pounds. But I will show you an experiment of a similar kind, in which we shall be able to measure exactly the force exerted."

Dr. Sinclair now selected from the apparatus which had been brought out for the purpose, an instrument which consisted of a thick glass cylinder, about four inches in diameter, open at both ends. Within the cylinder there was a block of wood with soft black leather upon its rim, which fitted closely to the glass, and required some force to move it up and down.

A strap hung from a hook in the block through the lower end of the cylinder, which had a rim to keep the block from sliding out. The upper end of the cylinder also had a stout rim, but it projected outward and served to suspend the cylinder on a wooden frame, which was mounted upon three strong iron legs.

Dr. Sinclair and William now raised the tripod upon three chairs, so that they were able to hang a chair to the strap in the block. When this was adjusted, the top of the cylinder was covered with a perfectly smooth plate of brass, into the centre of which was screwed fast a long narrow tube of India rubber, the other end of which had previously been screwed into the brass plate of the air-pump.

At her father's request, Alice now seated herself in the chair, which rested upon the floor. William Sinclair worked the lever of the air-pump, and immediately to the great amazement and delight of all the party, the chair with its fair burden began to rise, and continued to do so until the block had gone up from the bottom to the very top of the cylinder. As the chair first swung in the air, Alice seemed greatly inclined to spring out of it, but once assured by her father's word, she sat quietly enough, until the block descended, and the chair again rested upon the floor.

There were not a few then ready to make the magical ascent, and even little Fanny grew bold enough to go up. When the excitement was a little over, Harry said,

"But, papa, how is this experiment at all like my sucker?"

"The air-pump is the cord, the cylinder is the leather, and the chair is the slab. By means of the air-pump, the air in the cylinder above the block, which is properly called a piston, is gradually removed. When it is all taken away, the air beneath the piston presses it upwards with a force of fifteen pounds for every square inch in its upper surface. Now, if instead of putting one of you into the chair, we put in weights, we shall find out how much force the air beneath the piston can exert. If Harry and Herbert will fetch the old weights from the storehouse, we will try the experiment."

The weights were soon brought, and when one hundred, one fifty, and two fourteen-pound weights were put into the chair, the whole was raised. The addition of a seven-pound weight, however, made the force to be overcome by the air too great. The chair slowly descended, and the amount of the atmospheric force was properly declared to be about one hundred and eighty pounds.

"What amount of surface should the piston present to the air, to justify this conclusion, Harry?" said his father.

"Twelve inches square," was his inconsiderate reply.

"Twelve inches square! why, Harry, a piston of that capacity would lift a ton!"

"He means twelve square inches, papa, I'm sure," said his sister.

"Well," said Harry, "what's the difference between them?"

Amid not a little raillery, our impetuous young hero learned, for the first time, that although there is no difference between a square inch and an inch square, there is, upon the contrary, a vast difference between twelve square inches and twelve inches square!

CHAPTER XXVIII.

The Air-Pump—Harry Made Prisoner—Cupping—The Fly's Foot—The Barometer—The Grand Duke's Well—Toricelli—Measuring Heights.

"THAT is a very beautiful and excellent air pump, apparently," said Mr. Oldbuckle. "I have always been accustomed to the old form of the instrument, with two barrels, and with winch and rack work."

"I have one of them, now," replied Dr. Sinclair, "but although it cost me twice what this instrument did, I never think of using it. This is a Boston pump, the contrivance, I believe, of a Mr. Claxton. The cylinder moves upon the piston, and is worked by a single lever. It has the advantage of the old pumps, too, in the greater simplicity and durability of the valves."

Here Dr. Sinclair entered into a particular explanation of the parts of the air-pump, not for his excellent and learned guest's information, but for the instruction of the young people gathered around him. Having finished his explanation, he pointed out to the group, a visible vapour within the bell-glass, which was fastened by atmospheric pressure to the pump-plate.

Mr. Oldbuckle now said,

"Do you recollect, my dear sir, the beautiful lines of Darwin, which describe the operation of the air-pump, and refer, also, to the singular formation of vapour, you have just shewn us?"

"I do not recall them to mind, at this moment, and must beg of you to refresh my memory," replied Dr. Sinclair.

"That I will do with pleasure, for they always struck me as a most felicitous proof that poetry is not essentially divorced from any subject, however mechanical it may be. These are the verses:

'Now as in brazen pumps the pistons move,
The membrane valve sustains the weight above;
Stroke after stroke the gelid vapours fall,
And misty dew-drops dim the crystal wall;
Rare and more rare expands the fluid thin,
Till silence dwells, and vacancy within!'"

"They are very fine lines, indeed," said Dr. Sinclair, "and beautifully true to fact. The cold vapours, the growing rarity of the air, the extinction of sound, and the final vacuum, are all happily described."

"Alice has been telling me, papa, that you can make any of us sensible of the great pressure of the air," said Mary.

"Certainly, Mary, nothing is more easy," said her father. He took a glass which was open at both

Called upon Harry to close the upper orifice with the palm of the hand.—p. 305.

ends, and placing the larger mouth of it upon the plate of the air-pump, called upon Harry to close the upper orifice with the palm of his hand. This he could just manage to do, and while he was pressing it down, he suddenly felt himself relieved from the necessity of doing so, for his hand was externally forced, not only upon the cup, but almost into it, with an energy which made him fairly shout with mingled wonder and terror.

"Why, what is the matter, Harry?" said Mr. Oldbuckle; "your hand has borne the pressure of the atmosphere a long time, and ought to be used to it, now."

"Ah!" said Harry, as he looked at his released hand, upon the palm of which there was a bright red ring, "but I never knew it before!"

"Then you are a living proof of the adage—

'Where ignorance is bliss, 'tis folly to be wise;'"

and Mr. Oldbuckle added, "but you may congratulate yourself, Harry, that it was not your head instead of your hand, or certainly you would have had a fractured skull."

All the party now tried the experiment, persuaded successively by William Sinclair, who told them that the weight of the atmosphere was one of those extraordinary facts in science which required to be *pressed* into every one's consciousness. For his own part, he laid his cheek upon the mouth of the glass, and then working the pump slowly, he fastened himself to it, and his cheek was seen projecting below the thick rim of the glass. When he released himself, there was still a swelling upon his cheek, with traces of the blood which had been forced to the surface by the internal pressure of the air.

"This," said Gertrude, "is an illustration, I can see clearly, of the process of cupping, of which I have such an intense horror."

"And yet, my dear Miss Vivian," said Dr. Sinclair, "it is not such a very painful process, after all. The action of the cup is less violent than that of this glass, and the spring lancet does its work in an instant; when it is all over."

"Will you pardon me, my dear sir," said Gertrude, with an arch smile, "if I have the effrontery to confess, in your presence, that I am a convert to the new school of Homœopathy, which, you know, abjures all manner of blood-letting?"

"If I were a practising physician," was the Doctor's reply, "I might venture to argue with you, if only with the hope of securing you as a patient of my own."

"I should not prove very *patient* under either mode of treatment, I fancy," said Gertrude.

"I hope sincerely,—since I am not in the practice, now—that your patience will not be put to the proof very soon."

"Thank you for your kind wish," said Gertrude;

"and now, if you please, tell me if this principle of atmospheric pressure does not have something to do with a fly's ability to walk upon the ceiling, and upon the smooth surface of glass?"

"It has been frequently stated, and is perhaps generally believed," replied Dr. Sinclair, "that the cavity in a fly's foot, between the two pads which the microscope reveals, is exhausted of air by the muscular action of the fly, and is thus pressed against the ceiling. I am almost reluctant to call this pretty theory into question at this late day, but—"

"Surely, my dear sir, you are not going to do so with your 'but'?" said Mr. Oldbuckle, with a perplexed smile.

"But," resumed the Doctor, with a smile without the perplexity, "I am almost obliged to do so by my own microscopic observations, which lead me to suppose that this atmospheric action of the fly's foot is a myth, and that the fly's foot is fastened to the surfaces upon which it walks, by a delicate gum exuded from these pads or cushions. Such a gum is discovered upon them, and it has also been detected upon glass and other very smooth surfaces traversed by the fly."

"Really, you surprise me by your statement," said Mr. Oldbuckle.

"Another thing," said Dr. Sinclair, "which gives force to this modern idea, is that the fly is always cleaning its feet, as if to brush away atoms of the gum which have become dry and obstruct its progress."

"I must confess," said Miss Vivian, "that there is more poetry, if less philosophy, in the atmospheric theory of the fly's locomotion, and I am inclined to adhere to it in spite of Dr. Sinclair's microscope."

"I am much of Gerty's notion," said Edward Vivian; " besides, if we give up the atmospheric principle in the case of the fly, who knows but we may be called upon next to resign it in the case of the limpets, who are now supposed to cling to the rocks by means of these natural 'suckers'?"

"I will not quarrel with your conclusion, be it what it may," said Dr. Sinclair; " but I think there is a great difference between the limpet, which, when touched, fastens itself to the rock by an air-cell, and the nimble-footed fly, which would have to exhaust and refill its air chambers with amazing rapidity, if it did so at every step it takes along a polished surface, whereas one emission of gum would last it a long time in warm weather."

"You must some day show me the fly's foot-pads and this curious gum which issues from their pores," said Mr. Oldbuckle, "and then, perhaps, I shall resign my air-drawn theory."

" That it will afford me great pleasure to do," was his host's reply; and then, turning to Herbert, he asked him if he knew the meaning of the term, barometer.

Herbert's etymology was here at fault, and so Dr. Sinclair explained the term as derived from the

Greek, and signifying a weight measure, but applied now exclusively to the instrument used for measuring the weight or density of the atmosphere. He then took down a barometer, which hung in the library, and opening the lower part of the case, showed the young people the manner of its construction. It was a glass tube sealed at the top, but bent near the bottom into a little cup. The tube was about three feet long, and was filled to the height of nearly thirty inches with mercury, or, as it is more commonly called, quicksilver. Mary wondered why the heavy fluid did not all descend into the cup and overflow it, and there were others who felt the same surprise. Dr. Sinclair reminded them of the experiment in the laboratory when the water stood up in the tall bell-glass, which was open at the bottom, and told them that both results were produced by precisely the same cause—the pressure of the atmosphere.

He then asked Alice if she remembered who invented the barometer, and thus first measured the weight of the air.

"I believe, papa, it was a pupil of Galileo, but I have forgotten his name," was Alice's reply.

"Toricelli," said her brother; "wasn't it, Ally?"

"Yes, that is the name; thank you, dear Willie."

"Did you never hear the story of the Grand Duke's Well, Alice?" said Mr. Oldbuckle.

"I do not think I have, sir; will you be kind enough to tell it to me?" said Alice.

"The Grand Duke of Tuscany," continued Mr. Oldbuckle, " had ordered a pump to be sunk in some part of his pleasure-grounds, and was superintending the work himself, when the workmen having introduced the log-tubes to a depth of over forty feet, reported to him that the water did not rise to the top of the logs by several feet. He was perplexed, and related the circumstance to Galileo, of whom he sought an explanation of the wonder. Galileo's predecessors in philosophy had taught the dogma, that 'Nature abhorred a vacuum,' and hence when the piston made one in the pump-log, the water rushed up to fill it. Galileo did not adopt this ridiculous theory, but believed that the water rose in the log, on account of some attraction existing between the piston and the fluid. When, therefore, he found that the water refused to rise in the Grand Duke's pump higher than thirty-four feet, he concluded that, at that height, the weight of the water overcame the attraction of the piston. This explanation satisfied his noble patron better than it did one of his most intelligent pupils, a young man named Toricelli. He pondered the circumstances a long time, and soon after he left the school of Galileo, it occurred to him that the water must have rested at the height of thirty-four feet in the pump-logs, because there the force which raised it, was precisely balanced by the weight of the column. He immediately instituted experiments with quicksilver in a glass tube, and reasoned that if there was such a force at all operating on the water of the well, it would also sustain a column of quicksilver, at a height as much less than that of the water column, as the weight of the former exceeded that of the latter. He tried the experiment, and found it to be just as he thought. He filled a glass tube, three feet long, with quicksilver, and then covering the orifice with his finger, plunged it into a cup of the same fluid. To his great delight, he saw the quicksilver, after rising and falling several times in the tube, stand still at the height of twenty-nine inches. Then he concluded, instantly, that the pressure of the atmosphere upon the quicksilver in the cup was the force which kept it up in the tube, and that the weight of his column of quicksilver must be the exact counterpoise of a column of air of the same diameter, and of the whole height of the atmosphere. Toricelli was right, and his beautiful experiment showed conclusively why the water did not rise all the way up the pump-log. It proved that a column of quicksilver, twenty-nine inches high, is just the weight of a similar sized column of water, thirty-four feet high, and that the external pressure of the air is just equal to balance either of them, and no more in any case."

Alice thanked Mr. Oldbuckle for his entertaining history of the barometer, which Herbert and Harry both declared made the matter perfectly plain to them.

"But what are those marks and figures upon the frame of the barometer for?" said Harry.

"Those," said his father, "indicate the changes of the barometer, with the changes in the state of the atmosphere. When the air is quite dry, it has the greatest weight, and keeps the quicksilver at nearly thirty inches, from which it falls as low as twenty-seven inches in very wet weather, when the air is much lighter."

"I think the best use of the barometer on land," said Edward Vivian, "is to measure the height of mountains."

"How can you do that with the barometer?" said Harry.

"By noticing the diminished height of the column as you ascend into the air. The quicksilver is found to fall half an inch for every five hundred feet of elevation; so, if you were to take the barometer to the top of a high mountain, hitherto unmeasured, and the quicksilver fell five inches, you would know at once that its height was five thousand feet. I ought to add, however, that this rule is not strictly correct; for, although the quicksilver falls half an inch for the first five hundred feet, it falls a fraction less for every successive five hundred; and very accurate measurement, by this method, requires the use of particular formula."

"What an easy way to ascertain heights!" said Miss Vivian; "and though I never thought of it before,

I suppose this is the way in which the elevation reached by balloons is ascertained?"

"Even so, Gerty," said her brother, "and you will have to thank Dr. Sinclair, as well as all these young pupils of his, for much pleasing and valuable knowledge."

"I wish I never had a more unpleasant task to perform than to do that," was her earnest reply. "I do thank him with all my heart."

"And never was any one more happy to impart such information," said her gratified host.

CHAPTER XXIX.

More Philosophy for Miss Vivian—The Laboratory—Empty Jars—Oxygen—The Magic Taper—Combustion—Burning a Watch-spring—Oxyd of Steel—Sparkling Carbon—Carbonic Acid Gas—The Grotto del Cane—The Martyred Mouse.

"AS you insist upon leaving us to-morrow morning, my dear Miss Vivian," said Dr. Sinclair to his fair young guest, as she entered the library, after tea, "I think I shall trouble you with a little more philosophy, before you go. I wish you to take away only brilliant memories of Beechwood, and I have been preparing, during the afternoon, for a family lecture upon oxygen. Is it your pleasure that it shall be given to-night?"

"Ah! Dr. Sinclair," said Gertrude, with a smile of unaffected delight, "you are resolved to make my departure as painful as possible, by multiplying the charms of your happy home."

"That we may the sooner win you back to it, my dear Gertrude," said Mrs. Sinclair.

"Oh! Gertrude," said Alice, "do stay until Saturday, the end of the vacation."

"I can not, dear Alice," was Gertrude Vivian's reply; "for Edward's vacation also expires on Saturday, and there is duty to be performed at home.

But I shall carry with me quite as delightful memories of Beechwood as your kind papa and mamma could wish."

"But you have not told me, after all," said Dr. Sinclair, assuming a look of perplexity, "if I shall attempt to entertain you with philosophy to-night, or not."

"Pardon me, dear sir," she replied gaily, "I thought I had already manifested my delight at your proposal. By all means, philosophy to-night, if I may speak for the rest."

"Well, Herbert," said Dr. Sinclair, "I shall try what I can do, to-night, in the way of burning ten-penny nails for matches!"

Herbert remembered Dr. Sinclair's promise to that effect, and replied that he was impatient to see the wonder.

"I shall have to invite you all down stairs," said Dr. Sinclair, "for I can not very well make experiments with oxygen in this room."

"Oh!" said Alice, "I love to go into the laboratory. It is such a queer place, and has so many queer things things about it."

The party now went down into the laboratory, which was beneath the library, and of the same dimensions, except in height. It was comfortably fitted up, and a large fire blazing, upon the hearth, shed light and warmth over it.

Upon one of the two tables which extended through

it, there were several jars and bell-glasses, standing inverted, with their mouths in plates containing water. These Dr. Sinclair cautioned them not to upset as they contained, he told them, the oxygen gas, which he had prepared for experiments.

"Why, papa," said Fanny, "I can not see any thing in the glass jars."

"There is something there, nevertheless, my little girl, and though you may not see it, you will believe it, by and by."

Fanny looked still more closely at the glasses, but they seemed to her to be quite empty.

"The term *oxygen*, Herbert, do you know its etymology?"

"I do not, sir," he replied.

"Like the term hydrogen, it is from the Greek, *oxus*, acid and *gennao*, to make; oxygen, therefore, signifies to make acid, and when the name was first employed, it was thought that every acid contained oxygen. Though this is not the case, the name is still the best which can be given to this element."

"Was it not once called vital air, papa?" said Alice.

"It was, my daughter, and considering its relations to all kinds of life, the name was natural enough."

"To whom do you attribute the discovery of this element, Dr. Sinclair?" inquired Mr. Oldbuckle.

"The *first* discovery of it was certainly made by Dr. Priestley, of England, though Scheele, of Sweden, and Lavoisier, of France, both afterwards discovered it, without a knowledge of Dr. Priestley's observations."

"It was certainly a wonderful discovery," resumed Mr. Oldbuckle, "and opened a new world to the chemist."

"Yes," said Dr. Sinclair, "the discovery of oxygen gave new names to many things, and led to many vast results."

"I have not had much experience in the laboratory," said Mr. Oldbuckle, "and shall be glad to know how you obtain oxygen. I believe the old process was to heat manganese in an iron bottle."

"That is still a common process, I believe," replied Dr. Sinclair; "but no one who is well-read in modern chemistry would resort to it at this day. It is a tedious method, and yields a gas of uncertain quality. There are two far better methods of procuring the gas. One is to heat to dull redness, in a copper flask, the chlorate of potash; and a still more simple one is to employ the same substance, mixed with manganese, in a green glass flask, heated over a spirit-lamp. By this process, I have to-day obtained a quantity of the pure gas."

"Are those the only substances that contain oxygen, sir?" inquired Herbert.

"No, my dear boy; it is found in a vast number of substances, and is the most widely diffused of all the elementary bodies."

"I believe, sir," said William Sinclair, "that it constitutes about one third part by weight, of nearly all known matter, does it not?"

"You have understated rather than overstated its proportion to the entire mass of our globe," said his father, "for it composes nearly one third of its solid crust, eight ninths of all the water, and one fifth of the atmosphere."

"I thought you said the other day, sir, that it constituted one third of the bulk of water," said Herbert.

"I am gratified that you are so mindful of my words, Herbert, as not to mistake them. I did say one third the other day, but recollect that it was one third of the bulk. It is sixteen times heavier than the other element of water, and hence by weight, it constituted eight ninths of the water of the globe."

"What a very extraordinary fact it is," said Mr. Oldbuckle, "that nearly the whole weight of water consists of that which supports fire!"

"And the wonder is increased," added Dr. Sinclair, "when we remember what was also mentioned the other day, that the remaining ninth part of water is the most inflammable substance in nature."

"I seem to see," said Mr. Oldbuckle, "a new significance in the words of Scripture, 'The elements shall melt with fervent heat, the earth, also, and the works that are therein shall be burnt up.' Chemistry teaches us that a vast part of the whole earth is highly combustible, and the still greater portion of it, suited to support and quicken combustion. How simple and natural does the prediction appear in th's light, and how terrible will that great conflagration be!"

"I have often reflected, my dear friend," said Dr. Sinclair, "upon this theme, and it is, as you say, a very significant one. But we must not keep our young philosophers waiting, too long, for the sights, which have as yet more charm for them than the speculations of science."

Dr. Sinclair now took one of the smaller jars, which he had filled with oxygen, and carefully restoring it to its upright position, he quickly removed the plate, and substituted a light cover of card.

"Would the gas escape, papa, if you were not to keep the jar covered?" inquired Alice.

"I see that you think it ought not to do so, Alice," replied her father.

"Not if it is heavier than the atmosphere," insisted Alice.

"In a quiet room it would not escape," said Dr. Sinclair, "but here there is so much agitation of the air by our motion and breathing, and so much variation of temperature and density, that there is a probability of the oxygen's becoming partially mingled with the air. The oxygen is heavy enough, however, to be poured from one vessel into another, like water."

He now took a lighted piece of wax taper, fastened

into a ring at the end of a piece of wire, and having blown it out suddenly, he plunged it, while there was yet a spark upon the wick, into the jar of oxygen before him. With an audible report, the taper suddenly burst into a vivid flame, and burned with unwonted brilliancy. Withdrawing the taper, he blew it out again, and again plunged it into the jar, when the same result followed. Three or four times he repeated the experiment, until, at length, the taper was not relighted in the jar. This failure astonished the young people as much as the first success did, until Dr. Sinclair told them that the repeated kindling and burning of the taper, together with the heat of the process, had consumed and dissipated all the oxygen which was in the jar.

"That is a very beautiful experiment, indeed, Dr. Sinclair," said Miss Vivian; "it seemed almost magical."

"It would have been accounted so in old times, doubtless," said Mr. Oldbuckle.

"I do not understand it, sir," said Harry; "what lighted the candle?"

"You noticed the spark which still glowed upon the cotton wick of the taper, did you not, Harry?"

"Yes, sir, and I saw it flash brightly the moment it went into the jar."

"Well, then, my boy, you shall learn something new about combustion, which is nothing more nor less than a combination of some substance with this very element, called oxygen. There may be combustion without fire, or smoke either. You must know that a vast number of substances have a great liking for oxygen—the chemists call it affinity—and they are always ready to unite with it. Iron likes oxygen, but it can not unite with it when both are dry. If either of them is wet, then they unite, and the oxygen turns that part of the iron with which it is united, into what we call *rust*, but what chemists call *oxyd* of iron. The process is combustion of one kind. Other substances like oxygen, also, but can not unite with it except at very high degrees of heat. The carbon of wood, or cotton, or coal, is eager for oxygen, but it must be raised to a very high temperature before it can combine with it. This may be done by several methods, as by bringing the sun's rays directly upon it by a convex glass, by employing friction as travellers often do, by a discharge of electricity, by chemical mixtures, and by applying an inflamed body to it. The last is the common method. The moment the substance is hot enough for the heat to be visible to the eye, it attracts the oxygen furiously, and burns until it is consumed itself, or all the oxygen is exhausted. After this long speech, you will be pleased to see a very beautiful experiment which bears directly upon the subject."

Dr. Sinclair now placed before him a large glass bottle, which stood in a plate containing water. The bottle had no bottom, but a cork was fitted tightly in

Its neck. It was full of oxygen gas, as nearly pure as it could be obtained. He now called the attention of the young people to a watch-spring which he had twisted into the shape of a cork-screw, and fastened into a cork. Upon the lower end of the spiral, he had wound a fragment of thread, and dipped it in melted sulphur.

"What are you going to do with that cork-screw, papa?" said Fanny.

"Burn it all up, Fanny," said her father.

Fanny's little head shook with incredulity, but she said nothing more; and the Doctor, removing the cork of the jar with one hand, with the other ignited the end of the spring, and then plunged it into the jar of the gas. The effect was very beautiful, and to nearly all the group, quite surprising. William Sinclair had darkened the lamp, and yet the room was light with the dazzling brilliance of the jar. It was full of the most radiant sparks, and a very bright bead of light was rising gradually up the watch-spring.

"Yes!" said Harry, after a close inspection, "Yes, I declare, Herbert, the watch-spring is a-fire, and it will all burn up!"

"What do you think is the prospect for the ten penny nail, eh, Herbert?" said Dr. Sinclair, amused at the wonder which was depicted on the face of his young guest.

"I am quite willing to believe that you can burn it, sir," said Herbert.

"You shall believe, now, and *see*, by and by."

When the brilliance died away, the interior of the jar was covered with a yellowish crust, and the fragment of the steel spiral was also very rusty in appearance. Dr. Sinclair told Herbert that this was the oxyd of steel.

"What became of all the oxygen, sir?" said Herbert.

"It all entered into the steel; and if we were to collect the pieces of melted steel which fell—"

"See!" said Harry, "two of them are burned into the plate!"

"If," continued Dr. Sinclair, "we should collect all and weigh them with the unconsumed part, we should find its weight increased by just the weight of the oxygen consumed."

"That is a most interesting fact," said Miss Vivian, "and I am curious to know more about this gas."

"I will burn a piece of fine iron wire in this next jar," said Dr. Sinclair, taking in his hand a spiral wire attached to a cork. He introduced it, and it burned with intense rapidity, but threw out very few sparks.

"Why did it not scintillate, like the watch-spring?" inquired Gertrude.

"The very question I supposed some one would ask," said Dr. Sinclair, "and I will answer it by asking you another, Miss Vivian: what is made use of to convert iron into steel?"

"Charcoal, sir," said Gertrude.

"And it is the charcoal—the carbon, rather—of the steel spring, that outsparkles the pure iron. Here," he added, "is a piece of fine charcoal, prepared from box-wood on account of its hardness, which I shall now expose to an atmosphere of oxygen."

He plunged it into a jar of the gas, but it did not take fire, and indeed, remained as black as ever. The young people looked perplexed, but in a moment Alice exclaimed:

"Oh! papa, you are puzzling us. You did not raise the temperature of the charcoal before you put it in the gas."

"You are quite right, Alice. I will repair my error," said her father, withdrawing the charcoal, which he immediately held in the flame of a candle, until there was a faint spark upon one angle.

"Will that do, Ally, think you?" he asked.

"Yes, papa, I have faith in you to believe it will!"

The slight spark had no sooner touched the oxygen than it grew brilliant, and instantly spread over the whole piece, which glowed like a bright star, while the jar was completely filled with a shower of sparks, which elicited the admiration of all. In a few moments, it grew dim, and went out.

"Is all the oxygen consumed, sir?" said Gertrude.

"Converted, rather, my dear Miss Vivian, into another gas. Both the carbon and oxygen have changed form, and the united product is carbonic acid gas, of which I can only say, very briefly, that it is destructive to animal life. It is called 'fixed air,' because its great weight makes it settle in mines, and pits, and wells."

"Oh! is that the air which is found in the Grotto del Cane, in Italy?" said Gertrude.

"That is it, and the reason why only dogs fall victims to it, is that the stratum of the gas is just deep enough to reach their noses, while men breathe the good air of the cave above it."

Dr. Sinclair illustrated his remarks about carbonic acid gas, by taking a live mouse, which was confined at the end of a piece of wire, and introducing it suddenly into the jar where the carbon had been consumed. In a very few moments, the mouse almost ceased the struggle which he had been hitherto making to escape from his bonds.

CHAPTER XXX.

The Resuscitation—Too Much of a Good Thing—Atmospheric Air—Supply of Oxygen—Producing an Alkali—Fire from Ice—The Mock Sun—Sulphurous Acid—The Compound Blow-pipe—Burning a Ten-penny Nail—The Drummond Light—The Bude Lamp—A *Feu de Joie*.

"POOR mousey!" said Fanny. "Papa, wasn't it cruel to kill the little mouse?"

"Are you quite sure it is dead, Fan?" said her father, as he withdrew it from the jar of carbonic acid gas, and, the next instant, put it into another jar filled with pure oxygen.

"Oh! look! look! Alice," said Herbert, and Harry reëchoed the exclamation, while all the group gathered closer around the jar, when, to the amazement and delight of all, the mouse was once more making violent muscular efforts, and "yawning," as Fanny said, with desperate earnestness.

"'*Vita ex articulo mortis*,'" said Mr. Oldbuckle.

"Truly," replied Edward Vivian, "it is life in death."

Every one pronounced it wonderful, but before the exclamations had ceased, Dr. Sinclair had removed the mouse from the jar, and considering his freedom fairly won by his martyrdom, he set him free with no other injury than a wet coat. As he scampered off,

Mary asked her father why he did not suffer him to remain longer in the jar?

"Because I did not wish to kill him, Mary," her father replied.

"Why, papa, that made him alive again!" persisted Mary.

"And he would soon have died from excess of life, my child, if I had not removed him."

"And he would have furnished us a melancholy proof," said Edward Vivian, "that one may have 'too much of a good thing.'"

"That is quite above me," said Harry, shaking his head.

"Oxygen," said Dr. Sinclair, "is the great supporter of life, as we know; and, as you have just seen, it will sometimes restore the dead to life; but He who made it, and put it in the atmosphere, mixed it with four times as much of another gas, which has no power to support life or to sustain combustion. This other gas is called nitrogen, and its only use in the atmosphere is to dilute the oxygen and make it fit for our lungs and for combustion. If we had only pure oxygen to breathe, with our present systems, we should not live long. We should die in violent excitement. A fire, once kindled, would continue to burn until every thing was consumed. If we could imagine such a thing as an atmosphere of pure oxygen for a single day, what a wonderful sight there would be presented upon the earth. Men and beasts would be crazy with excitement and passion, stoves and furnaces and steam-engines would all take fire from the fuel within them, and the burning would not cease until the globe was consumed."

"May a kind Providence preserve us from such a catastrophe!" said Mr. Oldbuckle.

"It is a beautiful truth," said Dr. Sinclair, "that the proportion of oxygen in the atmosphere never varies. It is the same in the valley that it is upon the mountain-top, the same in the hospital that it is in the street."

"How is it, then, that the atmosphere becomes corrupted and unfit for respiration?" said Miss Vivian.

"It is made so by the substitution of foreign gases for much of the volume of the atmosphere. The foulest air of a crowded hall contains one part of oxygen for every four of nitrogen by bulk, though carbonic acid gas and other vapours may constitute the greater volume of the air in the room, and these are irrespirable."

"I think I understand perfectly your explanation," said Gertrude.

"There is one thing more to notice here," said Dr. Sinclair, "and it is, that no other proportions of these elements will unite to form atmospheric air. Two fifths of oxygen with three fifths of nitrogen make the exhilarating gas which intoxicates those who inhale it, and would destroy life if breathed for a long time."

"What a wonderful proof of design in the creation of the atmosphere this fact affords," said Mr Oldbuckle.

"I wonder, very much," said Edward Vivian, "that more use is not made of oxygen in cases of suspended animation from foul air, drowning, and other causes."

"I have always believed," said Dr. Sinclair, "that if oxygen could be administered promptly in such cases, it would produce magical results."

"Why could it not be so administered, sir?" said Gertrude.

"There are two principal reasons," replied Dr. Sinclair; "the difficulty of obtaining it except in a laboratory, and the general ignorance of all such matters among those who have to deal with such cases at the critical moment."

"I have read of some cases in which oxygen has been administered with happy results," said Mr. Oldbuckle, "and these are presumptive evidence of its general efficacy."

"Papa," said Alice, "will you please to tell me how the supply of oxygen in the atmosphere is kept up when it has to support such a vast amount of life?"

"Your question is a very reasonable one, Alice. It is estimated that a man consumes twenty-five gallons of oxygen every hour, and, then, it is required in vast quantities for combustion. The answer to your question is another proof of design in creation, and it is proof, also, that the Great Designer is full of benevolence. While the animal world is consuming oxygen, Alice, the whole vegetable world is supplying it. The lungs of animals convert it into carbonic acid gas, which is destructive to animal life, but by a wonderful provision it feeds the vegetable world, and the cells of plants re-convert it into oxygen, which the plants themselves do not require. If you will gather some mint, or other vegetable stems next spring, and, having put them into a bell-glass filled with water and inverted in a plate, place the whole in the sunshine, you will presently see little sparkling globules all over the sprigs, and they will gradually gather in the upper part of the bell, displacing the water from the space they occupy. They will be found upon examination to be pure oxygen gas."

"Really that is as wonderful as it is beautiful," said Gertrude. "How charming it must be to learn all such valuable truths as these!"

"I have shown you," said Dr. Sinclair, "how oxygen unites with iron to form an oxyd, with carbon to form an acid, and now I will show you how it unites with potassium to form an alkali, which is just the opposite of an acid."

He took from a small bottle a piece of bluish looking metal which he put into a pendent spoon attached to a wooden cover. Then touching the potassium with a glass rod that he dipped in water, it suddenly inflamed, and he plunged it into a jar of oxygen. Immediately a rose-coloured vapour filled the jar, which was kept very bright by the burning metal. It did not last long, and when Dr. Sinclair withdrew the spoon it was half-full of a white substance which he called potash.

"But do tell me, papa," said Alice, "how the metal which you call potassium, took fire when you touched it with the wet rod. I should almost as soon think of dipping a candle into water in order to light it!"

"I do not wonder at your surprise, Alice, which, however, I will endeavour to remove by explaining to you, that potassium has such a strong affinity to oxygen that it will take it from any substance with which it is combined. Hence it is necessary to keep it in naphtha, a fluid which contains no oxygen. When it is exposed to the air, it rapidly oxydizes, and even from water it absorbs oxygen so violently, that the heat generated sets the deserted hydrogen on fire, and the volatilized metal tinges the flame with a violet colour as you saw."

Dr. Sinclair now directed Harry to fetch a piece of ice, and when he had brought it in, he cut a hole in it with his penknife, and into it he put a globule of potassium, which immediately burst into a vivid flame, and consumed rapidly, while in a moment, the cavity, like the spoon before, was half-full of potash.

One of the glass vessels upon the table was a globe with a broad mouth to it, in which was fitted a cork. This was now brought forward, and again William Sinclair partially darkened the room. Dr. Sinclair exhibited to the young people a stick of phosphorus glowing in the darkness. He cut off a portion of it, and having carefully wiped it dry, he placed it in the pendent spoon from which he had removed the potash. The spoon was fastened to a cork like that in the mouth of the glass globe. Dr. Sinclair now touched the phosphorus with a hot wire, and as it began to burn, he introduced it into the globe. The effect was so dazzling that all the party were obliged to shade their eyes; the globe glowed like an artificial sun, and it seemed, for a few moments, as if so much intense splendour must produce a fearful explosion. It died quietly away, however, and the globe remained full of dense vapour, as white as snow, which Dr. Sinclair said was the vapour of phosphorous acid.

This experiment was followed by another, in which sulphur was burned in oxygen, with a deep violet-coloured flame and dense clouds of vapour. A little water was left in the jar before the combustion, and when it had ceased, Dr. Sinclair shook the jar until nearly all the dense white vapour, which had been formed, disappeared. He then poured out the water into two wine-glasses, and every one who felt inclined, tasted it, to discover that it was exceedingly sour with sulphuric acid.

"What was it that made the hydrogen soap-bubbles explode the other day, Harry?"

"Air, sir, I think you said."

"The oxygen of the air it was which separated from the nitrogen, to form a new alliance with the hydrogen."

"Have you any hydrogen gas now, papa?" said Alice.

"This large bag is half-full of it," he replied, "and this smaller one contains oxygen. I have prepared them in order to burn up that ten-penny nail for Herbert."

Herbert's ten-penny nail was now an object of great interest, though, individually speaking, it was only a myth.

Fanny's eyes grew large with wonder as Dr. Sinclair took a nail from the mantel-piece and said, "I will endeavour to burn this for you, Herbert, if you say so."

Herbert agreed to adopt that as the nail of his fancy, and inquired what the hydrogen had to do with it.

"Very much," said Dr. Sinclair; "it must supply all the fuel we require. When a jet of hydrogen gas is ignited in pure oxygen, it is one of the hottest flames that can be produced. If the two gases are burned together, in the proportions in which they exist in water, the resulting flame, though very small, is hot enough to melt flint, and to burn the hardest metals. The apparatus employed to produce this effect is called a compound blow-pipe."

Dr. Sinclair with the aid of his son, now adjusted to the two gas-bags a double jet, so that the gases should unite at the orifice of the jet only. Weights were put on the bags to press out the gas. The hydrogen was first ignited, and burned with a pale greenish flame. When the oxygen was let on, the flame grew small, and very white, and then Dr. Sinclair held the nail by a pair of tongs, in the minute flame. Instantly the point of it became of a white heat, and a perpetual shower of sparks flew in all directions, while, now and then, globules of melted iron fell upon the edge of the table and burst into a thousand scintillations. In less than three minutes, Herbert's tenpenny nail was consumed, and all the party joined in acclamation. Dr. Sinclair next exposed the point of a very fine file to the action of the flame. The scintillation was exceedingly vivid and abundant, far surpassing that of the nail, which, taught by the watchspring, Herbert and Harry had no difficulty in tracing to the carbon in the steel of which the file was made.

A piece of copper wire burned with a beautiful green flame without scintillation, and some flattened pieces of zinc produced flames of a dense white appearance. Platinum was next presented to the flame, and, although it resists the most intense heat of a furnace, it yielded to the minute but wonderful flame of the oxy-hydrogen blowpipe, and dropped in fluid globules from the jet. After several experiments of this kind, Dr. Sinclair took the stem of a common tobacco pipe of clay, and holding it in the flame, it soon glowed to a white heat, and sent out such dazzling rays into the room, that all were glad to veil their eyes from its splendour.

"Is not that what is called the 'Drummond light?'" inquired Mr. Oldbuckle.

"It is," said Dr. Sinclair, "though it is a very imperfect exhibition of it. There should be a parabolic mirror behind the jet, and, instead of pipe clay, a lime cylinder should be very nicely adjusted to the flame, which, in the best arrangements I have seen, issues from several jets, all of them curving towards the lime."

"Why is it called the Drummond light, Mr. Old buckle?" asked Herbert.

"Because it was first produced by the experiments of a British officer of that name, if I mistake not," he replied.

"You are correct, sir," said Dr. Sinclair, "for although the effect of the compound flame upon lime had been noticed, Lieutenant Drummond was the first to devise an apparatus for producing it to the best advantage."

"Why is not the Drummond light more used for illuminating purposes?" inquired Edward Vivian.

"It is too difficult to manage," said Dr. Sinclair,

"though it is employed in various ways, in some light-houses, I believe, and in the oxy-hydrogen microscopes."

"Oh! yes! Herbert," said Harry, "don't you recollect the Drummond light at the top of the Museum in New-York? It used to move round, and sometimes Broadway was brilliantly lighted by it, far above the Park."

"There is another very beautiful and more manageable oxygen light than this," said Dr. Sinclair. "It is called the Bude light, after its inventor, and I will afford you a rude illustration of it. In this lamp, which is called an Argand lamp, the wick is supplied with oxygen by the air rushing through its circular tube. If, instead of air, which contains only one fifth part of oxygen, we contrive to feed the flame with a current of pure oxygen gas, the result will be a furious and intensely brilliant combustion."

Dr. Sinclair now connected the tube of the oxygen gas-bag to the lower part of the lamp-tube, and instantly the flame of the lamp, which was burning high, and with much smoke, fell to half the height and became as white as the steel in the flame of the of the blow-pipe. The light was even more admired than that of the lime cylinder, not that it was so bright, but it was more steady.

"I remember very well," said Mr. Oldbuckle, "to have seen the Bude lamps erected in Trafalgar Square in London, a few years ago. They gave a most splendid light, and attracted a great deal of attention. I believe the new Houses of Parliament, also, are or were lighted by Bude lamps, which were so placed in the dome as to shed their light, while they were not visible from below."

"Do you wait, sir," said William Sinclair, "for the grand *finale* of this night's exhibition?"

"I believe we are ready for it, my son."

"I propose to fire a salute of musketry," said William Sinclair, "with a very novel description of cartridge," and he exhibited a large glass vial which was corked, though apparently empty. Dr. Sinclair tied some cotton fast to the end of a brass rod, and then dipped it in alcohol and set it on fire; meanwhile, William Sinclair turned up his coat-sleeve and bared his arm half-way to his elbow. He then opened the mouth of the vial in a tub of water, and placing his thumb over it, he sunk it to some depth in the tub. Taking the lighted wand from the hand of his father, he removed his thumb partially from the mouth of the vial, so that bubbles escaped from it and rose to the surface of the water. These he touched with the flaming wand, and they went off with a sharp quick report, which, when they came thick and fast, very greatly resembled a successive discharge of musketry, as heard in a *feu de joie*.

None of the young philosophers found any difficulty in understanding this noisy and striking experiment, when they learned that the "cartridge" was filled with the two gases already described, but Harry said to his father:

"Why did William keep the bottle so far beneath the water?" to which question his father replied:

"To prevent the gas in it from taking fire before its time. If it had done so, the vial would have been blown into a thousand pieces, with a loud report."

Highly delighted with what they had seen and heard, our happy party bade adieu to the laboratory, and returned to the library, ready for thanksgiving and repose.

CHAPTER XXXI.

The New Year—Fanny's Regrets and Reasons—Childish Philosophy—The Bent Spoon—An Optical Illusion—Bringing a Sovereign to Light—Explanations—Twilight—The Spectre of the Brocken—Departures.

FANNY'S New-Year's wishes to all the party at Beechwood were as prompt and affectionate as her Christmas greetings had been. The new year dawned with a clear light, and the sun rose in cloudless beauty after the storm of the previous day. It was natural that the young people should find in this a token of a bright and happy year, and that their salutations should be exchanged with eagerness and enthusiasm. The morning devotions of the family were not performed without a due recognition of the day, in the selection of the beautiful New-Year's hymn, commencing:

"Come; let us anew our journey pursue;"

and Dr. Sinclair offered grateful acknowledgments to God for his prolonged bounty, and besought his favours for the new year.

"Oh! I am so sorry," said Fanny, at the breakfast-table, " that you are going away, Miss Gertrude."

"Why, Fanny, have you just thought of it?" said

Alice. "We all said, yesterday, that we were sorry she was going home."

"Yes," said Fanny, "I know you did; but she wasn't *just* going, then, and to-day she is."

"Very good, my little girl," said her mother, "you are a true philosopher, Fanny; you won't borrow trouble, I see.

"What does that mean, mamma?" asked the little girl.

"It means that you are content to be sorry when the time comes to be sorry, without thinking about it beforehand."

"Fanny has the wisdom of a child," said her father, "and it would be well if we could all keep that wisdom, as we grow up, and as mamma said, just now, 'not borrow trouble.' "

"But Fanny," said Gertrude Vivian, "why are you sorry that I am going away?"

"Because I love you, Miss Gertrude, and because mamma is glad to have you here."

"Sufficient reasons, certainly," said her mamma; "and I am sorry, too, Fanny, that Gertrude must leave us, to-day."

"And are you not sorry that I am going, too, my dear little girl?" said Mr. Oldbuckle.

"Oh! yes, Mr. O'buckle, but then you will come back, very soon, and Miss Gertrude won't."

"Oh! yes, Fanny, Gertrude will surely come soon to see you," said Miss Vivian, "and your mamma has promised that you shall come with her, and Alice, and Mary, to see me at Viviardale, before very long."

"Shall I, dear mamma?" said the little girl; "oh! dear, how happy I shall be!"

"Fanny borrows pleasure, it seems, if she refuses to borrow pain," said Edward Vivian, who was interested in the conversation.

"Another proof of the happy instincts of childhood," said her father.

"Oh! mamma, see how you have bent that spoon!" exclaimed Mary, as her mother placed a tea-spoon in a glass bowl of water which stood upon the table.

"How bent it, Mary?" said her mother, with surprise, while the attention of all was directed to the object of remark. The spoon was half buried in the crystal fluid, and the handle of it appeared to be bent sharply in the middle. Dr. Sinclair immediately took it out and called upon Mary to notice that it was perfectly straight—a fact which she could not dispute, though she looked her astonishment.

"Why, papa, it looked to me as if it was bent!" said Harry.

"And so it did to me," said several voices in suo cession.

"And I must acknowledge," said Dr. Sinclair, "that so it did to me, also."

"How queer!" said Harry.

"But I would have you remember, Harry, and

Mary, also," said their father, "that appearances are often deceitful, and this is one of the numerous instances."

"An optical illusion," said Mr. Oldbuckle

"What is that, Fanny?" said her father, as if answering her perplexed look; and he added, addressing Mr. Oldbuckle:

"You must pay the penalty, my dear sir, of using hard words in the hearing of this little philosopher, and make them plain to her."

"Well," said Mr. Oldbuckle, laughing, "I will do my best. I mean by an 'optical illusion,' Fanny, a cheat put upon the eye, in making it seem to see what it really does not see; the spoon seemed to be bent, but it was not bent."

Fanny was puzzled, still; and Mr. Oldbuckle, having asked Mrs. Sinclair's permission to use a china bowl which was near him, took from his pocket the sovereign which had created such merriment upon the miser's plate, and dropped it into the bowl, saying as he did so, with a smile:

"There is a good deal more philosophy in a sovereign, than has ever been drawn out of one."

Every one laughed at his wit, but no one denied his words; and he proceeded to place the bowl so that Fanny and Mary could look into it, but not far enough to see the coin. He now took the waterpitcher in his hand, and poured water gently into the bowl, so as not to touch or disturb the piece of money. Before he had half filled the bowl, Mary exclaimed:

"Oh! there's the money—I can see it very distinctly!"

"Yes," said Harry, who had put himself in the same relative position to the bowl as his sisters occupied, "I see it, too! Mr. Oldbuckle must have moved it by the stream; or else," he added, with a doubtful look, "it has floated up on the water."

"It can not float, Harry," said Mr. Oldbuckle, "and I assure you that I have not moved it a particle!"

"What makes it appear, then, papa?" said Mary.

"The same cause, my daughter, which made the spoon appear to be bent. Your sister can tell you what the cause is, I fancy."

"I am sorry to say, papa," replied Alice, "that I have forgotten the term, though I know it is some property of light."

"It is that property of light which is called refraction;" said Dr. Sinclair, "and perhaps Herbert can tell us the etymology of refraction."

Herbert was very happy to reply immediately:

"It is derived from the Latin frango, sir, which means to *break*."

"Do you know where light comes from, Fanny?" said her father.

"Yes, papa, it comes from the sun."

"How does it come to us, Alice?"

"In straight rays, papa."

"Does it pass through all substances?"

"No, papa. It is thrown back from the surface of opaque bodies, but passes through transparent substances."

"That is true," said Dr. Sinclair, "but I want to know yet one thing more. Can you tell me what happens to the rays of light when they pass from the atmosphere into water, or any other transparent substance?"

"They are refracted, papa."

"Or, that Fanny may understand it better, let us say they are bent out of one straight course into another. The same thing happens when rays of light go out of water into the atmosphere. But tell me, Herbert, what enables us to see any object at all?"

"The light, sir," was his answer.

"Your answer is quite as definite as my question, Herbert, and therefore I ought to be satisfied with it, especially as it is indisputably true, but I meant to ask how the impression of any object is conveyed to the eye?"

The young people were silent, and Dr. Sinclair resumed:

"It is by means of the rays of light which proceed from it to the eye, and you must remember that the object always appears to be in the direction of the rays which come last to the eye. If, therefore, the rays pass out of one medium into another, between the object and the eye, the rays will be bent, and the object will appear in a false position. Now, who can apply these rules to the bent spoon, or to the piece of money?"

After a brief pause, Alice ventured to say with some hesitation :

"The rays which come to the eye from that part of the handle of the spoon above the water are straight, and those which come from the part below the water are bent out of that course by the water, and so the handle seems to be bent just where it enters the water."

"You have explained Mary's phenomenon very well, indeed, Alice," said her father, "and I hope she understands it; but you have not attempted to explain Mr. Oldbuckle's mystery."

"Since he has puzzled us, papa, I think we must expect him to tell us the riddle."

"The proposition is so reasonable, my dear sir," said Dr. Sinclair, "that I do not see how you are to refuse."

"I trusted," said Mr. Oldbuckle, "that the explanation would devolve upon you; but I will not refuse Alice's request. The sovereign was not visible to Mary, and others, at first, because the rays of light which proceeded from it, through only one medium, were cut off from the eye by the edge of the bowl. When I had covered it with water, however, the rays of light which proceeded from it took a direction through the water considerably higher than their former course, so that when they reached the air again, and continued on to the eye, they carried to it the image of the coin, which was really not in the straight line of vision. It was raised up in appearance, though not in fact, by the water. Now, if the water were removed from the bowl gradually, as by a small syphon tube, the coin would vanish from our view; and if Mary should retreat a little from the table, till she can not see it, I could make it visible to her, by pouring in more water to the basin, which would increase the length of the first rays through the water, and of course appear to raise the money higher in the bowl."

Mary, and indeed all the party, thanked Mr. Oldbuckle for his lucid explanation, and William Sinclair congratulated him upon having thrown a clearer light upon the phenomenon, than even the sun did.

"And yet," he rejoined laughingly, "without the sun's light, my explanation would have been dark enough."

"And it is to this curious property of light," said Miss Vivian, "that we owe the beautiful phenomenon of the twilight, I believe?"

"The gloaming of the Scotch: how poetical the word is, Miss Vivian!" said Mr. Oldbuckle.

"I like the English 'twilight' better, sir," said Gertrude, "perhaps from habit, and it may be from the frequent use of it by our poets, though I must confess that the Scotch term is the most musical."

"But, papa," said Harry, who was listening with interest, "what is the twilight? I know that it is the hour before sunrise, and that after sunset; but what makes it light at all, when the sun is not above the horizon?"

"The very thing that made the coin appear visible when it was actually below the rim, or horizon, of the bowl," said his father.

Why, papa," said Mary, "the sun's rays do not pass through water, do they? and become bent, do they?"

"Upon the ocean they do, literally, my daughter; but upon the land, the same effect is produced by the greater density of the air and the thick vapours upon the earth's surface, which make a different medium as really as the water. The sun's rays, when he is some distance below the horizon, are refracted, so that an image of the sun is still apparent to the eye of the observer."

"What makes the length of the twilight vary so greatly in different parts of the world?" inquired Miss Vivian. "I have heard Edward say that the Southern twilight is very short, in comparison with that of this region."

"The duration of the twilight," said Dr. Sinclair, "increases from the equator to the poles. The longest twilight at the equator is a little over an hour, while at the poles it lasts for two months, and thus the long night of the polar regions, which is just half the year, is gratefully relieved of more than half its gloom by the two long twilight intervals which precede and follow its six months' day."

"I think," said Gertrude, "that Mrs. Norton's apostrophe to the twilight is quite as beautiful as any thing in the works of our poets."

"Will you do us the favor to repeat her lines, Gertrude?" said Mrs. Sinclair.

"I am not sure of my memory," she replied, " but I will try:

> 'O Twilight! spirit that dost render birth
>   To dim enchantments, melting heaven to earth;
> Leaving on craggy hills and running streams
>   A softness like the atmosphere of dreams.'"

"They are truly beautiful, and beautifully true," said Mrs. Sinclair.

"'The dim enchantments,'" said Mr. Oldbuckle, "find a literal realization in the famous spectre of the Brocken."

The eyes of the young people seemed to ask what this famous spectre could be; and Dr. Sinclair begged his guest to give them some account of it, which he cheerfully consented to do.

"In the Hartz mountains of Germany," he said, "there is a summit which has become famous, from the frequent apparition of gigantic figures, in human shape. One traveller relates, that, having gone out about sunrise in the morning, from the hotel of the Brocken, he was startled to see upon a hill, two miles distant, a human figure of monstrous dimensions. Just at the moment when he caught a glimpse of this apparition, the wind threatened to blow off his hat, and he clapped both his hands to his head to save it. The giant shadow mocked his motions, and continued to mimic him, whether he bowed, or waved his hand. He then went and called the landlord of his inn, and they both proceeded to the spot whence the spectre was first seen. At first, nothing was visible, but in a few moments, lo! there were two colossal figures who bowed low to the salutations of our traveller and his host. The figures were sometimes very clearly defined, and then again grew dim and vanished, but presently reäppeared. I need not tell you, I suppose, that they were the shadows of the spectators, magnified to frightful dimensions, by the reflecting and refracting powers of the clouds and atmosphere, upon which they were painted by the sun, like the images of a magic-lantern upon the vapours of a chafing-dish."

Mr. Oldbuckle's account of the spectre of the Brocken suspended all the operations of the breakfast-table; and when it was finished, no one thought it worth while to renew them. They would all gladly have continued the interesting conversation, which had sprung up in consequence of Mary's optical illu sion, but the morning was stealing away; and Dr. Sinclair, knowing that some of his guests were desirous of reaching their own home as early as possible, rose to superintend the preparations for their departure. No one knew better than he did, how, in the exercise of a generous hospitality, to

"Welcome the coming—speed the parting guest."

In less than half an hour after breakfast, Edward Vivian and his sister were on their way to Viviandale. Mr. Oldbuckle had left for the Grove, and the Beechwood party, after vainly regretting their departure, were discussing plans for making the most of the two remaining days of the vacation.

CHAPTER XXXII.

A Sleigh-Ride—A Snow Landscape—The Railroad Station—A Late Train—Rate of Speed—Railways in England and America—English Engines—Brother Jonathan's Railroads—The Locomotive—Its History—The Return.

"WHAT do you say, children, to a sleigh-ride this beautiful morning?"

"I say yes, papa, with all my heart," replied Alice.

"Yes, sir, oh! yes, that is just the thing!" said Harry.

"Will you join us, William," said his father, "in an excursion to the Railroad Station, whither some business of importance requires me to go?"

"Oh! do, brother Willie," said Alice, as he looked up, a little doubtingly, from the pages of a new book to which he had resolved to devote the morning.

"Yes," said he, rising, "the book will last, but this capital sleighing will not continue long."

The preparations for the ride were soon made. The family sleigh was driven to the front gate by Mark Fletcher, and the whole party, excepting Mrs. Sinclair and Fanny, were soon bestowed among the buffalo robes which lined its seats. William Sinclair took the lines from Mark's hand, and the impatient horses scarcely waited for the flourish of the whip, which was the signal for starting. They were off with a bound, and the bracing air, with the gliding motion of the sleigh, exhilarated the spirits of all the party. The road was nearly level, skirting, for several miles, a small stream, which was now fast bound in the icy embrace of winter, and so buried in the snow that it was scarcely distinguishable from the highway, except where one or two rustic bridges carried the latter across it. The snow lay over all the ground, leaving no unsightly patches of barrenness to mar its beauty. The fall of the previous day had covered the branches of the trees, and bent the crowns of the young cedars towards the earth. The landscape was monotonous, but beautiful withal; and the universal hush which prevailed, provoked, rather than rebuked, the light laughter and eager conversation of Dr. Sinclair and the young people.

When they reached the Station, or the Depôt, as it is more commonly termed—though for what reason it is impossible to say, since the former is an English, and the latter a French word—a train of cars had just arrived, an hour behind its usual time. The delay was occasioned by the snow upon the track on the upper end of the route, which had, in some places, required the use of the steam-plough to clear it away. It was the morning passenger-train to the city, and there were seven cars, besides the baggage-car, attached to the locomotive. A freight-train was also waiting at the station, and such was its length that it

extended nearly over the turn-out track which it
occupied. The engines of both trains were letting
off steam as our party drove up, and the horses
manifested a little unwillingness to approach the iron
steeds of the railway; so Dr. Sinclair directed William
to turn them aside to a large shed which had been
erected as a carriage shelter. Here, they were un-
fastened from the sleigh and tied to a rack, while the
party proceeded to the passenger-house, upon a platform close to the track. Scarcely had they arrived
there, when the steam-whistle uttered its startling
signal; the passengers hurried to their seats in the
down-train, and with a few quick, laborious breath-
ings, the steam-horse started, with its immense burden
of human life, for the city.

While Dr. Sinclair was transacting his business
with the agent of the railroad, another passenger-
train came up, having passed the one going down, at
the next station below, which was five miles distant.

"It is only sixteen minutes," said William Sinclair,
looking at his watch, "since the down-train left. It
had to go to the next station, before the train which
has just arrived could leave; so that both of them
must have travelled very rapidly between the two
points."

"Yes," said Herbert, "forty miles an hour."

"Oh! no, Herbert," exclaimed Harry, "scarcely
twenty miles an hour. Five miles in sixteen minutes
is very slow travelling for a steam-engine, I think."

"Why, Harry," said Alice, "what a mistake. You forget that the sixteen minutes must be equally divided between the two trains, giving only eight minutes to each."

"Sure enough," said Harry, "I quite forgot that."

"The trains are running faster than usual," said William, "to make up for lost time."

"How fast do the trains travel on the best railways in this country?" inquired Herbert.

"About thirty miles an hour, I should suppose," replied William. "The average speed of the trains upon our American railroads is less than that upon the railways in England, probably by one fourth. The mail and passenger-trains there run at least forty miles an hour."

"Why do they run faster than our trains, brother William?" inquired Alice.

"The roads are better, and the engines more powerful, as a general thing," was her brother's reply.

"Why, I thought," said Herbert, "that the Yankees had the credit of excelling the English in steam engines."

"Only in marine engines, if they are entitled to it even in those. The American steamships and steamboats surpass the English steam craft in speed, more, I think, from the build of the vessels, than from the superiority of the engines. At all events, the English locomotive engines run at a greater speed than ours, though we must take into account the greater solidity and smoothness of the English roads, upon which much more money is expended than upon our roads."

While William was drawing this distinction between the English and American railroads, Dr. Sinclair had come up, unperceived, to where the group were standing, at the window of the passenger-house, and he made them all start by saying, as William ceased speaking:

"Brother Jonathan has twenty miles of railroad to build for every one that John Bull constructs, and a dozen engines to run for every one that his big brother keeps in motion. It is not to be expected, therefore, that he can build his roads as expensively, and equip them as completely, as the English roads."

The freight-train now resumed its course up the road, and another succeeded it upon the turn-out, occupying the position in such a way that the engine stood nearly in front of the passenger-house. Dr. Sinclair proposed that the young people should go and take a good look at the iron monster which performed such Herculean tasks. The engine was a new one, of the largest size, and it shone with all the glitter of its first polish. It was fitly named "Titan," as a row of brass letters upon the boiler indicated.

"Do you know any thing about the name which this engine bears, Harry?" said his father.

"I do not recollect any thing about it, sir, if I ever knew," Harry replied.

"And you, Alice?"

"I am in the same blissful state with Harry papa," said Alice, blushing.

"How is it with you, Herbert?"

"I remember, sir," he replied, "that Titan is a name which occurs in the classical dictionary, and I know that he was a giant; but I can not tell you any thing more."

"That is something gained, certainly," resumed Dr. Sinclair; "but it may be as well for you to know that the mythologists generally enumerate six Titans, the sons of Cœlus and Terra, though later writers reckon three times that number. The general account is, that they dethroned their father, and waged war with Jupiter for the government. The Titans were finally overcome, and cast into Tartarus. The name is a symbol of great physical power, and the adjective Titanic is frequently employed in our language in the sense of gigantic."

"Papa," said Mary, "I should like to know how the engine works."

"And so should I, very much indeed," said Alice; "for although I have an idea of the force of steam, I can not understand its use in this curious-looking machine."

"Your difficulty, Alice," said her father, "is a very common one. I presume that of the tens of thousands of people who travel upon railroads, not one in a hundred knows how the locomotive moves, and I could not hope to make it intelligible to you without the aid of a model."

"Why are two of the wheels so much larger than the other four, papa?" inquired Alice.

"They are the driving-wheels of the engine, and upon their size, which must, however, be nicely proportioned to the power of the engine, depends the rate of speed. On each side of the long horizontal boiler, you notice a polished steel cylinder, in each of which a piston moves, that turns the driving-wheel, by a crank. The two cylinders work together, and the driving-wheels move round upon the rail, while the pistons move once backward and forward in the cylinders. Steam, from the boiler, is let into the cylinders at both ends alternately, first to drive the piston forward, and then to drive it backward."

"What becomes of all the steam, after it has done its work, papa?" said Alice.

"It escapes from either end of the cylinder into the waste tube."

"Why have the driving-wheels no flange, sir, which I now, for the first time, perceive they have not?" said William Sinclair.

"They were at first constructed like the friction-wheels, with flanges; but, in the new engines, they are omitted, the flanges of the small wheels being considered sufficient to keep the engine upon the rails."

"That driving-wheel must be five feet in diameter, is it not?" said William.

"Scarcely less, I should suppose," said his father.

"Every revolution of it will carry the engine forward, then, more than fifteen feet, if the wheels do not slip," continued William.

"What should make the wheels slip?" asked Harry.

"The want of adhesion between the tires and the rails," replied his father, "and, at first, this was the grand difficulty in the locomotive. All manner of devices were adopted, such as rough edges, projecting knobs, cogged rails, and chains, to overcome a difficulty that really existed only in the imagination of machinists. By and by, it was found that the natural adhesion of the surfaces was adequate to keep the wheels from slipping, unless the rails were wet, or frosty, or greasy, in which case it is customary to sprinkle them with sand, which enables the wheels to take hold of the rails."

"How long is it since the locomotive was first invented, papa?" asked Mary.

"The first steam-engine upon wheels, which is the definition of a locomotive," replied her father, "was made in 1804, so that nearly half a century has elapsed since it was invented; but for many years it was a rude and inefficient machine, compared with this noble specimen of man's art."

At this moment, the engine gave tne usual signal of departure, and the engineer tried his boiler, which spirted a jet of steam and water in the direction of our group, and made some of them start with trepidation. In another moment, the polished arms began to move, the huge wheels turned round, and the ponderous engine moved on, followed by a train of freight-cars, of which Alice and Mary counted twenty-five in number.

"See, Herbert," said Harry, "how these heavy rails are worn and broken by the trains which pass over them."

"And can you suggest any other cause, my boy," said his father, "that contributes to the injury of the face of the rails?"

Harry could think of none; neither could Herbert, and I am not sure that Alice would have done so, had not her father varied the form of the question when he passed it to her, by saying:

"What effect must the rain and moisture have upon the rails, Alice?"

"They will become rusted, sir," she replied, "and—"

"Say 'oxydized,' my daughter, when you are sure that you will be understood; but go on with your answer."

"And the scales of the oxyd of iron will easily be crushed and peeled off by the wheels."

"Very good, indeed, Alice," said her brother William, "the idea never occurred to me until now."

"The injury done in this way to the rails is not inconsiderable," said Dr. Sinclair; "but," he added, taking out his watch, "do you know that we have been here nearly two hours? We must make haste back to Beechwood, or we shall be behind our usual dinner-time. I will show you, by and by, a model of a locomotive engine, by which you can study its parts more easily than you could from the engine, itself, which has a multiplicity of things about it to confuse the novice."

The ride back was even pleasanter than the morning journey had been, for the sun was shining out, both bright and warm. The snow was dripping plentifully from the branches of the trees, and the rays of the sun made the flakes and the drops sparkle like diamonds.

CHAPTER XXXIII.

Snow-Sports—The Telescope—The Tower-Chamber—History of the Telescope — Varieties — Lord Rosse's Telescope — The Moon—Her Revolutions—Telescopic Views—Surface of the Moon—The Moon-Hoax—A Star—Jupiter and his Moons—Addison's Hymn.

THE afternoon was devoted to sledding and snow-balling, and a merry time our young people contrived to make of it. The warmth of the sun had made the snow soft upon the surface, but the air was cold and the bottom of the snow was still too dry for the boys to succeed very well in their efforts to make a snow-man. They abandoned the design, therefore, and found their principal amusement upon the hill which had been the scene of their previous sport. William Sinclair had, for once, resisted their wishes, and was wrapped up in his attractive book, "The History of Henry Esmond." He was already fascinated by the portrait of Beatrix, and Esmond, himself, was beginning to exercise a strong degree of influence upon him. The snow had no attractions for him, comparable to the cozy sofa of the library, and the unfolding pleasures of Thackeray's glimpses of the times of Queen Anne.

At the tea-table, Dr. Sinclair announced his intention to devote the evening to the telescopic examination of the moon, a piece of information which afforded the party unalloyed pleasure. He had recently procured a reflecting telescope of considerable power, and, during the afternoon, he had been busy in adjusting it for the proposed examination. The telescope was placed in the chamber of the tower, over the library. The room was small, but still of sufficient dimensions to afford ample space for the instrument, and also for a small stove to warm the chamber. Between the three windows of the tower, there were cushioned seats for its visitors, and soon after tea, these were nearly all filled by the family.

"I must tax your knowledge, Herbert," said Dr. Sinclair, "for the etymology of the name which this beautiful instrument bears."

"Like its kindred word, microscope, it is from the Greek, sir; from telos—far, and skopeo—to see."

"And the word is admirably expressive," said Dr. Sinclair, "for by the telescope we are enabled to see truly afar, not only upon the surface of our globe, but into depths far beyond its atmosphere, even."

"To whom do you attribute the invention of the telescope, sir?" inquired William.

"To Galileo, beyond a doubt," was Dr. Sinclair's reply; "for although the pretty story may be true, that some children, who were playing in the shop of a spectacle-maker in Holland, magnified objects by putting two spectacle-glasses together, no one applied the discovery to scientific purposes, before Galileo."

"I have heard a story to the effect that Jansen, a spectacle-maker of Magdeburgh, discovered the principle, and constructed telescopes, which he sold at a very high price, before the close of the sixteenth century."

"Such a story is to be met with in books, I know," said his father; "but if there were any telescopes constructed before Galileo's instrument, made in 1609, they must have been toys only.

"Was this the form of the first telescopes, papa?" asked Alice.

"By no means," said her father. "The first telescopes were like the spy-glass in the library, and were called refracting telescopes. The instrument we shall use to-night is a reflecting telescope, and was first devised by Mersenne, a Frenchman, about the middle of the seventeenth century."

"Pardon me for interrupting you, sir," said William Sinclair, "but I have always understood that Sir Isaac Newton was the inventor of the reflecting telescope."

"Newton constructed two in 1692; but he was certainly anticipated twenty years by Mersenne; and in 1662 a young man named Gregory published a proposal to construct a reflector, which he did not do, for want of means. Sir Isaac Newton varied from the plans of Mersenne and Gregory, improving on both, and hence the reflector is sometimes called the Newtonian telescope."

"What is the difference, papa, between them?" inquired Alice.

"It is very wide, my child. In the refracting telescope, the spectator looks at the object directly, through two lenses, one called the object-glass, and the other the eye-glass. In the reflecting telescope, he sees only the image of the object, reflected from a concave metallic mirror or speculum, at the bottom of the tube, to another plane mirror, and from the latter to the eye-glass at the side, or at the edge of the mouth of the tube."

"I was very much interested, recently," said William, "in a particular account of the huge telescope erected by Lord Rosse, at his magnificent estate in Ireland."

"I read the account in the *London Illustrated News;* that is the one you allude to, I presume," said his father.

"Yes, sir, that was it. It was described as occupying a vast space, inclosed by massive stone walls fifty feet high, seventy feet deep, and more than twenty feet asunder. The dimensions were so extraordinary for a telescope chamber, that I fixed them in my memory."

"I think the speculum of the Rosse telescope is six feet, or about as long as the tube of my modest reflector," said Dr. Sinclair, laughing, "but then my

Lord Rosse could afford to spend a handsome fortune upon this single instrument."

"Now, Fanny," said her father, "suppose you creep down this tube for me, and wipe the speculum."

"Oh! papa, I couldn't do that," said the little girl

"What is the speculum, papa?" said Mary.

"It is a concave mirror of metallic composition, a mixture of copper and tin, which takes a high degree of polish, and which reflects the image of a star or planet, when its rays enter the tube and fall upon the speculum."

"The moon is not full, to-night, is it, papa?" said Alice. "It does not seem to me to be quite round."

"This is her thirteenth day, Alice. Can you tell me when she will be full?"

Alice was at fault, having evidently forgotten what she must have learned from Mrs. Marcet, that the period from one new moon to another is twenty-nine days and nearly thirteen hours, and that the time of full moon is just one half of this period.

"So," said Dr. Sinclair, "the moon will rise full on Saturday night. It is better, however, to examine her surface with the telescope before she becomes full, because it presents more striking points than when we see her full illuminated face."

"Do you recollect, Alice," said her brother, "how long it takes the moon to complete a revolution upon her axis?"

"I fear I have forgotten all my astronomy," said

Alice; "the diameters, and distances, and periods, were always hard to remember."

"It is the more easily recollected, perhaps," said her brother, "that it is also the period of her motion in her path around the earth. She accomplishes both in twenty-seven days and a half."

"Why papa said, just now, that the time from one new moon to another was over twenty-nine days, did you not, sir?" asked Harry.

"I did, indeed, Harry, and there appears to be a singular discrepancy between my statement and your brother's, and yet both are true."

"I do not see how they can both be true," persisted Harry.

"Then we must clear up this difficulty before we go on, my boy. The moon goes round the earth every month, eh, Harry?"

"Yes, sir; so I have been taught."

"And does the earth remain stationary all the time, Harry?"

"No, sir, the earth goes round the sun," replied Harry.

"Well, now, my boy, suppose you had to run around a coach in a circle, upon a highway, and you could do it when the coach was still, in one minute, would it take you any longer to run around it if the coach was going at full speed?"

"Yes, sir, I am sure it would, a good deal longer."

"I think so, too, Harry; and since the earth is flying in its orbit at the rate of sixty-eight thousand miles an hour, it takes the moon over two days longer, to get completely around it, than it would if the earth were at rest."

"Here, Harry," said his brother, "look at my watch; you know that at noon, both hands are precisely together, and it takes the minute-hand one hour to go around the dial. Are the hands together again at one o'clock?"

"No, indeed, they are not," said Harry. "The hour-hand is at one, but the minute-hand is five minutes behind it."

"And it will be six minutes, before the minute overtakes the hour-hand. So the moon goes round the earth in something more than twenty-seven days; but before she comes into the same position to it again, she must overtake the earth's motion, and this takes two days more."

"I think I understand it fully," said Harry, with a gratified look.

Here Dr. Sinclair interrupted the conversation, to afford the party a view of the moon, through the telescope. Fanny was first raised to the high stool, and directed to look through the eye-glass at the edge of the tube.

"Oh! papa," she exclaimed, "how pretty it is! it is as bright as the fire, except some ugly-looking holes."

"They are ugly holes, I have no doubt, Fanny,"

said her father, as he lifted her down from the stool.

Alice succeeded Fanny, and, one after another, they all looked at our fair satellite through the telescope. The entire disc of the moon was not visible at once, but the whole field of view was occupied by one portion of it, upon which the eye beheld a strange variation of brilliancy. There were spots of large size that seemed to be entirely unilluminated, and others partly in shadow. These were surrounded by rings of very bright light; and Dr. Sinclair explained to the young spectators that the shadowy portions were low, and the bright portions elevated parts of the moon's surface. The black spots, he said, were deep cavities, and might be the beds of dried-up seas, or the craters of huge volcanoes.

The unfilled edge of the moon appeared very luminous, and there were two or three bright spots apparently separated from the main limb. These Dr. Sinclair particularly pointed out, and supposed them to be the peaks of high mountains, which had caught the sunlight, while their broad bases were yet unillumined. This view, he told them, they could not have enjoyed, if they had waited until the moon was full.

"How high are the mountains in the moon, papa?" said Alice.

"Not so high as some of the mountains on the earth, probably," said her father; "but considering the fact that the moon is vastly smaller than the earth, they are exceedingly lofty. And then they cover the whole visible hemisphere of the moon, and if her other half is as rugged as the one we see, it must be a perfect Alpine world."

"Has not the other side been examined, sir?" said Herbert.

"No, Herbert, and for a very simple reason. The moon never turns her other hemisphere towards the earth. She turns upon her own axis, in just the same time that she takes to move round the earth, and so we never get a glimpse of the other side of the moon."

"Papa," said Alice, "I was just thinking that if the moon is inhabited by human beings, and they ever travel from one hemisphere to the other, the traveller who should come from the other side to the one we see, would be amazed to behold the earth shining with such a broad bright face in the sky."

"How much larger would the earth look to him than the moon does to us, Alice?"

"I do not know, papa, but it must be much larger."

"Yes indeed, it must—at least thirteen times larger," said her father, "and that would be a sight worth going from one hemisphere to another to see."

"Unless the adventurer had to climb over volcanic mountains, or to traverse valleys full of lava, like Ice land, which, I think, the moon must resemble somewhat," said William Sinclair.

"But, papa, do you think there are people in the moon?" inquired Mary.

"Why, Mary, have you not heard of 'the man in the moon?'"

"Very often, papa, and seen his face, too."

"A real man, Mary?" said Fanny, whose eyes were very wide open, at this part of the conversation.

"Look at the moon, Fanny," said her father, "and tell me if you see nothing there like a face."

Fanny looked, but her imagination, not yet quickened by stories of "the man in the moon," was not prompt to detect his lineaments in the curious disposition of light and shadow which prevailed there. At last, with Mary's aid, the little girl confessed to seeing something like eyes and nose, and mouth, belonging to "the man in the moon."

"But, to answer your question seriously, Mary," said Dr. Sinclair, "it is not probable that there are human beings in the moon, for two reasons, which, although they are not absolutely known facts, are exceedingly great probabilities. The moon, it is supposed, has no water, and, worse still, no atmosphere; and if it had both of these, it is such a wild volcanic globe, that even Iceland, which William thinks must be something like it, would be a paradise of beauty compared with its fearful chasms, craters, and its rugged mountain ranges."

"Was there not a great excitement once, in this part of the world, sir, produced by a famous moon-story?" inquired William.

"Yes, my son, and if you would like to read it, I can gratify you, for I saved a copy of the *Sun* newspaper, in which it was first published, pretending to be copied from an Edinburgh scientific journal."

"I have heard so much of it, sir, that I should really like to read it. Was it not very ingenious?"

"In some points it was, without exception, the most ingenious hoax I ever met with; but the preliminary description of the telescope, with which its details were developed, was fatal to its success with the man of science. The great majority of people, however, were taken in, and the winged inhabitants of the moon, inhabiting indescribable Edens, were not myths to the multitude."

At Fanny's request, Dr. Sinclair now directed the telescope so as to present to her eye the image of a star. To her surprise, however, it was not magnified, and she said:

"Why, papa, it doesn't grow any."

The result astonished nearly all the young people quite as much as it did Fanny. They saw the star shorn of its dazzling rays, but not a whit larger than it appeared to the naked eye. They could scarcely believe the explanation which Dr. Sinclair afforded them of this strange result. He told them that the fixed stars were so many millions of miles distant, that scarcely any telescope yet constructed served to magnify them to the eye. He then moved the instrument, until he was able to embrace the planet Jupiter in its range; and first showing the star in the heavens to Fanny, he directed her to look into the telescope.

She was now more bewildered than ever to see "a small moon," as she called it, with three stars close to it. After the others had enjoyed this beautiful view, and observed particularly the belts or stripes upon the disc of the planet, Dr. Sinclair told them that it belonged to our own system, and was not a fixed star, like the one they had seen just before.

Alice inquired why they did not see the four moons of Jupiter, to which her father replied that one of them was in eclipse behind the planet.

The hour of ten had now arrived, and Dr. Sinclair thought it best to put an end to the lesson and observations of the night. When they descended into the library, they sung, as part of their night devotions, the beautiful hymn by Addison:

> "The spacious firmament on high,
> With all the blue ethereal sky,
> And spangled heavens, a shining frame,
> Their great Original proclaim;
> The unwearied sun from day to day
> Does his Creator's power display,
> And publishes to every land
> The work of an Almighty hand.

Soon as the evening shades prevail,
The moon takes up the wondrous tale,
And nightly to the list'ning earth
Repeats the story of her birth;
Whilst all the stars that round her burn
And all the planets, in their turn,
Confirm the tidings as they roll,
And spread the truth from pole to pole

What though in solemn silence all
Move round the dark terrestrial ball?
What though no real voice nor sound
Amid their radiant orbs be found?
In reason's ear they all rejoice,
And utter forth a glorious voice;
For ever singing as they shine,
The hand that made us is divine!"

CHAPTER XXXIV.

Alice's Wish—Dr. Sinclair's Consent—Waiting for Mr. Old
buckle—His Arrival—Lord Rosse's Telescope Again—The Microscope—The Wonders of a Fly—The Spider's "Hand"—A
Flea—Wonderful Leaping—Various Woods—The Skin and its
Pores—Fanny's Hair—Points Contrasted—Other Objects—Animated Nature Displayed.

"PAPA," said Alice, as she entered the library, after she had attended to her after-breakfast duties, "will you show us the microscope this morning? Herbert wishes to know how to use his when he goes home, and we shall all enjoy it very much."

"I have no objection, at all, Alice," said her father; "though, if you will wait half an hour, Mr. Oldbuckle will probably be here, as he sent me word this morning, that he should soon be over."

"Then we will wait, papa, by all means, for I am always glad to have Mr. Oldbuckle with us, when we are playing 'Philosophy at Home.'"

Nearly an hour passed by before Mr. Oldbuckle came, but the young people had found pleasant occupation with books, and did not feel any impatience. As for William Sinclair, he had become so much interested in Henry Esmond's fortunes, that Alice had some doubt whether even the wonders of the microscope would divert his attention therefrom.

When their excellent friend from the Grove arrived, he had some English news to communicate to Dr. Sinclair, and when the budget was exhausted, Alice asked him if he would like to join them in a microscopic lesson. He cheerfully assented, and inquired what new topics they had investigated in his absence. When Alice told him that they had been to the railroad, and had a conversation on steam-engines, and that they had also made a visit to the moon, he exclaimed:

"The steam-engine and the moon, all in one day! I am afraid you are hurrying so fast, that you will lose sight of some of the wonders by the way."

"We saw a great many, at all events," said Alice.

"Yes," added Dr. Sinclair, "they did not see all; but if they will only remember those they did see, the lessons will not be lost."

"That I am sure they will not be upon such pupils," and the old gentleman smiled affably upon the young people around him, and he immediately added: "But did you talk about Lord Rosse's great telescope at Parsonstown?"

"It received 'honourable mention,' sir," replied William Sinclair, "and we would have awarded it 'a gold medal,' if we had possessed one of sufficient merit."

Mr. Oldbuckle laughed at William's allusions to the jury awards at the great Crystal Palace, and said,

"I visited Lord Rosse's estate in 1849, and had the pleasure of repeated observations in his monster telescope—a name which is not only just in itself, but also necessary to distinguish it from the other great telescope erected upon his grounds."

"I did not know," said William Sinclair, "that there was another."

"I might have said *others*, with truth," continued Mr. Oldbuckle, "for there were three, at the time of my delightful sojourn at Parsonstown, to which the degrees of comparison might well be applied—great, greater, greatest. They are grouped together, the smallest in a temple with a dome, and the two larger ones open to the weather, but surrounded by lofty Gothic walls. The larger of these was scarcely completed, before Lord Rosse conceived and commenced the construction of the 'monster telescope,' which is more than twice the dimensions of the other."

"Why, I should think all the astronomers in the world would congregate at Lord Rosse's estate," said William.

"All who go there, and they are not few," replied Mr. Oldbuckle, "experience a generous hospitality from the noble proprietor, or in his absence, from his intelligent steward."

"The 'monster telescope,'" said Herbert, "must have cost a vast sum of money, I should think."

"I do not know how much," said Mr. Oldbuckle, "but I have understood that the noble lord has expended, altogether, nearly two hundred thousand dollars in the furtherance of astronomical observations."

"And purchased therewith a world-wide meed of fame and admiration," said Dr. Sinclair, with a little of his friend's enthusiasm.

"What a pity it is," said Mr. Oldbuckle, "that Lord Rosse's magnificent estate and his glorious observatories are not erected somewhere beneath the clear blue skies of this country."

"Why so, Mr Oldbuckle?" said William; "I did not give you credit for being so much of a Yankee as to desire to rob Great Britain of such ' a fair jewel in her crown.' "

"I will answer you," replied Mr. Oldbuckle, "in the language of Brutus, altered for the occasion ·

'Not that I love Britain less, but science more;'

and I must add, to make myself intelligible, that the atmosphere of Ireland is so humid, that it is exceedingly difficult to obtain observations there, while here our skies are clear, and instead of one night in a week, upon an average, we have three or four, perhaps, suitable for astronomical purposes."

"We have as yet," said Dr. Sinclair, "no Lord Rosses in this country, whose princely fortunes enable them to build monster telescopes; but American enterprise is extending even to the objects of science, and already numerous well-furnished observatories have been established, while American machinists supply respectable reflecting telescopes at moderate prices."

"I must beg the pleasure of inspecting your new instrument, upon some early occasion," said Mr. Oldbuckle; "but now, my dear sir, do not let me keep you and these young philosophers any longer from that little twin brother of the telescope, the microscope."

"I have already made one exhibition of this instrument to the young people," said Dr. Sinclair, producing his microscope; "but we confined our attention to the subject of crystallization, and even in that department, we made but a meagre show. I propose this morning to take a more discursive range, and I could wish earnestly that I had an oxy-hydrogen microscope, with which to startle and amaze these eager spectators."

"You have an instrument of much beauty, certainly, in this compound microscope," said Mr. Oldbuckle.

"It is one of the best, for its cost, which I have ever seen," replied Dr. Sinclair. "It was made by Harrison, of Hull, whose instruments you have doubtless heard of; and with the addition of Resse's high power lens, and other appliances, cost me less than fifty dollars."

Dr. Sinclair now adjusted the microscope, and explained, as far as it was necessary, its various parts. He then opened a small case, from which he took a dozen slips of glass, about two inches long, and three quarters of an inch wide. These slips were double, being fastened together at the edges, and between them, at intervals of half an inch, were "objects" for microscopic use. Besides these slips, or "slides," as Dr. Sinclair called them, he laid upon the table small forceps, glass cells, and other appliances, ready for use.

"This slide," said Dr. Sinclair, "is devoted to the house-fly, and contains three examples of the wonders which that familiar insect carries about in his body."

"And shall we see the fly's sucker, sir?" said Harry.

"You are not converted, then, by my remarks, to the glue theory, Harry?"

"I think it is so much more romantic to believe that the fly has a sucker in its foot, than that it fastens itself to the ceiling or to the window-pane by gum," replied Harry.

"But only think, Harry," continued his father, "that if the fly makes a philosophical experiment every time it puts its foot down, it must do this at least ten thousand times in a minute!"

"P-h-e-w! that is rather a staggerer!" said Harry.

"But here is the fly's foot," resumed his father;

"I will put it into the focus of the object-glass, and you may all examine it in turn."

"Oh! what an ugly-looking object!" said Alice; "four great joints, two sharp claws, and two things which look like wings."

"They are the pads, Alice, upon which the fly walks," said her father.

"I see no gum, papa," said Alice.

"That is not strange, for the specimen is old and dry, and there might have been none exuded from the pores, which you may see, when the foot was prepared."

When the fly's foot had been duly examined by all, Dr. Sinclair pushed the slide forward, and brought the eye of a fly into the field of vision.

"It looks to me like a piece of coarse lace," said Mary.

"Or like a piece of honey-comb, I should say," was Harry's observation, as he obtained a glimpse of the object.

"The eye of the fly is compound," said Dr. Sinclair, "and patient examination will show that there are four thousand divisions, or distinct lenses, within that exceedingly minute object, and every one of these points is capable of distinct vision."

"If the microscope did not reveal marvels at every glance," said Mr. Oldbuckle, "we might afford to stop and wonder at such as this."

The other object upon the slide was the proboscis

of a fly, with which it sips up fluids from the table.
and which exhibited its interior cavity very distinctly.

The next slide revealed further curiosities of the
insect world, of which nothing was examined with
more interest than the foot of the spider. This
appeared armed with formidable claws or fingers,
and Dr. Sinclair inquired if any one recollected the
mention of these in the Bible. As no one answered
his question, he reminded them that king Solomon
says, in his book of Proverbs, "The spider taketh
hold with her hands;" a very graphic description of
the manner in which this voracious insect seizes its
victims.

Harry thought the flea greatly resembled a lobster;
and its curiously curved back, its six stout legs and
thighs, and its shell-like scales, which arm it like a
coat of mail, somewhat justify the comparison.
Fanny declared that a flea would frighten her more
than ever. Dr. Sinclair told them that the large
thighs of the insect contained the strong muscles
which it required, to perform its extraordinary leaps
of perhaps a thousand times the length of its body.

"Why, if a man could leap in that proportion,"
said William Sinclair, "he could spring over the
Catskill mountains at a single bound!"

"Yes," said Mr. Oldbuckle, "seven-league boots
would be at a discount; and of the locomotive, even,
one might say—

'Othello's occupation's gone!'"

The next series of objects embraced six sections, cut from twigs of various trees and shrubs. These were cut across, and so thin as to be transparent. Some were circular, showing the whole section, and others were quarters of a circle from a larger section. They all presented a very singular and beautiful appearance. The outer rim, which is the rind of the wood, displayed a number of layers or folds; next to this was a broader rim or band, not unlike fine network in its appearance, which is the bark of the tree. The next section exhibited the sap-wood; the next, the harder wood; while in the centre was the pith column. The whole surface was covered with cells or vessels, in which the sap circulates. No two varieties of wood were alike, and the harder wood, such as the box, displayed a closer arrangement of its cells, than the woods of softer fibre.

The next objects which were presented, were three varieties of skin, so disposed that the secretory pores were visible, like minute needle-holes. With a specimen beneath the lens of the microscope, the young people could not cavil at Dr. Sinclair's statement, that a square inch of the human skin contains nearly fifteen thousand of these distinct tubes! A variety of specimens of hair was next examined, and the large hollow tube, into which the microscope converted a hair, taken from one of Fanny's golden curls, greatly astonished the little girl. Some of the specimens, the hair of the bat among them, displayed little tufts or fringes, at regular intervals along the tube, which latter appeared to be filled with colouring matter. A transverse section of a porcupine's quill afforded much gratification. It exhibited radii of a whitish substance, which Dr. Sinclair said was marrow.

"Now, Mary," said her father, "which do you think is the finer—this cambric needle, which mamma has just lent me, or this thorn which I cut from a rose-bush, just now?"

"I think the needle is much the finer, papa," said Mary.

"You shall see the points of both, side by side, in the microscope," said her father, "and then you shall tell me again."

"Oh! papa," she exclaimed, as she saw the two objects protruded before her eyes, "what a difference! one is a great, rough, black rod, and the other is perfectly smooth and bright-coloured, though of equal size."

"The latter is the thorn—a point of God's fashioning," said her father, "and the former is man's work, which certainly suffers in comparison."

"What a mass of huge twisted ropes," said Harry, as he looked at a piece of lace; and a piece of the finest linen cambric seemed to him coarser than any cotton-bagging he had ever seen.

"These," said his father, "are more of man's handiwork, which, it seems, does not bear microscopic examination."

"Oh! papa, what a beautiful object!" was Alice's exclamation, as a fish-scale was subjected to the microscope. It glittered like a mass of mica, and exhibited a complicated structure. The dust of the lycoperdon, a species of fungus, which grows in the form of a puff-ball, was next presented, and the scarce visible particles were converted into round orange-coloured globules, not unlike mustard-seed.

"We will take a glimpse of animated nature, now," said Dr. Sinclair, "if Harry will get me the vinegar-cruet."

"Oh! papa!" said Mary, "you do not mean to say that there are animals in vinegar?"

"Certainly I do, my child; but of that you can have proof without the microscope. Most strong vinegar contains a little eel-like animal, which is visible to the eye in a strong light."

Harry now brought the vinegar-cruet, and Dr. Sinclair held it up to the light, proving the truth of his words. He then poured a little of the fluid into a glass cell, which he closed by sliding a piece of glass over it. It was then placed in the microscope, and the whole field of vision was occupied by six or eight large-sized eels, or snakes, as Fanny called them, which writhed about with the wildest contortions. Mrs. Sinclair looked at them with a shuddering sensation, and said she did not generally give way to squeamishness, but she hoped she should forget the vision when she had occasion again to use vinegar.

"Show us the mites in cheese, papa," said Harry.

"We have no cheese old enough," said his mother.

Dr. Sinclair laughed, and told Harry to make another visit to the pantry, and to bring some of the dust off the rind of the cheese, and if he could find a fig, to bring that also."

"Oh! papa!" said Mary, "please don't show me ugly living things in figs, or I shall never eat another."

"My store-house will be the richer for that," said her mother; and she added, laughing, "Figs are one of Mary's weaknesses."

When the cheese-paring and the fig were brought, Dr. Sinclair exposed minute fragments of the first to the magnifying lens, and there was a scene of terrible rioting upon the glass. A dozen uncouth-shaped creatures, whose globular bodies were provided with eight arms or legs, were tumbling over one another, and over the fragments of cheese-dust, equally magnified.

"The warmth of the sun has quickened their motions," said Mr. Oldbuckle, as he glanced at their gambols.

"What do you call these creatures, sir?" asked William.

"They belong to the acari tribe," said his father, "while the vinegar-eels are called infusioræ or animalculæ."

The fig-dust was put beneath the lens, in spite of Mary's playful resistance, and it revealed a degree of animation scarcely less remarkable than that of the cheese.

The dinner-bell rang in the midst of their microscopic investigations, which all the party were loth to exchange for the gratification of grosser tastes, than those which science ministered to.

CHAPTER XXXV.

Infusioræ —Wheel Animalculæ — Flint-Shelled Infusioræ —Fossils—Flint — Chalk —Polishing Slate —Fossil-Flour — Dirt-Eaters —Eating Slate-Pencils—Microscopic Blood—The Wisdom of God—Thoughts of To-morrow—Pleasant Intelligence—Mr. Oldbuckle's Adieus—The End of Harry's Vacation.

IMMEDIATELY after dinner, the microscopic examinations were resumed. Dr. Sinclair told the young people that his exhibitions of the infusioræ, or animalculæ, were greatly restricted by the season, as the water of stagnant pools, or slow-running ditches, in which vegetable matter was constantly steeped, yielded them in the greatest variety, and these were now inaccessible.

"This cup," he continued, "contains an infusion of hay, which has been steeped in water since yesterday, and which, in the temperature of this room, should now yield us abundant animalculæ. I will expose to the microscope a drop of it, which, to the naked eye, appears to be full of only films and sediment."

"Oh! what a singular sight!" exclaimed Alice, as she placed her eye to the instrument. "There are hundreds of curious little animals, some round and some egg-shaped, which seem to be swimming about, just for play."

Alice's description was not exaggerated. These minute monads were of many forms and of many colours; and such is the infinite variety of these animalculæ in water, that it would require a volume to describe them.

"Of what use are such insignificant creatures as these, sir?" said Harry.

"If I can not answer your question, particularly, my boy, I can assure you that God has made nothing without a purpose; and every one of the millions of infusioræ is of some service in the great economy of Nature."

"I presume that they furnish food for animals of a higher order than themselves, do they not?" said William.

"Beyond a doubt," replied his father, " and patient watching would probably reveal to us instances of the destruction of the smaller by the larger of these animalculæ."

"There can be no question," said Mr. Oldbuckle, " that this infinitely multiplied animal life is nourished by the putrifying vegetable matter from which it springs, and thus, perhaps, the air is preserved from corruption, to a vast extent."

"If this infusion were allowed to stand for several days," resumed Dr. Sinclair, " there would appear new varieties of animalculæ. These are called monads, and they would be succeeded by parameciæ, and those by rotiferæ, or wheel animalculæ, of which, it is ascertained, there are not fewer than two hundred kinds."

"Why are they called wheel animalculæ, papa?" inquired Alice.

"Because when in motion they spread out, from their mouths, rays that resemble the spokes of a wheel; but," he added, "it is not in water alone that we find these animalculæ. They exist in myriads in the air, in mould, in vegetable cells, in the smut of wheat and other grain, and in a great many other forms."

"How truly does the poet exclaim," said Mr. Oldbuckle:

> 'Full Nature swarms with life: one wondrous mass
> Of animals, or atoms organized.''

"I will now call your attention," said Dr. Sinclair, "to varieties of animalculæ not now possessing life, but affording evidence of its abundant existence in past ages. They are called the flint-shelled animalculæ, and the race is not extinct. Countless myriads of them dwell in pools, in ditches, and in the sea. They are of unsurpassed beauty of form, some of them resembling the ancient lyre, and others are circular and covered with rays. In this slide are minute fragments of flint, chalk, and coral, which I will present successively to your notice in the microscope."

"But what have flint and coral to do with animalculæ, papa?" said Alice. "Surely there are no animals in such a hard substance as flint!"

"No living animals, I grant," said her father, "but do not be incredulous when I tell you, that the hardest flint you ever saw is composed of myriads of the shells of once living animals, invisible to the naked eye."

"Oh! papa!" said Harry, "that is hard to believe."

"It is nevertheless true," said his father, "and you may believe also that chalk and lime, and much of the slate, are all composed of the fossil remains of animalculæ."

"What are fossil remains, papa?" asked Alice.

"The term fossil is applied to all petrified remains of animal or vegetable life, of former periods of the globe. Thus coal is a fossil, and bones of animals dug up, are called fossils. Marl, and lime, and chalk, are also fossils of animalculæ. But look at these fragments of flint in the microscope, and observe the variety of forms they present."

"Those star-like fossils," said Mr. Oldbuckle, as he glanced at the object, "are exceedingly beautiful."

"They are the shells of animalculæ that existed many ages ago," continued Dr. Sinclair; "and these and kindred forms, now constitute rocks and soils in different parts of the globe. These chalk fragments are composed of exceedingly curious fossils, called foraminifera."

"Oh! what pretty shells!" said Fanny, when her eager eye caught sight of them. "They are full of holes, and I think I should like to string them for beads."

"I am reminded," said Mr. Oldbuckle, "of the saying of the early naturalists, 'Omnis calx ex vermibus,' (or, to translate, for the benefit of the young people, 'All chalk is made by worms,') and there is a vast degree of truth embraced in it, which the microscope reveals to us."

"In Prussia," said Dr. Sinclair, "there is found a fossil called polishing-slate, which is entirely composed of the shells of infusioræ, so exceedingly minute that a piece of the stone, not larger than a thimble, or a common marble, contains ten thousand millions of distinct animals, and the weight of all the vast multitude would not exceed fifty grains!"

The astonishment of the young philosophers was growing at every step of the examination, and would find expression in a variety of ways. When Dr. Sinclair concluded his account of the polishing-slate, Harry ventured to say that he thought that was the climax of animalculæ wonders.

"Let me see if I can not excel it," said Mr. Oldbuckle. "I have read descriptions of a species of earth in Swedish Lapland, which is found under a vast bed of decayed moss. Four fifths of this earth is composed of fossil animalculæ. It is called berg-mehl, and in seasons of scarcity of food, which occur frequently in that far northern country, the poorer classes of the people mix this earth with their flour, and consume it as food."

"Oh! Mr. Oldbuckle!" said Alice, "do you believe that?"

"There is no reason to doubt it, my bird; and one of the Chinese missionaries records the existence and similar use of this earth in China, in seasons of scarcity."

"Can it nourish them, do you suppose, sir?" said Herbert.

"What do you think of it, Dr. Sinclair?" said Mr. Oldbuckle.

"I think not," he replied; "but it probably serves to fill the stomach and prevent the sensation of hunger. Moreover, it is stated that the use of this fossil flour, without meal, is soon fatal to life; but," he added, after a slight pause, "the Laplanders or the Chinese are not the only people in the world, that eat dirt."

"What other people commit such a barbarism?" inquired Mrs. Sinclair.

"Americans, my dear," replied her husband.

"You amaze and perplex me exceedingly," she rejoined.

"I saw, during a visit to the South, and while in the upper part of Georgia," continued Dr. Sinclair, whole families of very poor people, whose complexions were of a deathly whiteness, and their hair resembled flax. I was told that they acquired this appearance by eating clay habitually, and they go by the name of 'dirt-eaters.' I remember conversing with Professor Agassiz, on this subject, and he expressed a curiosity to examine the clay or dirt which these people were accustomed to eat, presuming that it is composed chiefly, if not altogether, of fossil infusioræ."

"What a revolting idea these dirt-eaters suggest to the mind," said Mrs. Sinclair.

"I have known boys and girls too," said Dr. Sinclair, "who are not exactly like these 'tow-heads' of the back-woods, who nevertheless injured their health by eating blue-clay, slate-pencils, and even pipe-stems."

"Oh! papa!" said Alice, "I know some girls who eat up their slate-pencils so fast that they can rarely keep a supply on hand."

"And these girls," said her father, "are devouring fossil animalculæ, which if they knew, perhaps, they would cease the evil habit."

"I shall certainly tell some of them about this conversation," said Alice.

"I do not wish to tantalize you, my children, with references to wonders which I can not now show you," said Dr. Sinclair; "but I can not help expressing my regret, that I could not obtain a living frog, to afford you a view of the circulation of blood in its foot. This is justly regarded as a crowning wonder of the microscopic exhibitions, especially when shown upon the screen of an oxy-hydrogen microscope. The red colour of blood is entirely owing to the presence of little globules, or corpuscles, which float about and are full of deep red fluid. If the web of a frog's foot be placed under the microscope, these globules are seen coursing rapidly through the veins or blood-vessels, and upon the screen of a solar or gas microscope, the effect is very beautiful. A tide of these red, oblong corpuscles rushes over the screen, and then they enter the smaller vessels and are carried off out of view. As I can not show you this sight, I will invite your attention to a drop of blood which I will generously sacrifice upon the altar of science for your instruction."

Dr. Sinclair pricked his finger with the point of a needle, and rubbed the slight wound upon a slip of glass, so as to spread the blood over its surface. He then put the glass into the microscope, and bade Alice look at it.

"Why, papa," she exclaimed, "the globules are quite round, and not oblong, as you described them in the frog's foot."

"They are round and small in the human blood," replied her father, "and if you notice clearly, they are also concave."

When all had examined the blood upon the glass,

Mr. Oldbuckle asked Dr. Sinclair if he had any more wonders to reveal to them?

"I believe I have done, my dear sir," he replied, "though I have not glanced at the thousandth part of the marvels which the microscope reveals. I hope I have succeeded in impressing the minds of the young people with the astonishing variety, beauty, and wisdom of God's works; the very smallest of which declare his glory as effectually as the magnificent sun which shines in our system."

"Your examinations with the telescope, yesterday, and those with the microscope, to-day," said Mr. Oldbuckle, "have brought before these young minds, the extremes of God's creative power; and I am reminded of the words of the eloquent Doctor Chalmers 'While the telescope enables us to see a system in every star, the microscope unfolds to us a world in every atom.' Truly did the Psalmist exclaim—

> 'Oh! Lord, how manifold are thy works!
> In wisdom hast thou made them all;
> The earth is full of thy riches.'"

This was the last formal lesson in philosophy which the young people received during Herbert's delightful visit at Beechwood. The next day they were to return to the city; he to his own beloved home, and Harry away from his, to the duties of school-life, where he could not expect to find the paths to knowledge as pleasant as those in which he had been rair bling for a fortnight. As Herbert, however, was to share with him the tasks and trials of his school-hours, so he looked forward to a participation in the pleasures of his school-fellow's home; for, to the great rejoicing of both of them, the Rev. Dr. Russel had consented, at the earnest solicitation of Dr. Sinclair, to receive Harry into his family, during the rest of his stay at school in the city. Dr. Sinclair did not tell Harry and Herbert of this, until the former began to look sad with the thought that his vacation was at an end, and that he must leave his happy home and all its loved ones. It proved a great consolation to him, and he began, at once, to talk cheerfully of the next term.

"And Herbert shall come back with me, in July, shall he not, dear mamma?" said Harry.

"If he wishes to come, my boy," said his mother, "and Dr. Russel is willing, we shall give him even a warmer welcome than we did a fortnight ago this afternoon. Then we welcomed him for your sake, and when he comes again we shall welcome him no less for his own."

Herbert's eyes were full of quick tears, and his lip quivered, as he vainly tried to express the thanks and love which were overflowing his heart. Mrs. Sinclair's eyes were not less quick than those of Alice, to detect his emotion, and she turned to Mr. Oldbuckle, saying gaily—

"You must bear in mind, my dear sir, that we

shall be lonely enough, when all these young gentlemen have taken their departure, and let us see much of you at Beechwood, although our delightful lessons in home-philosophy may be suspended—not ended, I hope."

"I shall obey your injunction, my dear madam, most willingly. And now," he added, "I must bid my young friends good-bye, for I regret that I can not linger to tea, as I could wish to do. Good-bye, Harry, and good-bye, Herbert, my dear boys, both of you," said the old gentleman, giving a hand to each. "I hope I shall be spared to join you both again in scientific amusements, at Beechwood; but whether I am or not, my heart's benedictions rest upon you." Then turning to William Sinclair, he said—

"And I must bid you good-bye, too, I suppose, my young friend, which I do with the hearty wish that you may take the highest honours of your class, at college."

Mr. Oldbuckle's adieus were warmly responded to by William, as they had been also by the schoolfellows, and with less formal leave-taking of the rest of the family, he departed.

There is always sadness in the separation of those who love each other, and the family at Beechwood did not look forward to the morrow without pain. We will not linger till the last words were said, for we may readily imagine that they were spoken hur riedly, and that there had been gayer groups assembled upon the porch of the hall, during the past fortnight, than that which was collected there immediately after breakfast, the next day.

Dr. Sinclair and the girls accompanied William and the school-fellows to the station, and saw them depart upon the rail-way, in different directions, however; all of them bearing with them delightful memories of the pleasures they had enjoyed during Harry's Vacation.

www.ingramcontent.com/pod-product-compliance
Lightning Source LLC
Chambersburg PA
CBHW050844300426
44111CB00010B/1120